A PEACE AFTER
GRIEF

Stories For Those Who Grieve

Tristan A. Watson

Order this book online at www.trafford.com
or email orders@trafford.com

Most Trafford titles are also available at major online book retailers.

Printed in the United States of America.

ISBN: 978-1-4669-1148-2 (sc)
ISBN: 978-1-4669-1147-5 (hc)
ISBN: 978-1-4669-1146-8 (e)

Library of Congress Control Number: 2012902012

Trafford rev. 07/21/2012

 www.trafford.com

North America & international
toll-free: 1 888 232 4444 (USA & Canada)
phone: 250 383 6864 ♦ fax: 812 355 4082

Dedicated to my brother, Dell Wayne Watson Jr.
(1984-2004)
"Live life to the fullest."

Let us not forget all of the brave men and women who have lost their lives in war fighting to protect us. They are the true heroes and courageous souls who fearlessly fought on the battlefield to ensure our safety. Furthermore, let us not forget the valiant men and women who continue to fight for our wellbeing. Their bravery enables us to embrace peace and safety every single day. Thank you!

> "And God shall wipe away all tears from their eyes; and there shall be no more death, neither sorrow, nor crying, neither shall there be any more pain: for the former things are passed away."
> —Revelations 21:4

TABLE OF CONTENTS

INTRODUCTION

Letters of encouragement, words of comfort, and an array of warm embraces never really quite seem to remove the embedded pain centered within our hearts as we try to move past the hurt of dealing with the death of someone we have lost. I've often heard people say to not use the expression "someone we've lost," because we already know their physical body is no longer present in this world. However, everyone is entitled to feel how he or she sees fit if they are struggling to move forward with their life after experiencing the devastation of losing someone they loved or cared for.

It's no secret that death is ultimately a part of life, and as my father always says "we are all graveyard travelers." To some people this may be an insensitive expression, but for others this signifies nothing but the absolute truth. Within the last couple of years I've learned death doesn't have a respect of person. As naïve as it may sound, up until 2004, I still carried the belief that death was something which came much later in life, well over into someone's geriatric years. Conversely, when I found myself leaning over my twenty year-old brother's casket at his wake, I could no longer carry such a notion. Death strikes the elderly; young, middle-aged, Anglo-Americans, African-Americans, Hispanics, any and everybody.

Too many of us know the unfortunate circumstances of laying someone we love to rest. We know all too well the emotional and physical toll grief takes on us and others who share in our pain. We know the hurt we feel as we try to rest our heads at night, but all we can think of is the desire to have our loved-one back. It's important to never let the grief we feel be buried deep within us. Those of us who grieve deserve all the time we need to try to make sense of why we were chosen to go through such pain and heartache.

The death of a loved-one wasn't something I thought I would ever have to experience in my life. It sounds foolish for me to say, but dealing with death was something I thought other people went through. Never in this life did I think I would lose someone so close to me. Chapter six of this book is based on true events that happened in my life the night I lost my brother. I remember that night every day of my life, and in each one of these stories I spilled over some of the things I thought about at one time or another. Although these stories have different characters and different plots, the theme remains the same. Dealing with death!

I've never been a big fan of believing that time heals all wounds, and that things will get easier as the months and years pass. The pain can inadvertently go either way, causing people to reach an acceptance and healing period, or time can cause individuals to become deadlocked in their everyday life. One thing I learned after the death of my brother was that everyone deals with grief differently. Some people need to be around others. Some people want to be left alone. Some need counseling, and others may need different resources to help them cope with the death of a loved-one, or friend. Some people turn to their faith, and others may turn their back on their faith and religion. Everyone is different, and everyone is entitled to grieve how they see fit.

I came to the conclusion that grief affects everyone differently, and that there isn't a time limit on someone's grief. After my mother lost her son, people in my family expected her to accept it, and just move on. They criticized her and demeaned her spirituality, all because my mother had questions for God, and didn't understand why her twenty year-old son was taken away from her. Everyone automatically thought she was supposed to get on with her life, and pretend like she hadn't raised a child for eighteen years. It was easy for family members to pass judgment on her, because none of them knew the pain of losing a child. It was nothing for them to expect her to be in a recovery mode right away. It's easy for people to pass judgment on things they haven't personally experienced.

This is why it bothers me when people tell me they know how I'm feeling, yet, *their* brother is still alive. My brother was the one who inspired me to write this book. I didn't know how to react to death, or how to even move past it in the best way. I grieved silently after the death of my brother. My emotions were held internally after the night I lost him. I was like Andrea in chapter eighteen. I held on to hope, until I couldn't hold on any longer. I believed my brother was going to be okay, despite the doctor's constant monologues that his brain was damaged, and that he was having multiple heart attacks. I believed that God was going to heal him. For the first part of the week in the hospital by his side, I couldn't imagine my brother dying. It was inconceivable for me to even ponder that my brother *could* die, but after hearing the preacher, who came to be with our family during this time, starting to say, "If it's God Will," I still didn't accept death would ever come to my family.

I had to realize that our time here on this earth is very limited, and the people we share our lives with are limited as well. Spending eighteen years with my brother wasn't nearly enough time. Our time together has come and gone in the blink of an eye. I still remember those times we use to play together, how we got into trouble together, how we rode to school together, and how I was right by his side the night he passed away. It behooves everyone to treat each other with love and kindness, and to not focus on the trivial things in this life. Life truly is too short!

We, as a people, may come from different backgrounds, are different skin colors, have dissimilar religions, and may even look at life poles apart, but there's one thing every single person who has lost someone of significance in their life has in common; the pain and separation felt by a death. No one can deny the pure grief of having to go through this life with someone missing in his, or her, life.

Someone's grief cannot be measured against that of another person, because everyone grieves differently, and at different times. It may take a year, five years, or ten years for someone to feel the pain, as opposed to someone who spends their days and nights crying for the loss in his, or her, life. If I've learned nothing else in the past seven years since my brother's death, I've learned to allow each person his, or her, own space to grieve.

I hate death, and I hate that people we love must leave us at different periods in our life. I was emotionally damaged because my brother's death came as a shock. One moment he was having dinner with us, the next month he was laying in a hospital bed and fighting for his life. I was spiritually damaged because I prayed and prayed for God to heal him, and he died instead. I was confused. I thought that if I labored in the hospital Chapel, prayed earnestly, and believed in the power of God, my brother would survive. When he died I naturally had questions. However, I never walked away from my religion, or became disrespectful with God in any way.

It wasn't hard to understand what death meant. I knew my brother was gone forever, that's why I spent that night in the hospital crying uncontrollably. I didn't understand why my brother had to die, but I understood that death meant he wasn't coming back.

For some people they see death as a beautiful thing, and an early transition into an everlasting peaceful after-life. Some people see death as a tragic work of Satan. Everyone is entitled to believe how they see fit, but death is death, and it's painful for those of us who are left behind and have to simply cling to pictures and memories. It would be ideal for every person to come to a place in their life where they could just accept the death of a loved-one, or friend, and simply move on. It may be a long process for someone to come to a place where they can fully accept death and all its complexities.

A Peace after Grief is meant to help those who feel like no one understands what they are going through, and let them know that there are people out there who have suffered the same kind of hurt they are going through. It's only after we've grieved, that we can whole-heartedly receive a peace. I believe that obtaining peace after someone's death, can surface once an individual has surpassed his, or her, grieving stage, and is willing to embrace acceptance of that person's death.

Being at peace with someone's death is different for each person. Some people may never reach a stage of peace, but through prayer it is possible to live a peaceful life after having accepted that a loved-one, or friend, is gone from this earth. No one should be told when his, or her, grieving period is over, everyone grieves differently, and there isn't a time limit on grief.

To those who grieve, it may not seem like it right now, but it is possible to receive a peace after grief.

Brother

By
Tristan Watson

You are in Heaven now, and life is hard to bear,
I wish we could have had more time to share.
You will never be forgotten, never.
It's hard, but I hope it will get better.

You were everyone's guidance here on earth,
You had a humble spirit of self-worth.
Believing was your survival in life,
You lived life to the fullest with no strife.

A display of smiles is what you showed,
You helped others on life's winding dark roads.
You were of peace and kindness every day,
To help me, no matter what, find my way.

You were truly blessed, prized like none other.
You will always be in my heart . . . Brother.

CHAPTER ONE
That Day In Memorial Hospital

Clouds in the sky, a mighty wind, bitter coldness in the air, and no trace of sunlight. Today was just like any other day. I had become accustomed to these depressing days that had become a part of my life for the past two years. I found myself wanting to trade places with my twelve year-old son, Parker. At least when he looked outside and saw the sky covered in gray, he was happy. Any day he woke up and felt no pain, was a good day for him. I, however, didn't see each day as a blessing. In many ways I inadvertently had given up on a season of sunshine and happiness. I truly believed in my heart there was nothing left for me.

I can remember sitting outside my church one Sunday and talking to my pastor about the problems in my life. He stayed with me for hours listening to me talk about how I felt, how I was depressed, and how I didn't feel like going on. As I was crying and opening up to Pastor Davis, he really had me believing he felt sympathy for me, and I even thought there was a look on his face which suggested, how in the world could God do this to you? How naïve I was. Pastor Davis couldn't have been less interested in what I was feeling. After I spewed everything I wanted to say, he humbly turned to me and said, "You shouldn't be focused on you. Your son is the one laying at death's door."

I couldn't believe that a man of God lacked empathy and compassion for one of his own members. I didn't understand what he meant. I was grieving and aching for someone to comfort me and tell me that everything was going to be all right. I wanted him to reassure me, and prophesy in the name of Jesus that my son would beat this disease and live in health. He didn't do that for me. My pastor let me sit on the cold and wet ground crying out of control, telling him my deepest fears, and he didn't even pray for me, or my distress.

"Pastor, excuse me," I uttered. "How could you say that to me?" I questioned. He looked at me stern-faced, and said it again. "You shouldn't be focused on you!" I was even more heartbroken by his supposed words of comfort. "God has stricken your son at a young age with this disease," Pastor Davis said. "Your son needs you to pray for him and stop questioning why this has happened, and realize you're not the one dying, he is!"

"Am I not allowed to have questions for God?" I exclaimed. "I will never understand how so many bad things can happen to one person," I replied.

"You feel as if you're exempt from heartache, pain and suffering?" Pastor Davis asked.

"Not exempt, but overlooked in a sense, sir. What did I do to deserve this?" I muttered.

"Nothing," he replied. "Everyone has trials, and hard times they must endure. The question is how will you handle it?" he declared.

After two years, I finally came to the realization of what Pastor Davis was talking about. It was hard for me to accept the fact that, who am I not to go through life's up's and down's. My son didn't need my depression, anger, and bitterness. He needed my love and prayers.

It took me a long time to get to a place where I could understand what I needed to do as a mother with a child suffering from Leukemia. When my son was diagnosed at ten years of age, I knew my life was over. In my mind, all I knew was a devastating disease and a young boy, equaled death. It didn't matter what the doctors said, I knew my son was going to die.

I remember sitting up at night crying, trying to fall asleep and thinking about my baby trying to fight a disease he didn't deserve. That's what made me angry more than anything. Why didn't I get cancer, or some other god-awful disease? Why was it Parker? A little boy whose only joy in life was playing with his toy car collection his father gave him before he passed away. Parker had been through enough already at such a young age. Losing his father when he was seven years old, having to grow up with no brothers or sisters, and now, living with Leukemia! It wasn't fair.

Parker was the cutest little boy. He could light up a room with his rosy red cheeks, ocean blue eyes, and a smile that could make anyone melt. He doesn't look the same anymore. His full, rich, blonde hair is gone, his skin is pale, and he doesn't smile that much anymore. I cried to myself thinking about my poor son, and if he would overcome this illness.

In an effort to help relive my feelings of being a failure as a mother, I began to rescind all the questions I had for God, all the complaints, all the negative emotions I felt, and I focused on my son, and not me. Pastor Davis gave me harsh advice at the time it seemed like, but I took it, and applied it. Parker didn't need a sappy, whiny mother. He needed me to be strong for him, to wipe the tears from his eyes, hold his hand when his body would rack with pain, and he needed me to tell him everything was going to be all right. He needed me to comfort him, and encourage him.

Last summer I received a visit from an old friend who had moved away just shortly after I had lost Daniel. She was my rock during what I considered the most difficult time in my entire life. I never thought tragedy would come to me again after losing my husband. She was my comfort. When she found out about Parker, she didn't hesitate to come see Parker and I.

"Hello Lucinda," Ann said, as she drove up into my driveway.

"Hi Ann," I replied.

She got out of her shiny red convertible without even closing her door, ran, and hugged me. As she was hugging me, I could feel a warm dampness on my right shoulder. She was crying.

"Oh Lucy, I didn't know what to say. I'm so sorry," Ann cried. We began to cry together, right there in front of my house. I didn't care. That affectionate, loving, compassionate embrace was what I needed that hot summer day.

Ann stayed an entire two weeks, helping me around the house, going to church with me, and even helping me pay some bills. Ann was more like a sister to me than a friend. When I hurt, it was as if she could feel my pain. It was as if she knew exactly what I was going through.

I can remember on the last day of Ann's visit, she wanted to see Parker one last time. We drove to Blessed Memorial Hospital expecting Parker to be up. I should have known better, he was tired from all the medication and treatment he was getting. Ann didn't care that he was asleep she still wanted to see him.

Ann's actions scared me. She made it seem as if she wanted to say good-bye, as if she was never going to see Parker . . . ever again. I had worked to hard trying to put those feelings of death, loneliness and grief behind me. I spent months trying to muster up faith and optimism, and even Ann, my best friend, was not about to ruin my progress.

"Ann, girl, stop it with that good-bye stuff! Parker is going to be up and out again," I told her.

"I know," Ann muttered, "can I have a few minutes alone with Parker, Lucy?" Ann requested.

"Okay," I said. In that instant as I was leaving out of Parker's hospital room, those old feelings of doubt, and uneasiness returned.

As I looked through the long rectangular glass on Parker's door, I could see Ann holding Parker's left hand, and resting her head gently on his stomach. He was fast asleep, but there was Ann with her eyes closed, holding Parker's hands, and looking as if she knew something was going to go wrong. I couldn't help but begin to cry. I couldn't understand how someone with no children could feel such a deep connection to a little boy.

Ann kissed him on his head, hugged him as best she could, and walked out of his room not looking back.

That night, before Ann was to leave tomorrow, we sat in my favorite restaurant talking about anything, and everything, in our lives. Ann told me she wished she would have married and had children. She told me she regretted living alone. I told her she wasn't too old to still make her desires come true.

"It would've been nice to have had someone to share the holidays with, take trips with, someone to come home to, and a loving child to kiss and hug and raise," Ann began to tell me. "But after the pain you've experienced, I don't know if I would be strong enough to endure what you've gone through," Ann said. "You're a strong woman, Lucy!"

"I'm not strong, I'm just a realist," I told Ann. "There is no way possible for me to bring Daniel back or to magically cure Parker. I'm forced to move on. I don't want to, but I have to."

"You are strong. Not many mothers can bravely handle the day-to-day stress of life, and balance the fear that at any moment their child could die," Ann said. "I certainly wouldn't be able to do it."

I knew somehow Ann was trying to ease my mind by making me think I was some kind of super mother. If she only knew the truth. If she only knew I spent months throwing pity-parties for myself, that I lived in denial, or that I even stopped going to church for awhile. If Ann knew the truth, she wouldn't dare suggest that I was strong. I knew myself I wasn't a strong person, or the kind of mother Parker needed. Truth is he's stronger and unimaginably brave for his age!

When he first was diagnosed two years ago, the news didn't take him by surprise. I mean, he didn't know anything about Leukemia, or how this illness could be deadly. From the look on his face as I was explaining it to him, he understood that he was sick. To him being sick meant a couple days away from school, some saltines, a seven-up, and some pink medicine in a bottle. I only wished this disease could be healed with my mother's old remedy for an upset stomach, or some vapor rub for a congested chest.

But not this time. My son could die and there was nothing I could do to help him. Parker was the kind of child every mother wishes she had. I've heard his teachers describe him as, "the child they prayed for, but didn't receive." Not only was Parker a humble, quiet, loving child, he was intelligent and fun in his own right. It wasn't fair that I might have to possibly live my life without my one and only child.

As the night ran on, Ann stayed up with me until I began to fall asleep. I didn't want her to go because I knew once she left my life would never be the same.

"How are you dealing with Daniel's death?" Ann asked. I was stunned that she had brought up my husband. A peaceful night thus far was interrupted by an unpleasant emotion I was not ready to discuss.

"It's been awhile, I'm slowly healing," I answered. I couldn't figure out why she was asking me this question. Could she possibly know something about Parker? Was she trying to prepare me for the worst?

"He was the love of your life right, Lucy?"

"Yes he was."

"You always think about him don't you?"

"Every day I go to Memorial," I replied.

"Listen, I'm not trying to scare you, or get you upset with me. But you do have a life insurance policy on Parker, right? You didn't have one on Daniel."

I hesitated, I knew she wasn't going to appreciate my answer.

"No, Ann, I don't," I answered.

"Lucy, it's been two years now, you should have got one by now. You don't want to be in the same situation you were in when you lost Daniel," she said kindly.

All I could think about was how wrong Ann was. If I secured a policy, that meant I was giving up and that I didn't believe my son was going to get better. How was I supposed to have faith, and trust that Parker would get better if I was going off and preparing for the worst? I was not living in denial; I was having faith for the first time in a long time. I trusted that Parker would get healed in a way Daniel wasn't.

I had met Daniel at a restaurant. I used to wait tables, and he would come in every Friday night, sit by himself in the corner booth and order a chilly-cheeseburger, large order of onion rings, a small order of fries, and a medium iced tea.

I felt so sorry for him, I just knew he was going to have clogged arteries, a bad heart, high cholesterol and a weight problem by the time he was thirty-five. Who cared though, Daniel was a handsome man with a bright future. He was a recent college graduate with a degree in Biology. He was going to be a doctor he told me.

It was a good thing he was smart, because he needed something to balance the fact that he had very limited social skills. I mean the fact that he was sitting alone every Friday night made me believe that he had no friends.

I would take his order and glance over at him every few minutes to see if he would be watching me. Sure enough, every time I would glance over at him, he would swiftly turn away from looking at me. He finally told me one night, "You don't think I come here every week for the food do you?" he blurted out.

I replied, "Well, yeah, of course. I thought you just really loved chilly burgers," I said. From that moment on, we were never apart!

As Daniel tried his hand at getting accepted to medical school (in between his busy schedule) we got married, and moved into a two-bedroom house in a middle-class neighborhood. We were only married five months when I found out I was pregnant. I still to this day think that Daniel blamed me for his educational struggles all the way until his death, but he never showed it.

Daniel absolutely loved and adored Parker. Their relationship was like none other I had ever witnessed between a father and son. I grew up with two sisters, and we borderline hated our alcoholic father. Parker was the splitting image of Daniel. My husband spent the weekends playing with Parker, taking him shopping, and reading to him at night. In a way I was jealous of their relationship, but Parker still loved me just the same. I could tell by his hugs and kisses on my cheek, and his beautiful smile.

I didn't want to have any more children because I didn't want Daniel to feel as if he had to give up on his dreams, due to the fact that he was stuck with having to go out and support a large family, and being depressed while he did so. I understood all too well how important it was for him to be a doctor. Eventually, I got medically fixed.

It took Daniel a long time to get accepted to medical school, but he didn't give up. He accomplished his goal. I can still see his face, and how happy he was when he finally got accepted. That night, we celebrated his victory with pizza, cake, and a movie. This would be our last family celebration together. Of course I didn't know that at the time, but in a way I should have known that nothing good lasts forever. Additionally, Daniel never got to finish medical school.

I thought I was entitled to happiness. I thought that God had finally shined on me. I believed the rewards of having a loving, caring husband, and a beautiful little boy, were the gifts I deserved after having suffered for years as a little girl.

I didn't have much in life, and I didn't want much. I wasn't college educated, and didn't have many material possessions. Just me having a wonderful life in my home was all I needed. It didn't last though. I remember the night I received a call from Daniel's friend Arlin, who told me what had happened to Daniel.

I was in bed waiting for Daniel to come home after spending a night out with his friends on a cold Friday night. I don't know how many times I slept peacefully on Friday nights, knowing that Daniel was out having a good time with his friends. However, this particular Friday in November, changed my life forever.

Arlin called me at two o'clock in the morning, telling me to hurry to Memorial Hospital downtown. I kept asking him what was wrong. He wouldn't tell me. In a calm uneasy voice he simply said, "You need to get to Memorial Hospital right now! It's Daniel." I wouldn't allow myself to ponder that anything was terribly wrong. I wasn't about to think that my husband was in danger. Little did I know he was.

As I rushed into the hospital, holding Parker's hand, I asked the lady at the nurse's station on the first floor, if she had any information on a Daniel Hawthorne. In the midst of her searching through paper work, I kept a steady eye out for Arlin, hoping he would see me and take me straight to Daniel. I didn't see him anywhere.

After the nurse informed me where to go, and where Daniel was, I sat quietly, hoping for some good news. Daniel had been in a car accident. He was run off the road by an eighteen-wheeler truck. His car ended up in ditch. The wreck was so bad Daniel had to be cut out of his car. Arlin told me Daniel wasn't even on the road for five minutes, before he ended up in the ditch.

Nothing could have prepared me for the devastation and pain I would endure that night! There was nothing they could do for him . . . Daniel actually died on his way to surgery.

I remember the heaviness in my heart and the anger inside me. I had to explain to Parker what happened. He cried day and night, trying to understand that he wouldn't see his Daddy's face anymore. He didn't want to talk to me for awhile, but I understood. Daniel was not only his father, but also his best friend. My best efforts of trying to console him were meaningless at best, because I was grieving myself.

The only man I ever truly loved, and wanted to spend the rest of my life with, was gone, taken away from my son and I forever. Death is forever. The pain of Daniel's death was so hard because it wasn't until his funeral that I realized what forever and ever meant. He was gone forever, never to come back to me again.

I could have never imagined that a couple of year's later tragedy would come back into my life. I didn't understand what I had done that was so horrible to make me have to suffer once more. One death in my lifetime was enough.

I tried to make life as easy and loving for Parker as I could. In many ways I tried to become his father. I was his new reading partner at night, we now shopped together, and almost every Saturday night I found myself lying on Parker's bedroom floor playing his favorite video game. I couldn't replace Daniel, but I sure did try to be the best substitute I could.

He keeps his daddy's picture in a standard nine by twelve picture frame on his bookcase against the wall. It hurts me to go in his room sometimes, and see Daniel's pretty blonde hair, smiling face, and baby blue eyes looking back at me. I wish Parker would just take that picture and stuff it in his closet somewhere.

Ever since he put that picture up, he never cries. Or at least I've never seen him cry when looking at the picture. It was the hardest thing for a long time having to adjust to life with just Parker and I. I wanted so badly to sell the house and just leave town, but I didn't want to be selfish to Parker. He shouldn't have the only home he has known taken away from him. So I stayed! I stayed for Parker.

Ann left the next day bright and early, she had to get back to her life. Her questions about Daniel and life insurance had stuck with me all night. So much so, that I barely got any sleep. As Ann was getting ready to pull out of the driveway, I rushed to her car. I had to ask her a question.

"Will I be giving up hope if I get this policy?" I asked.

"No Lucy," she answered. "There's nothing wrong with being prepared," Ann explained.

"I love you, Ann."

"I love you Lucy. Trust in God, and kiss Parker for me."

That day Ann pulled out of my driveway and left town. She wouldn't know how much I would need her.

I thought at the time of Parker's annual physical check-up everything was fine with his body. I did notice, however, he would get these dark purple spots on his arms. I wasn't sure what it was, but in my mind it couldn't have been anything *too* serious. I actually waited a whole month, until the day of Parker's actual appointment, before I reported to the doctor about those spots on his body.

I can recall one Sunday evening Parker became gravely ill, almost to the point where he couldn't stand up straight. I thought he had a bad stomach virus. I got him the usual stomach medicine to coat his stomach, but after the pain didn't leave, I knew he needed to see a doctor.

Leukemia has to do something with the blood cells, or bone marrow. I don't know, I forget. All I know is that after the doctor ran what seemed like a weeks-worth of tests, he diagnosed Parker with Leukemia. That day as I left the hospital with Parker, I myself, wanted to die.

It took some time before Parker began to feel the effects of all the treatment he was being given in order to combat his illness. Some months were better than others. Sometimes Parker was allowed to stay home for a couple days, other days he would end up right back in the hospital. I remember him throwing-up quite a bit, and sleeping for half the day.

At first Parker was able to go to school and maintain a healthy normal fourth grade lifestyle. However, his good days became far less, and he eventually had to leave school. I had to reduce my work hours, and I could only work on the weekends at the restaurant. I would spend the whole week with Parker night and day, trying to make sense of what was happening to him.

Parker soon found he was unable to get around on his own without the assistance of a wheel chair. I had to be brave around him, and hold my tears back until after he was asleep. I couldn't let him see me be emotional, because my poor son wouldn't have had any strength to draw from. It was up to me to see to it that he knew he could depend on me, no matter how distressing the circumstances were. I had to be his rock.

After he lost his ability to walk, Parker soon would lose his hair. He was such a brave little boy, the way he was able to look past his appearance. I guess kids are different than adults in that way. I don't know what I would've done if I would have lost my hair. I guess when you're fighting for your life, outer beauty isn't as important as trying to survive.

I spent months being anxious and fearful that Parker would soon ask me why this had happened to him, why was he going through this. He never did. I guess after his father died he became withdrawn, and held heaviness in his heart. I wanted to talk to Parker about his father, and answer his questions. I wanted to try to help him understand death. I didn't understand why Parker wasn't asking me questions about the terrible things that had become a part of his life.

Maybe I needed to talk about those things for myself. Maybe I was the one who didn't know how to deal with the heartache and pain. My son has never been the same. He was supposed to have the best childhood, filled with love, laughter, and joyful memories. Not so. Instead, he's facing a life threatening illness which can claim his life any day.

As the months went on, and Parker was in and out of the hospital, I didn't know how to be a good mother anymore. I was emotionally and physically drained from all the late night hospital stays, the medical expenses, those sleepless nights, as well as having to watch Parker try to adjust to life from limited, to no mobility, and seeing his face filled with sadness. It was too much for me to handle!

I stayed up many nights trying to figure out how I could actually cure Parker. I truly believed I had what it took to make Parker well again. What if I sold the house, and used the money to get the best doctors and most advanced treatment for him? What if I brought the pastor in on the weekends to stay with Parker, and pray over his body? I even thought about quitting my job and being at home or at the hospital with him all day. I thought to myself that if Parker saw that I was giving up my life to be with him, he would fight harder to get better.

My thinking was coming from the mind of a scared mother who was in fear of losing her child. I saw a flaw in all of my scenarios I had played over and over in my head. There was nothing I could do to keep my mind from pondering over all these things. Nothing I came up with seemed plausible.

When Parker turned twelve in March, I just knew he was going get better. I thought he was older and his body was stronger. However, the doctor explained to me Parker was actually worse. His body was rejecting the treatment he had been on for some time.

"I don't understand sir, how can his body be rejecting the very thing he needs in order to get well?" I asked the doctor.

"Parker's body has become susceptible to other types of infections because the blood cells he needs in order to do his fighting have become compromised," the doctor explained.

"I don't understand," I said.

"Well, what your son has is plain and simple, it's a form of cancer," he replied.

"Cancer!" I said in disbelief.

"Yes," he responded.

After that day when the doctor told me my twelve-year old son had cancer, I knew I had to work harder, and have more faith. I wasn't giving up on my son, or his miracle. I needed a miracle. It seemed as if time was not on my side. It had been nearly two years and I thought

Parker for sure would be up and playing, and would be able to go to school again. The doctor basically told me Parker was taking a step back.

I was willing to do whatever was necessary to keep Parker alive. Any type of transplant he needed, I was going to do it. However, the only thing I could do for Parker medically was give him blood. Even with the bone-marrow transplant, Parker still didn't fully recover. I was in deadlock. There was nothing else I could do for Parker. I felt like a failure.

I cried myself to sleep many nights thinking how I caused my son to get Leukemia. It was all my fault; no one was to blame but me. I knew I had caused my own son to become ill. If I hadn't waited nearly four weeks to get Parker in to see the doctor when I noticed his bruises, and the sickness which had over-taken his body, the doctors would have been able to have caught the Leukemia. I knew it was my fault. I knew why I was being punished as well. I didn't act like a good mother should have.

As a result of my bad parenting, I took a leave of absence from the restaurant in May, and had my mother moved in with me full-time. She had traveled some two hundred miles to come to be with me and Parker in the final stages of my son's life. At the time I didn't know that. I just wanted to be closer to Parker, and I needed my Mom to run things at home for me.

My mother had been to the hospital several times to see Parker, and he was always glad to see his grandma. He knew she always had a present for him. She would always bring a new toy car, a videogame, or some spending money. My mother was the kind of mother I wanted to be.

She raised my sister and I all by herself after our father died. She was strong, independent, brave, and loving. I tried to imitate some of her qualities and characteristics, but I could never quite be just like her. I remember even telling her once, how I tried to be like her. She would always try to make me feel better by telling me I was a better mother than her. I knew she was stretching the truth. I still loved to hear it though.

My mother was there for me when I lost Daniel. She sat and cried with me for days on end. She came and lived with Parker and I for several months after Daniel's death. Between her and Ann, I was able to move forward with my life a little bit easier.

When my mother found out about Parker I could hear her crying uncontrollably on the other end of the phone. Parker was her only grandchild, and I knew she loved him. It was hard for her to accept the fact that her ten year old grandson had Leukemia. I think she took it as hard, or if not more, than I did. She immediately came to see us. Ever since Parker had been sick, she came to every birthday, holiday, and at least one weekend each month.

My sister was another support system for me. I just wish she lived closer. She and her husband lived in New York. They don't have any kids, because he doesn't want any. I guess my sister loves him enough to overshadow her desire to have children. Well, I don't know that for sure. Maybe she doesn't want kids either. It could be her decision as well. All I know is that having at least one child makes this life worth living.

During the summer months Parker came home and he lived the best way he knew how. He was happy to be home, but I couldn't put that bright smile back on his face. He had become so ill he needed a wheel chair to get around. I guess he was used to being a busy body. He spent the majority of his days in bed, and really couldn't keep very much food down.

As he would lay in bed sleeping, all I could think about was this beautiful little boy who used to be so full of life and have so much energy, and now he was weak and frail. What kept me optimistic was the fact that I knew Parker would be well again. I didn't know when, but I know he would.

Finally, in September, Parker went back into the hospital. His three-month stay at home would be the last time he would ever sleep in his own bed again. Parker just couldn't get better. His poor body couldn't fight anymore.

That whole month I didn't leave his side. I let my mother keep things running at home, and I never left Parker.

One cloudy, rainy, cold day in November, I left Memorial Hospital. I left Parker sleeping and I went to take care of some business pertaining to work, and an insurance matter. My mother and I traded places. She went and spent the day with Parker, and I carried on the whole day taking care of different things I hadn't gotten a chance to attend to. It was a calm day. I figured it would be some hours before Parker would wake up again. So I took my time. It wasn't until I was back on the road heading towards the hospital that I received the call that changed my life forever.

My mother called me and told me to hurry back to the hospital. She wasn't frantic, or in an uproar. She was calm and in a low voice simply told me, "Lucinda, you need to hurry back to the hospital." I didn't think anything was wrong with Parker, because I had already declared in my mind and heart that he was going to be okay. Nonetheless, I hurried to the hospital. My mother wouldn't go into details. I kept asking her what's wrong. She just kept insisting that I get there.

I arrived at the hospital, rushed to the elevator and reached the fifth floor. I was in the elevator with my eyes closed, holding my hands together as I was saying a fast, but sincere prayer. Luckily, the elevator ride gave me just enough time to say a prayer and collect my thoughts.

As the doors opened I cautiously stepped out and stood right in front of the elevator. I put my hand over my heart, and as a mother, I knew something was wrong.

I walked to Parker's room holding my head down. I stood in front of his door, and before I gathered the courage to enter, someone opened the door. I slowly raised my head up. It was my mother standing right in front of me. She shakes her head, and I fell into her arms.

I began to cry so much I could no longer see my mother's arm wrapped around me. I remember falling to the ground in my mother's arms. She fell with me. I could feel her warm tears landing on the top of my head. All I could do was scream "Parker! Parker!" I cried. "No, Parker! Come back, Parker!" My own tears blinded me.

I remember one of the nurses, and my mother pulling me up from the floor and having to firmly hold me up from falling down again. They brought me into Parker's room. There he was lying in his bed. His eyes were closed with a light red glaze over his eyes, and a pale complexion on his face. He was gone. My baby boy had died of Leukemia.

After the funeral home came and picked him up, and the staff cleaned out his room, I rushed to see his doctor.

"What happened?" I asked.

"His body couldn't fight anymore, Ms. Hawthorne," the doctor informed me. As I continued to cry I kept trying to get the doctor to give me answers. I wasn't satisfied.

"Why did it happen all of a sudden? I thought he had time?" I asked.

"He fought as long as he could, but the treatment wasn't even enough to pull his body back to help him overcome the many things he was suffering from," the doctor stated.

I had to ask the doctor one last question in order to give me peace of mind, at least for that night.

"If I hadn't waited so long to get Parker to the hospital when I first . . ."

Before I could even finish my sentence the doctor interrupted me and said, "This is not your fault."

I hugged the doctor for what seemed like an eternity, and thanked him for all he had done.

As the night was running thin, I had to go back to Parker's room one last time. I stood in the empty room staring at where his old bed used to be, imagining him laying in the bed looking at me. Now he was gone! My son was gone from my life, and there I was facing the same set of circumstances I had when I lost Daniel. Parker was gone from my life forever, never to return to me. It was that day in Memorial Hospital that changed my life.

My mother drove me home from the hospital, and stuck by my side for the rest of the night. She slept right next to me, and she heard me crying the whole night. I knew this was the first night I would be living the rest of my life without my beautiful son. I didn't know how to push forward. My faith was shaken. I had so much faith that Parker was going to get better. No one could have ever told me my son was going to die of Leukemia at age twelve! I was filled with anger and rage. I didn't know where to focus my sadness, pain and devastation.

At Parker's funeral, I saw people I hadn't seen in years, especially Daniel's family. Here we were again, gathering together to say good-bye to another family member. I remember after the funeral how I let feelings of guilt flee from my mind. I no longer beat myself up over the fact that I wasn't there the last few hours of Parker's life. Those two months I had taken off and was by Parker's side day and night, was my good-bye and acceptance period someone explained to me. I was able to devote my undivided time and attention to my son. I was able to spend that time with him and love him. That period of time was getting me ready to accept the fact Parker wouldn't be with me anymore. Though I didn't realize that at the time.

After a few months had passed, I sold the house and moved in with my mother. I couldn't stay in a house where my husband and son once resided. It was too painful for me to live in a home and be constantly surrounded by memories. I had to leave.

I don't think I'll marry again. I couldn't bear the hurt again if something ever happened to the one I loved. As far as children—Parker was, and will always be, my only child. I will remember him and Daniel until the day I die.

My pastor made it a special point to tell me that Daniel and Parker are in Heaven now, with each other, and waiting for me. I cried when he told me that. So now, I live my life determined to get there and see my family once more.

I understand people have to go through certain things here on earth, and I'll never understand why my family was taken away from me; but I am glad I did *have* a family at one time. I dwell on the good moments, not the bad. I focus on the happy memories. I think about Parker and Daniel every day. I push forward with my life, even finding myself laughing and smiling some days.

No one could ever replace the two loves of my life, and I can't wait to see them again. I'm not bitter or sad. I'm grateful, and blessed to have known two beautiful souls.

CHAPTER TWO
A Need For Release

I started writing all of my thoughts and feelings in a little journal that I considered to be one of the most personal items I possessed. At the time, as I was going through high school and college, there wasn't an outlet for me to convey all of the emotions that I had been going through. Talking to my parents about what I was feeling, was not something I could do, being that my mom was a religious fanatic, and my dad was more spiritual than religious, plus he was a traditionalist through and through. There was no way I could tell anyone what I had finally figured out after years of struggling and denying to myself, what I was within . . . rather, who I was within.

My older sister was a little understanding, but I couldn't possibly tell her who I was. She wouldn't have been *that* understanding. I knew her thinking, how she operated, and what she believed. My best friend surely would've stopped hanging around me. He would've been disgusted with me. I know this because he once jokingly made some harsh comments about people who liked the same sex.

I don't know why, I just didn't tell everyone my secret. They eventually all found out anyway. There was no use in trying to hide and cover-up anymore. What I had been hiding for years was finally brought to the light. However, it wasn't by my choice. I was forced to reveal the most private information about me to people who claimed to have loved me, but only ended up judging me and condemning me to hell.

I couldn't come up with the reason why I felt the way I did. I wanted it to stop. I wanted to be normal and be just like every other red-blooded American male. I don't know how many times I wished I could've been the jock with the most friends, the intelligent guy with a serious girlfriend, or just a normal straight guy who loved girls.

My desires weren't the same as my male peers. I couldn't see myself loving a girl the way my dad loved my mom, or how my sister's boyfriend loved her. I was a weird teenager who had a dark secret. I didn't want anyone to know what I thought about at night, or how long I had been hiding behind a straight persona, or what my true desires were when it came to my sexuality.

I worked hard to the bitter end to keep my secret buried within me. Despite my best efforts, my hard work didn't payoff. After I was exposed, there was no sense in hiding anymore. Everyone soon learned I was a nineteen year-old homosexual male.

As far as my mind can remember I never did anything to lead people to assume I was gay. I did my best to act, look, and be a straight male. I followed everything to the letter.

I was a semi-active athlete, I talked to girls, mismatched my clothes, along with a host of other things. I can honestly say I did my best to conceal all the feelings and emotions I was having at a young age. No one knew about me and my tendencies, I know they didn't. No one could have ever guessed that I was living a double life. Everyone in my life found out by accident. An accident I know my mother wishes never happened.

However, it's like my grandma used to say, "Everything happens for a reason." She didn't believe in accidents, mistakes, or coincidences. She believed something as simple as a bad hair day had a purpose, and was supposed to happen to some poor soul. Nevertheless, she also believed in the most extreme. Death! Death was a reward for the righteous, and a punishment for sinners. Through my grandmother's eyes I know she would've considered me a sinner to the core.

I didn't always have feelings for the same sex. I can remember a time or two when I actually thought I was normal. Or maybe I always did, and I suppressed my feelings. I take myself back a year and a half ago to the days where I was actually happy, and thought I had finally found peace within myself. I was wrong. It was during a breakfast conversation that I realized I could never tell anyone just who I was.

"Jeremy, get down here, now!" yelled my mother. "You're supposed to be at school in thirty minutes. This breakfast is the best meal you're going to eat today. God only knows what kind of crap that school cafeteria is serving," she continued.

I kept thinking in my mind how excited I was that I would be going to college next fall. I wanted to escape my mother, father, and perfect sister. I mean honestly, I had to have been given to the wrong family. Between my mother's ranting and raving, and pressure to live holy, and my dad's forceful push to be some great ball player, and living in the shadow of my ridiculously intelligent, outspoken sister, my home life was anything but dull.

"Thanks mom, once again for this wonderfully, fantastic, delicious, home-cooked breakfast, I know you spent minutes making," I said sarcastically.

"Well, I know you need your strength to stay awake in class so you can continue to bring those mediocre grades home," my mom answered back. I liked our relationship, nothing boring about it.

Even though my mother and I didn't see eye to eye on most things, which heavily plagued me, I knew she always loved me. For one, she always said it, but I knew she meant it and she would do anything I needed if I asked her.

"Where's dad?" I asked.

"He left early this morning," my mother replied.

The relationship with my father was more straight forward, but with unreachable high expectations. I knew he was fairly disappointed in me. I spent four years in high school never really staying committed to one particular thing. I did enough just to keep my father off my back, but he would've liked to have seen me be more involved and become a basketball player, and get a scholarship to college.

Not in my plans! I spent a couple of semesters playing a little of everything. I knew I had to keep him happy some kind of way. My last semester in high school though, I didn't play anything. I took time for me. My dad could eat dirt for all I cared. I decided I wasn't going to try to please him anymore.

I wanted to remove as many stress factors as possible. One of the biggest stressors in my life at that time was my father. I eliminated him quick, and thought his concern about my life would fade to gray. No such luck.

"So, Jeremy, what are you and what's his name up to tonight?" my mom asked.

"I'm not sure," I replied.

"Well, just don't be getting into trouble!" My sister walks in on the tail end of my mother's words, and quickly asserts her rude comments into our conversation.

"Trouble, you don't have to worry about those two getting in trouble together, they'll be too busy hooking-up with each other," my sister said comically.

I chocked on my milk, and my mother frowned in disgust.

"What, Denise?" my mother said angrily.

"Mom relax, its okay if you have a gay son," my sister explained. "There are worse things in the world."

I wanted my sister to shut up so bad; I wanted the infamous topic to cease.

"That is not even remotely funny, Denise. That is one of the worse things in my book. No son of mine is going to be gay," my mother firmly stated. "Plus, Jeremy knows he'll go straight to hell."

I paused within myself for a second. Hell! I could really go to hell for being who I am? The same way a murderer could? I thought to myself how extreme that punishment was, to be on the same level as someone who took another person's life. Talk about fair.

"Mom, please, I'm not gay, and I don't know why you're getting so upset!" I exclaimed. "And Denise, can you learn to choose your early morning breakfast topics more wisely next time," I asked. She nodded her head yes, and left the kitchen smiling.

I thought to myself, could my own sister know about my sexuality? She had to know something. Just had to. On the surface she seemed cool with the fact that she might have a homosexual brother. It didn't seem to bother her. My mom, on the other hand, proved exactly why I could never tell anyone what I was battling with.

I figured my mom would pretty much disown me. That day at breakfast removed any doubt and wavering thoughts I had about coming clean. I couldn't. The best thing for me to do was to continue to live in secret, and maybe, just maybe, I could get rid of these feelings. This was probably just a phase anyway, being that I actually never really knew what all I was accusing myself of becoming. I didn't know anything about what it meant to be attracted to the same sex. I learned to repress my emotions and feelings. I held everything within me. I watched myself, and tried to be the best teenage male I could.

Time had passed since that day at breakfast with my mom and sister. I had to be careful not to give off the impression that the topic bothered me. If I lead on with it, or proved that I was in some way uneasy about it, my mother and sister would've suspected something. I wanted to learn the art of becoming unbothered by other people's emotions. I didn't want people to cause me to become anxious during certain circumstances.

I finished my last semester in high school and waited two long months to go to college and experience life for myself. I spent the summer days working, and I spent the night hanging out with close friends. I didn't have causal friends. I only had close friends I knew I could count on, and trust. Maybe it has to do with the fact that I'm a loser at heart. It didn't matter to me that much, just as long as I had a way out of my house when I needed it.

That summer was the best summer of my entire life, because I knew nothing in my life would ever be the same again. I knew I was heading toward bigger and better things. It was always my dream to go to a prestigious Ivey-league school, but I wasn't able to achieve it. Instead, I ended-up attending a small school about three hours away from my home, not my ideal place, but it was *away* from home. I was satisfied for the most part.

The week before I was to leave to go to college, I remember my mother and father sitting me down and having a conversation with me. I didn't want to have it. I just knew there was going to be some talk about holy this, and holy that. It was the same boring thing over and over. I managed to muster up enough strength to listen through my mom's speech about remaining true to who I am, and not be influenced to do things I know were wrong.

"Jeremy, you want to live your life free from shame and sin," my mother said. "You're at a point in your life, where what you do will pretty much follow you for the rest of your life. Don't do anything in college you know your father and I would be against. Please."

"Mom, you don't have to act like . . ."

I was suddenly cut off by my father.

"Jeremy, don't argue, just accept what your mother is telling you," dad said.

"Thanks, Michael, but I have this conversation under control."

I wanted to leave so bad. I was so sick and tired of being treated like a little child. My parent's always thought they had to tell me what to do, like I wasn't smart enough to figure it out on my own. That really bothered me.

"Mary, maybe you should tell him what you told me last night," my father said. Here we go, I thought.

"Jeremy, your father and I, just want you to know we're proud of you. I mean, sure, you didn't get into the college you wanted, and you didn't make the kind of grades like your sister, but that doesn't matter. We still love you just the same."

"Yes, son. You have your own accomplishments. There's no need to compare yourself to your sister," dad said.

In my mind I was thinking, it wasn't me comparing myself to Denise. It was them, not me.

"Are we finished," I asked.

"We love you, Jeremy," my parents said.

As I was getting up to leave, something just came over me, and I found myself saying, "I love you all too." What a weird moment for me. I knew I loved my parents, but I hadn't said it in a long time. Did

I really mean it? I couldn't understand. Maybe it was just the heat of the moment kind of thing.

After my parent's heart to heart talk, I went to my friend Dean's house. Dean and I had been best friends since grade school. Although we are two completely different people, or I should say, grew up to become two completely different people, we remained friends. He was the brother I never had. There was no one like Dean. I can honestly say I had a true best friend.

Did I trust Dean with the most important secret in my life? I would have to say no. This piece of information about me was life altering, and I knew in my heart there was nothing but negative repercussions to come. Besides, I didn't want to be another statistic in the eyes of society. Another teenager hiding who he is. I didn't want the frustration.

"When do you leave," Dean asked.

"In a week," I replied. I could sense a hint of either sadness or jealousy in Dean's tone.

"That's cool," Dean said. "Are your parent's going crazy?" he asked.

I figured I'd lie to throw him off a little. Dean already knew how overbearing my parents were, and how intrusive they could be.

"No, they've already accepted the fact that I'm leaving?" I said hurriedly.

"You lie," Dean laughed. "I know your parents, especially your mom. She probably sat you down and gave you a pamphlet on sex education," Dean said jokingly.

I had to laugh myself.

"Whatever," I said.

I felt sorry for Dean. There he was, a high school graduate like me, but no future goals. My best friend was happy working at the local burger joint as a long-term plan he had set for himself. His dad was a manager at the cable station. As far as his mom, who knows where she is? It was just Dean and his dad.

"You want to hang out tomorrow," I said.

"Yeah, after I get off work," Dean replied. "Maybe you can come with us when I go to school? Ride with us," I suggested.

"We'll see," he said.

I left Dean's house that night more upset than before. He had put me in a bad mood, and I didn't want to be bothered with anyone. I didn't understand why Dean was acting so weird. What could he possibly be angry about? He was way better looking than me, he was semi-popular, had more friends than I did, and he had a pretty girlfriend. Some people don't know how good their life is.

With three days left until it was time for me to go to school, I tried to do some soul searching, or what I thought soul searching might be. I was cleaning out my room, and going through lots of old photos, elementary writings, high school projects, and other miscellaneous things. I found myself throwing away old memories. I didn't think it was relevant for me to keep holding on to things I no longer had a use for. Besides, by me cleaning out my room, it meant my mother wouldn't need an excuse to go through my things in the name of trying to keep a clean house.

As I was going through a particular bright green rectangular plastic tub in my closet, I stumbled across a small black diary of some sort. I didn't know what it was, or if it was even mine. I opened it up and instantly remembered how I came into possession of a girl's diary.

Actually, it wasn't a diary. It was a daily journal, as my Aunt Tracy put it. She had given me this journal when I entered middle school. She said as I was approaching my teenage years, I needed a personal outlet to express my thoughts, feelings, and emotions. I took the gift and stuffed it in my closet as soon as I got it. I thought to myself, why in the world would a teenage boy need a journal to write about things in his life. I thought, how stupid, my aunt was just being cheap.

I never used the journal, and felt kind of bad. It was a nice leather journal though. I could never tell Dean I had this so-called 'journal,' he would make fun of me for sure. Of course my mom and sister thought it was just the greatest thing in the world. My dad shrugged it off, but I know he was thinking the same thing I was. Boy and journal don't go hand in hand.

I took out the journal and flip through some of the pages. Now that I was eighteen years old, I thought differently than when I was twelve. I actually thought I might try this out. As the night leaped into the late hours there I was, in my room, on the floor, writing my heart out. I was writing about everything I could think of. I didn't care about dates or times, I was just writing.

I talked about my first day of high school, my first kiss, my first dance, and the problems with my parent's. Anything that I thought was significant in my life up until this point, I wrote about. It felt good to release some of the pressures and problems I had been dealing with. Still, there was one major problem that I couldn't release. I wanted to talk about what I was feeling, but I couldn't bring myself to write about it in such a public way. No telling who was going to see this journal, if by chance I lost it someday.

After I finished writing for that night, I stuffed the journal in my suitcase to take with me. I looked around in my room, and reflected on some good memories of me as a little child. I wanted so badly to go back to being a little kid again. Things were much simpler in life. Problems were non-existent. I knew I had a long way to go before I would be problem-free again.

I remember the trip up to my college. My dad drove, and my mom and sister sat quietly. I kept looking out of the window hoping I was going to have a pleasant first year experience. I did everything right, I thought. In my mind I did everything right. I was humble, respectful, helpful, and giving. Surely life wasn't about to hand me an array of problems I couldn't deal with? Only bad people who hurt others, or who live bad lives, are the ones who have problems. How naïve I was to believe I was removed from having to deal with the heartache, pain, and suffering of life.

I remember us arriving at my dorm, unloading everything, and then getting something to eat. The day went by smoothly. I could tell my parents were a little sad, even my dad acted like he was going to miss me. As the time drew near for my family to say good-bye, I remember every detail down to the last second, before my family left.

"We love you Jeremy," my mother cried. My mother hugged me tightly as she cried, and hurried to the car. If I didn't know how much she loved me, I knew in that moment she did.

"Take care, son, love you," my dad said quietly. He hugged me and went to the car.

"I love you too dad," I said. I was confused. I thought my dad was disappointed in me, because I wasn't the kind of son he wanted. I actually thought he couldn't stand me. Now he's showing affection and emotion. I didn't understand. The last time I can remember my dad telling me he loved me, I had to be at least five years old.

"Jeremy, mom and dad are counting on you to succeed, and to make something of yourself. College is a new experience for you, and it's full of opportunity. Get your education, and don't do anything you know they would be against," Denise told me.

I really didn't know how to respond to my sister's dramatic good-bye speech. On one hand I felt as if I should've been emotionally moved, but on the other, she was just probably being sardonic. Leave it to Denise to take a touching moment and ruin it with her derision.

I knew my sister. I knew she genuinely loved me. It's a shame people have to go away and leave their families before they realize how much they are loved and appreciated. I should've left at age ten! As I turned away from looking into Denise's intense brown eyes, I looked up in the sky and suddenly realized that I was about to be left alone to engage in an experience I knew would in some way complete me.

College was the time for me to figure out who I was. I was excited that I was finally getting the chance to explore. For so long I had been confused about the kind of young man I was becoming. This time, away from home, was my time to see just exactly who Jeremy was.

"Bye," I told my sister. I hugged her good-bye, and watched her leisurely make her way to the car. There I was, standing on the top step outside my dorm hall, with my family all in the car slowly pulling away. It was as if time was standing still. It took forever for my family to drive away. As I began to turn to go inside, I took one last look at the car.

My mom's hand came flying out of the window. She shouted, "We love you, Jeremy!"

I threw my hand up and smiled at her. She smiled back. They drove off, and I was alone. However, I was happy . . . to be on my own. Making my own decisions at last. It was time!

That same night, I decided to clean my small closet of a room. I mean, the room was barely enough for even one person to move around and be comfortable. How in the world were two people supposed to cohabitate in this jail cell?

I cleaned off my side of the room, and made sure nothing was in the way of my roommate. I didn't know what to expect. I didn't know if he was going to be a meathead jock, a sloppy partier . . . neat and geeky, or just normal like me. What was I in for? I didn't know what to expect. My answer would come the next morning.

As I rolled out of bed at eight a.m., I woke to three gray suitcases, a brown duffel bag, and a roll of posters lying on the bed next to me. My roommate's stuff was here, but he was nowhere to be found. I hurried up and got out of bed, dressed, and prepared myself to meet him.

About two hours later, a tall skinny Black boy walks through the door. He stares at me for a second, and then he smiles.

"Hey man!" he said.

"Hey," I replied.

"I'm Kirk," he stated. "What's your name?"

"I'm Jeremy." I was nervous. I was getting ready to share a room with a black kid. I wasn't racist, or at least I didn't think I was a racist. I didn't know just yet.

"So we're roommates," Kirk said.

"Yeah," I muttered. I wasn't sure about how to take the conversation.

"Relax," Kirk told me.

"I'm fine," I replied.

"What are your hobbies?" Kirk asked.

"Well, right now, I like to write," I told him.

"For real?" Kirk uttered.

I didn't know how he took my answer. I didn't know if he thought I was some kind of little girl or something. I sure wasn't about to tell him I had a journal.

"Writing is my hobby too," Kirk stated.

When he said that, I knew we at least had one thing in common. It was my duty to try to become Kirk's friend. I didn't want to mess-up a potentially good friendship, because of my own opinions, and that of others, negative perceptions about African-Americans.

I wanted to see Kirk the way I wanted to see him. Not through someone else's eyes.

From that initial meeting in August, Kirk and I did become friends. Not in the way Dean and I were friends, but on another level that I was comfortable with. I spent the entire semester building on that friendship.

As the fall semester of my first year in college came to a close, I thought I was in a good place in my life. I was happy, I thought. I had been successful academically, and I was on my way home to spend the holidays with my family. Conversely, the wonderful holiday season I had hoped for didn't quite turn out the way I wanted it to. In fact, this was the last holiday season I would ever spend with my family.

When I arrived at home, of course everyone was glad to see me. Believe it or not, I was glad to see them too. I spent the night writing in my journal all the things that had taken place for me as a college freshman. I even found myself writing about some of my first experiences. I didn't want to, but something in me needed to release this information some kind of way. I couldn't tell anyone, so the next best thing was to write it down. Doing so, was one of the worst mistakes I ever made in my entire life.

It was right after New Year's Day, and I had spent the night at Dean's house. When I came in, my mom was waiting at the front door for me, with my journal in her hand. Before I could even shut the door, my heart was racing, I turned bright red, and I began to sweat profusely.

My mom stared at me with an overpowering, mean, angry look plastered across her face. She holds up my journal and throws it at me.

"I can't believe this Jeremy, I can't believe this disgust and filth you put yourself in!" my mother exclaimed.

"What are you talking about mom," I said.

"You're going to act stupid son!" My mom yelled. I had never seen my mom this mad before. I kept trying to play over and over in my head what could she be possibly talking about. I never would have guessed that she knew my secret. There was no way my mom knew about my sexuality. Yet, it instantly came back to me. I wrote everything down about who I was. I revealed it myself in that stupid journal.

"Wait until I tell your father," mom said angrily.

"Mom, clam down please," I said. My mom didn't listen to me, and she turned her back to me and began to walk to the kitchen. She kept walking faster and faster and I found myself running after her. I followed my mom into the kitchen where she began to yell my father's name at the top of her lungs.

"Michael!" my mom shouted. "Michael! Michael, where are you?" she called. All I could do was stand there in the kitchen with my eyes staring out of the window. I was sweating, my hands were wet, and I felt sick to my stomach. My dad already made it plainly obvious for over eighteen years I wasn't the kind of son he wanted. Now, he was about to find out his only son was gay. I could've died right where I was standing.

I didn't know how this happened. I was so mad at myself. I saw my dad rush into the kitchen with a worried look on his face. I remember looking at my mother forcefully telling my father how I was going to hell. I blocked out the first part of their conversation and studied the hostile look on my mom's face. She was as red as a cherry lollipop.

I was mad at myself, because I thought I did a good job of hiding my personal things. I was wrong. I beat myself up because I inevitably told the world about me. I wasn't trying to. I was just trying to release some of the issues that seem to have weighed me down. There was no one I could've talked to abut everything that I was feeling. There was no one there for me. The only way I knew how to feel at peace with myself was to write it out. This proved to be a big mistake.

As I finally tuned into my parent's heated discussion about me, I turned to my dad. He looked at me and started shaking his head. There it was. The disappointment my father had labeled me with was finally justified in his eyes. I actually gave him the ammunition. He was searching for a reason to have disdain for me, and I ended up giving it to him. All I could do was look at my parent's go back and forth in conversation.

"He's gay, Michael," my mom said. "He doesn't even realize what kind of danger he's in," she added.

Here she goes again with all this danger and hellfire. I was completely over my mom's dramatics. If I were going to hell, at least I would've lived being who I wanted to be.

"Why do you want to be gay, Jeremy?" my dad asked. "I thought you liked girls?"

"I do, I did," I answered.

"But now you don't?" Dad replied.

"I'm confused dad. I thought I was one way, and now I'm a different way," I explained.

"I hope you know there's nothing even remotely positive about being a young gay male," dad stated. "Me and your mom don't know where we went wrong."

"Dad this has nothing to do with you and mom," I tried to explain. "This has to do with me and who I am. I'm tired of not being able to live a free life. I'm sick of it."

"A homosexual lifestyle won't make you free son," dad said.

"I can't even look at you right now, Jeremy!" Mom shouted. "You literally disgust me at this very second. All that we've done for you this is how you treat us."

My mom stormed out of the kitchen. I could tell she was upset. I recall a time when she pulled my sister and I into the living room one day, and started reading all of those scriptures about people sleeping with the same sex, and how we were never to engage in those kinds of things. My mom made it her mission to scare me with all of her teachings about how homosexuality is an abomination in the eyes of God, and how being attracted to the same sex is nothing but the devil working in people's minds. I understood all of that. But my mom was really beside herself because she probably felt all of her so-called hard work went down the drain. She still ended up with a gay son.

"Do you realize people are going to make fun of us," my dad said. "Having a gay child is nothing a parent brags about, or is proud of. I'm taking you to prayer meeting first thing tomorrow. We're going to pray this off you in the name of Jesus."

My dad removed himself and left me standing in the kitchen, my heart on the floor, my pride gone, and my brain working overtime. I was even more confused than ever. I at least thought my parent's would be a little bit more embracing than they were. They were both harsh and didn't even ask why, when, or how. I realized my parents weren't proud of me like they said they were. They were actually embarrassed of me.

The rest of the time I was home for the holidays until school started again, my mom and dad were cold and unpleasant to be around. I never thought I would see the day when my parent's would be mean to me intentionally. Parents shouldn't act like that towards their children, unless they turn out to be cold-blooded murderers, thieves, or chronic drug abusers. I wasn't any of those. I was just a normal teenage boy trying to figure out his sexuality.

It was my parents who made it a big deal. They are the ones who chose to treat me different. When my sister found out, she didn't care too much, she was accepting of my decision. She asked how mom and dad found out. I told her mom was cleaning my room and she found my journal, and read it. I don't know how many times I told her she didn't have to clean my room. She did it anyway.

My dad's prayer meeting wasn't at all a success. I still felt the same way, and having three to four spiritual leaders throwing holy water on me, and reading the Bible to me, wasn't exactly going to help me in the slightest.

I later burned my journal, returned to school, and tried to forget about my problems back at home. It had been almost a month and I hadn't received one phone call from my parent's or my sister. I came to the conclusion they were all upset with me. I had spoken to Dean a couple of times and told him what happened. He took it better than I thought he would. He just asked that I not try to like him, or try anything on him. I was offended, but glad he accepted me.

Two months went by, I had still heard nothing from home. I felt alone and isolated. I didn't know how to fix the situation. I wasn't doing well in school, and I had no one who could understand me. I didn't even have my parent's anymore. They hated me. What's the point of living I thought?

One night in March, I wrote a four page letter addressed to my family, and Dean. I stayed up all night thinking about life, and how much I had disappointed my parents. I wish I could've taken it all back. I wish I could've tried harder to fight what I was feeling. It was too late. Everyone would soon know that I was gay. I couldn't take it anymore. I didn't want the shame and guilt constantly on me. I didn't want to be alive with everyone knowing my secret, and it wasn't as if I could turn to my parent's either. I needed to end my problems. And I did!

I left my family. It started when the local news station announced that, "An eighteen year-old freshman hung himself from the community shower in his dorm!" A four-page letter rested on my bed explaining to my family why I decided to end my life. I felt alone.

A whole year had passed, and the news that a young college freshman had hung himself was still the talk of the town. No one could believe what had taken place, or why no one reached out to help me. Guilt soon followed my parents. Mom and dad lived in a state of disbelief, and my mom was in and out of the hospital being treated for depression, and minor breakdowns. She lost her mind when she found out that I committed suicide.

She blamed herself because my letter stated that all I wanted was acceptance from my parents, and to release all the pressures that were weighing me down. I needed a release. The only way I knew how, was to end my life. It took mom a little over a year to finally accept the fact that I was not coming back. She still struggles from time to time.

Mary looked intensely at a room full of grieving parents, and with tears streaming down her eyes as she stood by her chair in a circle, she held her hand over her heart.

"My son was a loving and caring person. I hate myself that I didn't accept my son for who he was," Mary stated. "I joined this grief group hoping to find comfort from others. But I haven't found that comfort. And I never will. I didn't let my son live his life. I even stopped talking to him for a period of time. That's not what a mother does," Mary explained.

"To all you parents who have children that need acceptance and understanding, give it to them. Accept your children for who they are. Don't let them go through this life thinking they're alone. One of the worst things in the world is to lose a child. I bear this hurt every day since Jeremy killed himself."

"His note stated that he was alone," Mary cried. "I didn't even get a chance to say good-bye, or talk it out with my son. I regret it every day. Life is too short and precious to lose a relationship with your child over petty matters."

"My husband and I, wish we could take back all the hurtful things we said to Jeremy. The fact that he was gay didn't mean he wasn't our son. We should have loved him in spite of his sexuality, accepted him, and we should have kept praying for God to deliver him from his lifestyle. I hate the choices I made. Love your children, love them, love them, no matter who they are!"

"It's too late for me, but we shouldn't let another child kill themselves because they're afraid, alone, confused, and feel as if they have no one to help them. I say this to any parent, it's not worth the pain. Just love your child." Mary cried.

I hate that my family has to endure life without me, but I just didn't feel like going through this life not being accepted. I forgot to live life for me. I let others influence my decisions, and I didn't love myself enough to push through the hurt. There's nothing good that came from my death, but I was able to get my release.

34

CHAPTER THREE
The War Within

The year was 1967, and my son had been sent to fight in the war. There was nothing I could do to stop it from happening. The military didn't care my son had plans to go to college to be a doctor, and heal people one day. Or, that he wanted a big family. The military didn't care that my son was one of the most brave, loving, and humble people I knew. The only thing circling around in their minds, was figuring out a way to end this death pool called *war*.

I grew up dirt poor in a little small town in Texas, where the population was no more than about three hundred people. I loved growing up in a small house with my mommy, daddy, and three sisters. At times we had no running water, no food, no light, or clean clothes to wear, but we all loved each other. If I took nothing else away from my childhood, I knew how to love family.

Despite my pleasant home life, I decided to marry when I was eighteen. I moved out of my parent's house, and took a job cooking, washing dishes, and cleaning an elderly couple's home. I met my husband Wade, in my junior year in high school. We fell in love right away. He made me feel like I was the most beautiful girl in the world. He showed me what 'true love' really was.

After Wade and I finished school, he told me he wanted to marry me. I thought he wanted to go to college or something, being that he was a smart boy. He told me he couldn't afford college and he had no interest in going. I told him, with as much smarts as he had in mathematics and science, he'd be a plum fool not to go to school.

Wade wanted to work as a plumber, or something. He wanted to fix stuff. Instead, he ended up taking a job working on infrastructure. Roads and rail network, stuff like that! Wade told me our life wasn't going to be easy, and he never promised me we were going to have lots of money. I understood that. I just loved Wade so much. He was all I wanted. Our lives were tough! We spent the first year of our marriage living in Wade's parent's house. They threw us in an attic-like room above the main level of the house, and the house itself only had two rooms. One of the rooms was for his mom and dad, and one for Wade's younger brother, who was a teenager.

I felt more love at my own home, and asked Wade, "Could we move in with my parents?" He would always tell me, "Hannah, baby, the man is supposed to take care of the wife. What would I look like, living with *your* parents?" In my eyes we couldn't do much worse, living with his parents wasn't showing much independence either. Nonetheless, I kept my mouth shut, and continued to live with his parents despite my uneasiness.

My dream, since I was a little girl, was to become a doctor. I wanted to make people better. I knew I had it in me to be a good doctor. I even tried to get enough money together to pay for a couple of classes at the local college, situated a couple of blocks away from our house. Just as soon as I got the money saved, a more pressing matter came up, and I would have to shovel the money over to Wade. I eventually gave up on my dream.

No matter how much we tried to save and put money away, we could never stay above water. It was always one thing or another. I learned fast the struggles of married life, and all the things my parents went through. I thought there was only one way to makes things better.

I became pregnant with my first child when I was nineteen. I was nervous and excited at the same time. I instantly loved my baby boy from the very first second I looked at him, and he looked at me. I didn't know how to be a mother. I didn't know the first thing about *being* a mother! Wade sure as heck didn't know anything about the role of being a father. We learned though! We learned what it meant to be good parents.

Before I knew it, I had another son two years later. My boys were my life! Nothing else seemed important to me. The only thing I wanted to do was be with my husband and children.

I had two beautiful boys, Joshua and John. I spent the years raising my boys the best way I knew how. I resorted to the same child raising tactics my parents used to raise me. I loved being a mother. There was no other job I wanted to do. I only wish I could have had more children, but I became gravely ill after John's birth, and the doctor advised me to quit having babies. I listened, and spent as much time as I could with my children.

Life doesn't teach someone how to be a parent! Being a good parent comes with time and patience. My sons turned out to be two humble young men. Joshua was just like Wade, adventurous, ambitious, and outgoing. John is more like me, reserved, and bookish.

One thing Wade and I instilled in our two sons was to love each other unconditionally, and to form a close bond. I wanted my children to be close, and not let anything tear them apart. I guess family was important to me for some reason. Maybe it's because of my own upbringing, and how I was taught to love my sisters.

When Joshua and John entered their early teen years, I thought life was only going to get better. Never did I think I was going to have to endure one of the worst tragedies in the world. I would often think to myself how lucky I was to have such a loving, caring, and close family. It seemed as if nothing in the world could tear us apart. I lived a humble, thankful life.

It had been three years since my life was disturbed and interrupted. I'll never forget that hot July afternoon when I was in the store, and Ms. Henson stopped me, to talk about her son who was getting ready to join the Army. Thinking back to our conversation, I didn't mean to be so cold to her, but I wasn't caring. I figured there wasn't much for her to do as a mother, if her son wanted to join the Army. All I could think about was my sons weren't going to do something as foolish. Joshua had plans to become a doctor, and John wanted to work on airplanes.

Ms. Henson cried in front of me that day in the store, because she felt her son was going to die if he went on to join the Army. I felt sorry for her, but only to a certain extent. I didn't know how to react to her. As long as my sons weren't going, it really didn't matter to me that other people's children were going into the Army.

I did my best to give Ms. Henson some hope. After she cried to me that day in the store, I had literally forgotten all about our conversation. It wasn't until 1965, that I realized I wasn't going to be able to forget about the military, like I had done with Ms. Henson. 1965 was a bad year! As the Vietnam War became heated, more than 100,000 U.S. troops were fighting there, and it seemed there was no end to this war.

Families in our neighborhood didn't understand this war, and what we were fighting for. Everyone who had sons grew more afraid that any day their son would be called off to go to combat. I wasn't fearful at first, because there was no way Joshua was going anywhere. I wouldn't allow my mind to even go to that place.

Joshua was an average height, skinny, brown haired, eighteen year-old, who knew nothing about war. I knew my son would never make it in war. There was no way Joshua could survive this violence that was taking place in our world.

What I thought to be true turned out to be a lie. When mothers on my street were telling me how their sons were being shipped off, I couldn't believe it. The government was getting too close to my family. I saw mothers and father become angry and depressed. Wade told me not to worry that even if Joshua were called, he wouldn't be able to pass the physical tests and all that stuff. The military didn't want some five foot eight, one hundred and forty-pound kid, fighting in their war.

Wade gave me a little hope for a short time, but I just felt something inside of me that wouldn't allow my mind to be at total ease. Something kept torturing me. Deep down I knew Joshua was going to war. I knew my son was going to go fight in Vietnam, and there wasn't a thing I could do about it.

It was on a Wednesday afternoon in October 1966, that Wade strolled in the house quiet, and looking vexed. He walked through the living room searching for something. I stopped what I was doing and approached him.

"Wade, what's going on?" I asked, "Who are you looking for?"

"Where's Joshua?" Wade asked.

"He has gone to the store, he should be back any minute," I replied.

Wade dropped an envelope on the dull brown rectangular coffee table. I inched closer and closer to try to get a peek to whom the letter was addressed. I couldn't quite make out where the letter was from, but it looked important and official. Then, all I could see was Joshua's name on the envelope. Wade took a seat on the coach reaching out to pick up the letter. He didn't want me to see it. What he didn't know; and what he was trying to protect me from, I already had known what it was, and I now knew it was a letter telling Joshua he was needed to serve. All I needed was Joshua to get home, open the letter, and confirm my fears.

Thirty minutes passed before Joshua returned home from the store. He walked in smiling, with an arm full of groceries as if he didn't have a care in the world. I directed his attention to his father, and I signaled that his dad had something important to give him.

"Son," Wade exclaimed.

"Yes sir?"

"Come on in here and open this letter," Wade instructed.

Joshua handed the groceries to me, and calmly walked over to Wade in the living room. My heart began to pound at an irregular beat. I turned red, and I could no longer feel my legs. I was more scared for Joshua than he was himself.

Joshua sat down next to Wade and swiftly opened the letter. As he threw down the envelope, he began to read the letter as if he was under some kind of time constraint.

"What's the letter about son?" I inquired.

Joshua didn't answer me the first time. He glanced over the letter once more and tears filled his eyes. At that moment, I had my confirmation. My oldest son was leaving for Vietnam!

After Wade and I sat and consoled Joshua for almost the entire night, I couldn't quite understand how I was feeling about all of this. I didn't know whether or not to be upset, angry, or grateful. Naturally I was angry and upset, but there was a part of me that didn't know if I should be proud of the fact that my son was going to go protect our country. I tried to experience the pride and gratefulness, but those emotions would always be overshadowed by bitterness, rage, and disgust. I couldn't believe out of all the young men in this world, my son was chosen.

This was one battle I was going to lose. I couldn't be the mommy to run and save the day. I couldn't threaten anyone. I couldn't protect Joshua from this mean world. I felt helpless. My mind was in conflict, and I produced my own war. I had a war within myself, because I didn't know for the first time as a mother, how to help one of my children. I didn't have an answer to fix this problem, it was too big . . . and it bothered me.

My son was hurting and there was absolutely nothing I could do to help him. Joshua was to report for training in December, and he would be leaving sometime in the winter of next year. I held on to Wade's words of hope that maybe Joshua wouldn't be healthy enough, but it didn't help. Joshua turned out to be one hundred percent healthy. He was in good shape, and the doctor couldn't find anything that would exclude him from going to war. There was nothing else left for me to hope for! Come January 1967, my son was leaving.

The next couple of months raced by, and I spent every waking moment with Joshua. We did more things as family than ever before. I didn't want the bond between Joshua and John to be broken either, so I made sure he and his brother spent all the time they could together.

I remember at the end of December, writing a letter to the Governor of Alabama. I wrote a six-page letter to the Governor's Office, on why my son shouldn't go to war. I wrote about Joshua's plans, and I talked about his family life and his friends. I didn't tell Wade, because I knew he would try and stop me. I mailed the letter, but I never got a response. I thought the Governor could pull some strings and help my son get out of having to go. It didn't help. Joshua was already away at training.

One cold, but sunny day, I was pulling up in the driveway, when I saw Ms. Henson sitting on the grass reading a letter. I waved and spoke to her, but she didn't reply. It wasn't like her not to respond to me. I knew something was wrong. I closed my car door, put my purse on my arm and headed over to Ms. Henson's house.

"Hello, Ella," I said.

Ms. Henson looked up at me with a single tear rolling down the left side of her face.

"He's gone," she said.

"What do you mean?" I asked.

"Toby already left for the military," she explained.

At this point, I knew exactly how Ms. Henson felt. This time I wasn't so quick to brush her off. I sat down on the grass right next to Ms. Henson and let her explain to me all her hurt and frustration. I could relate to dear old Ella.

"Joshua is being sent too, Ella," I told her.

"Your baby is leaving too?" Ms. Henson asked.

"He should be leaving sometime this month," I said.

"You're a lot more calm than I thought you would be, Hannah," she said.

"Everything is inside me right now. I'm trying not to think about it too much. I'm still hoping to get a last minute miracle," I replied.

It was all too real for me. I knew the dangers of war, and the fact that more troops were being called for and sent out, was not a good sign. It told me that they're all dying over there. What if Joshua died? What if I lost one of my children? That thought scared me. I was trying to move past those thoughts, and I didn't want to think about the negative.

I stayed with Ms. Henson until the evening time that day. We shared stories about our lives, and what we wanted to do when our sons came home from the war. I asked Ella why her son wanted to go and join the military. She couldn't give me a clear answer. All I know is, she said it was something Toby had wanted to do for a long time.

In my mind I couldn't understand why someone would go voluntarily to fight in a war? A war in which the government themselves were confused about. Why, I thought, would someone give up their freedom willingly? I couldn't understand. Maybe it wasn't for me to understand. Maybe it wasn't any of my business to be worrying about someone else's child, when mine was getting ready to head to a war zone.

Come the end of January 1967, it was time for Joshua to leave, and go over to Vietnam. I didn't fall sleep at all the night before. I stayed awake crying my heart out. I couldn't find rest, and my mind and body wouldn't let me. I kept thinking about all the bad things that could go wrong over there, and all the terrible things that were going to happen.

Before Joshua left, we all gathered in the living room for a prayer. I held on to Joshua's hand tightly, and didn't close my eyes as Wade was praying. I kept looking at both my sons. Fear, anger, and hurt ran throughout my body. More so fear. Wade prayed longer and harder than ever before. By the time that prayer was over and done with, we were all crying. We hugged each other tightly, and repeatedly said we loved each other.

I couldn't let go that day. I just couldn't. We all rode in the car as Wade took Joshua to his destination for departure. We got out and hugged some more. I fell to pieces when I saw Joshua and John hugging each other tightly, as if they never were going to see each other anymore. I couldn't help but become flooded with emotion.

As we pulled away from Joshua, my eyes never left him. I watched him standing there dressed in his uniform, looking back at me. I wondered if he wanted me to rescue him, or if he wanted to help me be at ease. I didn't know what he wanted. I know I wanted him to come back home! He wasn't even out of the country yet, and I wanted him back already.

As the months passed, more and more people became outraged at the duration of this war. Families were losing loved ones, more young men were being shipped off, and people were growing restless and confused. People wanted to do something, but didn't know what to do. I remember reading about a small group of college students in Washington, organizing a march, with petitions of signatures to give to President Johnson, to tell him to put a stop to this war.

I knew their efforts would be in vain. There was no stopping this war. Young men were dying daily over in Vietnam, and there was nothing anyone here in the United States could do to stop it. Our voices weren't loud enough, and important enough. Our voices here in the United States weren't reasonable enough to make peace. The only thing we could do as Americans was wait. Wait to get bad news . . . wait to see if our loved ones were coming home. Only thing we could do was *wait*.

More months passed by, and still no word from Joshua. I don't even know if any of the letters I wrote to him even reached him. I went to work day after day, pretending as if I wasn't scared out of my mind. I was however. I couldn't even think straight half the darn time. Nothing we did as a family felt right anymore, because we were missing somebody.

I began to notice all of the turmoil taking place here in the United States during this time. It was hard to describe the absolute chaos here in Alabama. People tense from the war, blacks being treated like the scum of the earth. I tell you, I ain't never seen someone being hated because of their skin color. I thought to myself, how darn ignorant do you have to be, to hate someone over a skin pigmentation? I thought that was about the most brainless thing in the world. Nothing seemed to get better either.

Late one night, I stayed up with Wade. We sat in the dark, with the windows raised and wet towels over our heads and neck. July heat in Alabama will just about kill you. It was on this July night that I began to live my life in fear. Wade looked at me and told me something frightening.

"That there Congress is bull-headed and stiff-necked! They got them boys over there fighting in a war that should have ended a long time ago," he exclaimed.

"We'll be mighty lucky if we ever saw Joshua again," Wade said.

I knew what he meant, and I couldn't stop being afraid from them on.

It was in late August when we finally heard from Joshua. I rushed home with the letter in my hand and read it aloud to Wade and John. He had written a three-page letter telling us what it was like over there, and how he was doing. Through his letter he sounded okay, and that's what I was glad about. As long as he was alive and okay, that's all I needed to know.

After that, only one more letter came from Joshua. By the end of September, I didn't hear from Joshua anymore. I cried myself to sleep so many nights with Wade's arms wrapped around me. I tried to be strong for John's sake, but it was no use. I couldn't be the kind of mother I wanted to be because I had one son missing. Life was never going to be the same ever again. The thing that hurt the most was that Wade was right, we didn't know if we were ever going to see Joshua again.

I was a mix of emotions, and I began to be at war with myself again. I went over in my mind all the things that I could have, and should have, done differently for Joshua. I beat myself up all night reflecting how I could have made life better for him. He was a much stronger person than I gave him credit for. In both of his letters, he never once complained about being over in Vietnam.

We made it through our first Thanksgiving without Joshua, and was getting ready to prepare for Christmas without him as well. I had never experienced this kind of separation from one of my children. It was hard to live my life knowing that I had a son who was in the war. Nothing I did seemed to ease the hurt and pain. Nothing anyone did could help me stop thing about the bad things of war. I was okay, just as long as Joshua was okay.

"When is Josh coming home mom?" John asked me.

"Johnny, I'm not quite sure," I answered. "It could be a while before we see him again."

"Yeah, but how long is that?" he insisted.

"Well I don't know, son. Why don't you write him, son," I said.

"You sure that's a good idea?" he asked.

"Your brother would love that."

I could tell that Johnny was just as scared as I was, when he asked me when Joshua was coming home. I didn't want to lie to him, and tell him it would be soon, or make him believe I knew a date. The best thing for me to do was be honest and tell him that I didn't know. It was hard for me to give him false hope, especially since I didn't know myself.

We made it through Christmas too, that year, and I was beginning to accept this as a way of life right now. I was a mother who had a son at war. I had a son at war, and I couldn't do anything to bring him home. All I wanted was a safe return home for my son.

I would catch Wade crying at times when he thought he was alone. I would see him, and comfort him the best I could. It was unfair. Why couldn't my son have remained here? Why did he have to be the one to leave? I never understood what Wade and I did so bad that would cause us to have to go through this kind of pain, of having a child at war.

In keeping up with the latest on the Vietnam War, it seemed things were getting a lot worse, not better. Every time I turned around, someone else's child was being shipped off. I didn't care about anyone else's son. Only Joshua mattered to me. When I prayed at night, it wasn't for Ms. Henson's son, or for the Brown family across the street, or for the Smith family, who had two sons fighting. My prayer was for Joshua alone. As selfish as it seemed, I didn't care. Don't get me wrong, I didn't want anything bad to happen to anyone else's child, but my son, *my son* was the only one who mattered.

I would soon learn all the good my prayers didn't do. My prayers went unheard. Maybe it was because I was selfish, and didn't pray for anyone else's son? I'll never know. However, come the beginning of 1968, I saw Ms. Henson getting out of the car with a couple of grocery bags in her hand trying to rush to her front door.

"Hi, Ella!" I yelled.

"Hello, darling!" she yelled back.

"Where are you off to in such a hurry?" I asked.

With the biggest smile on her face she said, "I got to go make my son his favorite soup!"

"What do you mean Ella?" I was confused. Toby was at war, why would she be making him soup. I thought the poor lady was losing it.

"I didn't tell you, sweetie?" Ms. Henson said.

"What?" I asked.

"Toby was discharged. He can't fight anymore!"

I stopped what I was doing and rushed over to see what she was talking about.

"How is he?" I inquired.

"Come on in, Hannah, and see him for yourself," she said.

I walked in with Ms. Henson, and looked around in her house as if I had never seen her blue walls, shiny hardwood floors, and her hundreds of fake houseplants. I followed right behind her into Toby's room.

There he was sitting in a wheelchair with one leg and one arm missing. I could barely look at him, because I didn't know if I was making him feel uncomfortable by staring at him.

"Hi, Toby," I cringed.

"Hello," he replied.

I gave him a hug, and turned and gave Ms. Henson a hug as well. I knew how she felt, I made that connection with her instantly. Even though her son was missing a leg and an arm, and was in a wheelchair, she was just glad that he wasn't killed, and that he was home. Not to mention, he was at home, and not in some hospital. She was thankful for the small things.

"Thank you for protecting us," I told Toby. "It takes a special man to be able to go through what you've gone through. I'm glad your home now."

Ms. Henson left Toby and I talking, while she started on his soup. Toby was telling me about his time in Vietnam, and what it was like. I was trying to paint myself a clear picture of just what it was that Joshua was going through. I thought maybe I could somehow feel closer to him, but it wasn't working for me.

I just knew that Joshua was going to come back home to me. If Ms. Henson's son came back to her, Joshua was sure to come back to me. The only thing I had trouble dealing with, was trying to accept if he was disfigured, or had no arms or legs. I felt stupid because I didn't know if I was going to love him the same. I know it's selfish and trivial, but I didn't know how we could be the same family as before if Joshua had body parts missing. I didn't want my son to have to go through life if he wasn't complete. It really bothered me.

After spending the evening with Ms. Henson and her son I had a good feeling that Joshua was going to come home. I had to forget about what he was going to look like. I couldn't focus on that anymore. I just wanted him home safely. Besides, Wade told me, our family was never gonna be the same again anyhow. Once a young boy goes off to war, his mind will be different. He isn't the same anymore. In a way, what Wade was saying made perfect sense, but there had to be something in Joshua that would remind me of how he once was.

It was now March of 1968, and I still hadn't heard anything from Joshua. All my letters went unanswered. I didn't know if he was alive, dead, or sick. I constantly wondered if he was coming home or not. All sorts of crazy things ran through my head all at once. It was tough trying to live like a normal family and carry on as if we didn't have anything to worry about. We did have something to worry about! We hadn't heard from Joshua in months. I became worried. What if he was dead? What if he was just another body thrown away somewhere, and no one can give an account of where he laid. I fell into a deep depression.

I couldn't stand to wake-up in the morning anymore! Everything that mattered to me wasn't important anymore. Nothing I did was a hundred percent anymore. I wasn't even a good mother to John, or a good wife to Wade. I became consumed with the weight of anxiety, anger, rage and depression. I didn't know what to do. There was nothing I *could* do.

Waiting and not knowing is what killed me the most. At least if he was alive, I knew he was fighting hard and there was a chance that he would be coming home. If he had died, I would know not to expect him, and I would know he's in Heaven. However, I didn't have that peace of mind. I was alive, but dead inside. I couldn't bring myself to focus on anything anymore. I just wanted some news. I wanted to know something about my son. How could this happen to me? Why would God be so cruel to me, and not let me know what happened to my son? I had all these questions, and no one had the answers.

Come late April in 1968, during a thunderstorm, I had the front house door open and the screen door was closed. I had been cleaning the house that day. It had been four months into the New Year and still no word from my son. I had given up on worrying. I figured he was just too busy. I thought if something was really wrong, I would have been notified or something.

On that day, that dreadful, cloudy, rainy day, I received the answer to all of my questions. I received the information I had been waiting six plus months, to hear. The news came through a gentlemen dressed in a green uniform with a tie. As I saw him approach the screen door, my heart sank. There was no need for him to tell me the news. I already knew! My son was dead. My nineteen year-old son was dead!

I listened to the gentlemen, while I stood in the doorway gazing outside looking at the rain hit the street drop after drop. Wade came up behind me and caught me, before I hit the ground. I could barely breathe. It was like the life had been taken out of me. I felt myself trying to catch my breath, but I couldn't. I was trying to gasp for air as I cried and cried. I remember tears flowing down my face, but it was a silent cry. I didn't yell, release angry words, or fly into a rage. I sat on the floor crying, with my husband's arms draped around me.

I guess I expected it, when I hadn't heard from Joshua since his last letter over seven months ago. I knew then something was wrong. Still, just having to hear the news that your son had been killed in combat would be tough on any parent. Wade tried his best to be strong, but he couldn't hold back his tears either.

We weren't as lucky as Ms. Henson to have our son come home. We had to deal with trying to cope with the loss of a child. What made me even more distraught was hearing that Joshua had died months earlier, but they didn't give us the information until now.

I had so much hate in my heart for the world, I couldn't even see straight. I was angry that the Government and the military took my son away from me. He should have never been sent to go and fight in a war at his age. What lamebrain would send young, eighteen and nineteen year-olds to go fight? I didn't understand. I didn't want to understand either. I was too angry to try to understand stupidity.

After Wade and I told John about his brother, he took it hard. He couldn't believe his older brother was gone. Life in our house was pretty stale, and bitter for a long time. We didn't celebrate any holidays for a while. Joshua wasn't here with us. We all felt the same way.

After a year had passed, and Joshua was buried, I finally decided to take some of his stuff away. The things John didn't want, we gave it away. It was too hard to look at his posters, books, and clothes. It was just easier to get rid of it. The things of value like his drawings, and uniform top, I tucked away in my closet.

There's not a day that goes by that I don't think about Joshua and how much I want him back. The only thing I can say that I'm glad about is that I know where he is. I know my son is in Heaven. It was tearing me up even more not knowing anything, but I know now.

It's been almost three years since Joshua died in Vietnam, and this war is still raging. I don't know if this war is ever going to end. No one wants to make peace. It's down-right shameful that we have to solve things through violence and retaliation. At least the black's aint got to be separated from everyone else now. A law of equality helped the black's, it's time to get some kind of agreement to end this war. Too many people are dying. Too many *innocent* people are dying.

It hurts too much to see where Joshua lays. I only go to his grave on his birthday. I never thought in a million years my son would be dead before Wade and I. I don't know if I'm more upset at the fact that Joshua died violently, or that it took months to let us know he was gone. I get livid every time I think about my son's life being taken away.

I'm still constantly at war with myself because I'm mad that I wasn't able to do anything to stop this from happening. There was nothing I could do to help Joshua. He didn't want to go, he wasn't ready. He was forced to give-up his life.

I suppose I should be happy that he served his country and that he was protecting us for a short while, but it's easier for me to hang on to the negative things about his death. If I focus on the positive, then I would accept Joshua's death, and I'm not ready too. It's been three years and I'm not ready to let go.

I know it's time for me to let go, and realize that Joshua is not coming back. Death is forever! I cry when I think about forever, and never getting to see his face again. Nothing in the world will bring my son back to me. I've found that my grief is different from Wade's and John's. It helps Wade to be around Joshua's things. I can't do that. I'll burst into tears if I see something that reminds me of my son.

I deal with my grief by spending more time with John, and staying away from Joshua's grave. When I'm not around things that remind me of him, I can manage to get through this life easier. Don't get me wrong, I'm not trying to forget about Joshua, but until more time has passed by, I'm not strong enough yet.

I hold Joshua in my heart, and I often reflect on his smiling face and the kind of young man he was. I still struggle with my grief. Who knows if I'll ever be over the grieving process? I do know that he's missed terribly, and I can't wait to see him in Heaven.

CHAPTER FOUR
A Driver Unaware

Misty was the kind of girl who had confidence, but she was a humble, caring girl. She was trustworthy, dependable, and worked hard at whatever she put her mind to. Misty wasn't the average teenager, who thrived on being rebellious, taking risks, and living a life dedicated to partying.

Misty had a loving father, who spent his life trying to give Misty the best in life. He worked hard day and night, sacrificing time with Misty so that he could provide her with a modest upbringing. Misty's mother left her and her father when Misty was five years old. Her mother felt trapped in a family lifestyle she didn't want. She had told Misty's father that being a mother and wife wasn't something she wanted to do anymore. She left early one morning never to return.

When Misty was seven years old, she stopped asking about her mother, and when she was going to return. It was as if Misty had erased her mother from her mind completely. She had to endure a childhood without a female figure in her life. There wasn't anyone to teach Misty how to become a woman, or how to have the kind of confidence it takes to love one's self. All of Misty's teachings about beauty and life came from her father.

Greg was Misty's father, he helped her grow-up to become self-sufficient, and to be valiant. Greg played the role of both mother and father. Misty was Greg's second child. He had a son from a previous marriage, but rarely did he ever see his son. As a result, Misty grew up alone and without any siblings. However, Misty didn't grow up inadequate, or bothered by the fact that she was the only child.

When Misty was ten years old, Greg remarried. In a backyard ceremony, Greg married an old flame he once knew from a town he used to live in. Her name was Karen. Karen tried to be a mother to Misty, but Misty wasn't too accepting of her. Karen tried her best, but between her laziness, her controlling nature over Greg, mixed with her overbearing tendencies toward Misty, the marriage didn't last long. Shortly after their one-year anniversary, the marriage was over.

After Greg's second failed marriage, he never pursued another relationship. Greg lived his life with his daughter. Greg had the greatest love for Misty. There was nothing that Misty could do to shake her father's love. Now that Misty was seventeen, and seemingly had her own life to live, she still maintained an unbroken relationship with her father. Misty tried her best to please her father, he was the one person she tried to make happy. Being that Misty was a teenager, and supposed to be living a feral life, she was different. Misty was responsible, held a part-time job as a cashier at a local grocery store, and achieved superior grades. Misty was every parent's dream child.

The comfortable home life Greg had known for quite some time was interrupted one cold Sunday night in January. Misty was a senior in high school, and about to graduate in four months. Her whole life was right in front of her. She had plans to go to college and eventually become an elementary school teacher. However, all her dreams would be cut short.

Working late shifts at the grocery store was normal for Misty on the weekends. Greg expected her to be late on Saturdays and Sundays, and he would always wait for her by the front door, looking out through the blinds to make sure she was okay. Once she walked in the house and said, "I'm fine dad, go to sleep now." Greg would head off to bed. Misty would always come home no later than one o'clock in the morning.

The drive from the grocery store to Misty's house was no more than ten minutes. There was no reason for Greg to pick her up at night, and on weekends, because Misty told her father she wanted her independence. Greg didn't go against his daughter's wishes. Against what he believed, he allowed Misty to keep her part-time job.

On this particular night in January, Misty was off work at twelve thirty in the morning, and she knew she would be getting home earlier than she had been previously. Once Misty started driving down the street, she noticed bright lights following behind her, extremely close. She began to speed up the car, but as Misty increased her speed, so did the other car. Misty even slowed down, but no matter what she tried, the car matched exactly what she did.

Although Misty wasn't scared at this point, she was a young inexperienced driver, and didn't realize that she should've pulled over and let the other car go. Yet, she didn't do that. Misty turned down her radio and took her cell phone in her hand, as if she was getting ready to call someone. She kept her phone in one hand, and drove with the other. Misty was only five minutes away from her home, and felt as if she wasn't in any danger.

As Misty was getting ready to cross the bridge that leads into her neighborhood, her car was side-swiped on the left, and hit the ramp on the right. As her car hit the ramp, the small black sports car twirls around, hits Misty's car, and crushes the driver's side door completely in. Misty was killed instantly. The driver of the other car struggled to release himself from his car, and as he does his vehicle sparks a small fire. Misty's lifeless body is trapped inside her car, with no chance of being removed without serious help. Even if Misty were still alive, it would've been too late for her. Had she needed critical medical attention, she wouldn't have received it for at least thirty minutes.

The driver of the other car is unable to release himself. He quits trying to remove himself, and sits in the wrecked car looking dazed. The small fire that had been kindled earlier soon died off. There was Misty's red four-door car, caved in on all sides, windows shattered, and Misty was trapped in her seatbelt.

It was past one o'clock in the morning and Misty wasn't home. Greg automatically knew something was wrong. He knew his daughter, and knew she was always in the house with a minute to spare. Greg feared the worst, and called Misty's cell phone. She didn't answer, and her phone continued to ring. Even though Greg was terrified out of his mind, he still had a little hope that nothing was seriously wrong. He didn't call the police; instead, he put on some jeans, a tee shirt, grabbed a coat, and got in his car and went looking for his daughter. There was no need to travel to her job, for as soon as Greg was ready to cross the bridge, he didn't get very far. He saw the street covered with police cars, fire trucks, an ambulance and emergency technicians. It was a horrific scene.

After getting a quick look at the scene, Greg looked around trying to see if Misty was involved. He spotted her red car. Even though the car was damaged beyond recognition he knew it was Misty. His tears streamed down his face faster than he could get out of the car. He swiftly opened his door, dropping his cell phone on the cold, sullied street, and without turning off the engine or closing his door, he tried to rush over to Misty's car.

Greg couldn't get to Misty. Police were standing all around this gruesome scene keeping everyone away who wasn't a part of law enforcement, or a part of the Fire Department. Greg tried to push his way through. He yelled, kicked, and fought all he knew how to get to his daughter, but he was blocked. No one would let him pass. Greg found himself pleading to anyone, and everyone, hoping they would allow him to see Misty.

"Please officer, that's my daughter!" Greg cried.

"Sir, you don't know that," the officer said.

As Greg continued to cry, he begged the officer to just let him see if Misty was inside the car.

"Please sir, please, please, please. My daughter is in that car!" Greg proclaimed.

"We can't let you sir this a police matter now," the officer stated.

"Officer, I need to see her. I need to know if it's her in that car," Greg said.

"I need you to wait back behind this line right now!" the officer yelled.

Greg couldn't contain himself. He was screaming, pleading, and arguing with the police officer, who threatened to arrest him if he didn't move behind the yellow line. Greg tried to find a way to get closer to see if it *was* Misty in the car. There was no reasoning with Greg, he was determined to see if that was definitely his daughter.

Going against what the officer told him, Greg broke through the tape and ran to the damaged red car as if he was running for his life. When he approached the car and looked in, he couldn't recognize anything in the car. The car was severely wrecked, and it was going to be a challenging task trying to get Misty out. Greg moved around to the back of the car to see if he could identify the license plate. He wasn't successful.

Greg made his way around to the front of the car and peered in, trying to see through the shattered window. Then he saw the identity of the person stuck in the car. He saw Misty's brown hair tossed to one side, with her forehead bloody and bruised. His final confirmation came when he same her grocery store shirt, with her nametag displaying the name, MISTY. Greg lost it at that point.

Before he could even find the strength to gather his emotions, multiple police officers ran up behind him, and wrestled Greg to the ground. One officer grabbed Greg's legs, another pulled his hands behind his back, and the other officer put his knee on Greg's head. Greg was buried underneath a host of cops, lying still on his stomach. He didn't fight back. He was sprawled there trying to get the picture of his daughter's lifeless, bloody body out of his head.

The officer that night didn't care that it was Greg's daughter in the car. They were upset that he had disobeyed their orders. As a result, they arrested Greg that night. He was put in handcuffs, and taken in a police car to the Police Station.

Greg wasn't put in a cell, he was left in handcuffs sitting in an interrogation room, waiting. He was left waiting for someone to come in and release him. It would be another forty-five minutes before anyone came to see about Greg that night. An older, gray-headed gentleman, walked into the square windowless room, took a seat and stared at Greg for a couple of seconds.

"Hello, Mr. Harper, how are you this evening?" the officer asked.

Greg sat in silence looking at the brick wall. There wasn't an expression, or any emotion, that the gentlemen could make out on Greg's face. He was stone-faced and cold as ice.

"You're not in trouble, sir, and you're getting ready to be released," the officer said.

Greg turned around, and looked at the officer. "I'm not spending the night in jail?" Greg asked.

"No sir, the officers were just trying to detain you because you were interrupting a police matter. You were standing right in the middle of an investigation," the officer explained.

"Do I even need to ask, or do you have the information I need?" Greg inquired.

"I think I know what you're talking about, and yes I do," the officer said.

Greg prepared himself and closed his eyes.

"The name of the girl in the car was Mystique Harper," the officer explained.

Greg immediately began to weep. He put his head down on the table and allowed his tears to hit the ground.

"We got her name from her license," the officer stated.

"How did you get her out of the car?" Greg asked.

"They had to cut out the roof and pull her out," the officer said.

"I can't believe it," Greg cried. "How could this have happened to my sweet daughter? I don't understand this," he cried continuously.

The officer paused for a second and looked at Greg.

"Drunk driver," he stated officially.

Greg looked confused. He didn't ask any more questions, he put his head back on the table and continued to cry. The officer tried to talk to Greg about teen drunk driving, and gave him some facts and statistics. After about fifteen minutes of explaining about drunk driving, he looked up from his papers and turned to Greg.

"We need you to come tomorrow to identify the body, Mr. Harper."

"You said it was her, right? You said you knew it was her from her license," Greg protested.

"We still need a positive identification from a relative," the officer said. "We'll give you a call tomorrow morning and let you know where to go Mr. Harper, please go home and try to get some rest . . . if you can." The officer offered to take Greg home, but Greg refused and called his sister to come and pick him up.

It was almost five o'clock in the morning, and while sitting in his sister's car, Greg replayed over and over again what had just taken place a few hours ago. He couldn't comprehend that just that morning he was talking with his daughter, then he was on his way to bed waiting up for her, and now she was dead! His beautiful seventeen year-old daughter had died on this cold January night. There was no way he could believe it.

When Greg's sister Cheryl pulled up into the driveway, Greg asked if he could be allowed to sit in her car for a few minutes, he wasn't quite ready to go inside just yet. He handed the keys to Cheryl, and let her go inside the small, one-story house. It seemed as if Greg had stayed out in his sister's car for an eternity. However, his sister didn't mind. She knew he had just lost his child, so she didn't plan to leave his side for the rest of the night.

When Greg eventually came in, he slept on the couch and his sister slept on a dusty red reclining chair plopped right in the living room next to the coffee table. Greg was only able to sleep a few hours before he received a call from the police, asking him to come in at nine a.m. sharp that morning, and then the officers wanted to speak with him. Greg didn't shower that morning. He took off his clothes, put on some wrinkled jeans, and a blue collar long-sleeved shirt. He just slicked his hair back with water and headed downstairs. Cheryl fixed Greg some breakfast, and then they left.

Cheryl tried to hold a conversation with Greg, but he was short with his answers. Greg's mind was somewhere else. It was as if he wasn't present. His body was here, but he was somewhere completely different. Cheryl called her husband, and told him to meet her at the police station in fifteen minutes. Cheryl's husband was a policeman, and she wanted him to be with the other cops when they revealed to Greg what had actually happened last night.

When they arrived to identify the body, Cheryl asked Greg, did he want her to come in with him. "Do you need me?" Cheryl asked.

"No. I'm just going to go in there, and come right back out," Greg replied.

"As long as you're sure, Greg," Cheryl stated.

"I am. You've done enough, and I love you for it," Greg said.

He closed the car door, and walked up to the door of the building. When he entered, he could smell a strong, unclean scent, but he expected that. He approached a man waiting next to a door with a clipboard in his hand. Greg stepped up to him, introduced himself, and told the man he was here to identify his daughter. The man asked Greg for his daughter's name, looked down at his clipboard, and told Greg to follow him.

Greg walked through one long and dim hallway, very uneasily. He still had a drop of hope that maybe it wasn't his daughter. Deep inside his heart, he knew it *was* Misty. Besides, Misty didn't answer her cell phone last night, she didn't come home last night, Greg had seen the wrecked red car, and most importantly, he saw for himself, her long brown hair. There was no chance he could convince himself he had dreamed all of that. He knew the image he was about to see would be ingrained in his mind forever. The easy thing to do would be to let his sister go in and identify the body. Greg couldn't do that to himself. He had to have confirmation, and he needed to see his daughter one more time for himself.

Greg entered the room with the man. The man looked once more at his clipboard, and then went to a wall. He carefully pulled down what looked like a bed. He pulled it down and stretched it out. On this table was a body with a white sheet draped on top of it. The man checked his clipboard one last time, and checked the steel table that held the body.

"Are you ready, sir?" the man asked.

Greg stared at the sheet for a moment, and then looked at the man holding the clipboard.

"Yes I am," Greg answered.

The man stated that all he needed was a quick identification to determine if this, indeed, was the body of Mystique Harper. Greg nodded that he understood. The man swiftly pulled back the white sheet. Greg stood there with his palms and forehead sweating. The sheet lay on top of the young girl's chest. Greg leaned in and saw a brunette female, with spots of blood from the top of her head, down to her neck. Her hair had been cut to her ears, and every inch of her body displayed some sort of thick abrasions. Greg hardly recognized who she was. However, he knew enough to identify that indeed this was his daughter lying on the table. In one swift nod, yes, and with tears flowing down his face, he told the man that it was Misty.

Greg questioned the man about why his daughter's hair had been cut? The man said that he wasn't really sure, but when she was trapped in the car, one of the things that they had to do was cut her hair. Greg couldn't look at her any more, and requested that the man put the sheet back over his daughter.

Greg and the man discussed the funeral home in which Misty was to be taken to. Greg was informed of certain things he needed to do for the Mortuary. After Greg told the man which funeral home he wanted, the man stated that they would be on their way shortly. Greg said he had somewhere else he had to be.

Greg walked to the car, still dazed as to what was going on. He was trying his hardest to accept what was taking place. He didn't understand it. When he got in the car he didn't look at Cheryl.

"Are you okay, Greg?" Cheryl asked.

"I still just can't believe this. One minute I'm talking to my daughter before she goes to work, and the next minute she's dead," Greg cried.

"I'm so sorry, Greg. I'm so sorry," Cheryl said. She leaned in to hug Greg, and he fell into her arms in despair. She hugged him tightly, not wanting to let him go.

"It just happened so fast. I don't understand this," Greg sobbed.

"I don't understand either," Cheryl replied.

As Cheryl drove him to the police station, Greg stared out of the window trying to compose himself. He dried his eyes, and in a matter of seconds his sadness and confusion turned into hatred, rage, and anger. Greg wanted to know exactly what had happened, and who was responsible for his daughter's accident. Cheryl couldn't drive fast enough. Greg had to know who the person was that caused him to lose Misty. He wanted answers.

Cheryl pulled into the parking lot of the police station, and before she could turn off the engine, Greg opened the door, got out, slammed it shut, and raced inside the police station. Cheryl grew worried, and swiftly found somewhere to park and followed in shortly after Greg.

As Greg stood in the station, he waited patiently for Officer Walker to meet him in interrogation room number two. As soon as the officer was ready, he motioned for Greg to come in the cold, dull, rectangular room. Greg took Cheryl by the hand, and invited her into the room with him.

When they entered, there was a large silver, squared table in the middle of the room. Officer Walker sat across from Greg with a manila folder in front of him on the table. Greg and Cheryl took a seat side by side, and sitting next to Officer Walker was another officer. Officer Walker began to speak.

"I want to tell you sir, I'm sorry for your loss," Officer Walker said.

"Thank you," Greg replied.

"I'll try to be as sensitive as I can, but we need to tell you what happened to your daughter last night!" Officer Walker stated.

"Who caused the accident, officer?" Greg asked.

"I happened to be patrolling the area last night, when I responded to a call from the station about a severe wreck over near the bridge, on Height Avenue. I rushed over."

"Was my daughter still alive when you found her?" Greg asked.

The officer pauses for a moment.

"No, no sir, she wasn't. She was killed instantly."

Greg put his head down.

"Your daughter was hit by a drunk driver. The boy who hit her is over at University Hospital right now, getting non-life threatening medical treatment."

"Wait, he's still alive?" Greg shouted.

"Yes, he is sir. But upon his release, he will be charged with the death of your daughter," Officer Walker answered.

"Who is this punk? What's his name? Does he live over near me?" Greg demanded.

"Sir, at this time, until he is arrested, we can't release that information to you right now. All we can tell you is, that when medical personnel treated the young man, his blood alcohol level was three times the legal limit," Officer Walker informed.

Greg became enraged, and the veins in his neck bulged out.

"What kind of dumb answer is that? You can't release the information (Greg says sarcastically). This little low-life, ingrate, just killed my daughter, and you won't even tell me who he is!" Greg yelled.

"Like I said sir, all we can tell you is that we're waiting to arrest him at this point. He's a twenty year-old male," the officer said.

"I can't believe this!" Greg cried. "I suppose you have some bloody pictures, and the damaged car, in that folder you've got there? I don't want to see it," said Greg.

"There are other pieces of information I would like to share with you," Officer Walker proclaimed.

"Maybe you should just take a look, Greg," Cheryl stated.

"He doesn't have anything I want to know. The information I want, he won't give me," Greg answered.

"Officer, why can't you release his name, or any other information about him? We're the victims here," Cheryl asked.

"Legal stuff," the officer said.

Greg got up, and walked out of the room. He had become disturbed knowing that his daughter was taken away from him at the irresponsibility of someone else. He couldn't understand how Misty could be the victim of someone else's irresponsible and irrational behavior. Cheryl tried to comfort him, but Greg was so angry he wanted to physically hurt the boy that killed his daughter.

In his mind, he knew it wasn't a good thing to know who it was, because the way Greg felt, it would've caused him to have his own charges brought against him.

The officer walked out of the room to meet Greg.

"The car has been taken to the junk yard off Sycamore and Rinehart, you'll have to go there next Tuesday and meet with one of the guys there, to see if there are any personal possessions left in the car that you want, or what you want to recover," the officer explained.

"When did you say he was going to be arrested?" Greg asked.

"As soon as he is released from the hospital," Officer Walker answered.

"Why do I have to wait until Tuesday?" said Greg.

"We need to finish our investigation first, and then you may get any possessions she might have had in the car."

"I understand," Greg said.

"Before you leave, sir, I just want to tell you, I have a daughter of my own, and I know I would be just like you. So I sympathize. Trust me, we're going to seek justice for Misty. Believe me, we will," the officer said.

Greg felt little solace from the officer's heart to heart, but he had been eased in his mind only a small degree.

"This is just a sad case of an innocent person being a victim of a drunk driver, who shouldn't have been on the road in the first place," Officer Walker said.

"No, sir, this is a stupid case about an ignorant kid who didn't know what he was doing. He was a driver unaware," Greg added.

The officer hugged Greg and Cheryl, and wished them comfort. When Greg and Cheryl left the station, they got in the car and they both began to cry. It was official, Misty had died due to a drunk driver. *She* was dead, and the driver was still alive. How unfair, Greg thought. There was no justice in that.

The next two days flew by. Cheryl called most of the family, to inform them when, and where, the funeral was going to be. Most of Greg's family couldn't believe that sweet Misty was gone. Everybody knew how close Greg and Misty were, and how he did such a wonderful job in raising her.

Greg tried to reach Misty's mom. He tried calling an old telephone number he had for her a couple of years ago, but all he got was an automated voicemail message. He tried his hardest to find her, but he couldn't get a hold of her in time for her to come to the funeral.

Greg's son came into town. He really didn't have the best relationship with his father, but it was clear the two had a love for each other. His son Robert spent time at the house helping Greg store Misty's stuff. He didn't want to totally erase Misty from the house, but he didn't want to be constantly reminded that she wasn't here any longer.

At the funeral, Greg saw old cousins, aunts and uncles, friends, and others he hadn't seen in a long time. The funeral was held at a Catholic Church not too far from Greg's house. Greg cried during the service unable to hold himself together. He knew this would be the last time he would see Misty's physical body. It was hard for him to see Misty in a casket. A beautiful young girl, full of life, was killed, all because someone was driving while drunk.

During the service Greg kept playing over and over in his head how scared Misty must have been. He felt even worse, because he wasn't there to save her. The one night his daughter needed him the most, he wasn't there for her. Aside from the fact that his daughter was gone, which was reason enough to be angry, he was incensed because he knew something was wrong that night, and he moved to slow. If only he would've went searching for her earlier, or called the cops earlier.

Greg wouldn't let himself off the hook. He wished he could've traded places with Misty. He figured that he had lived his life and there was nothing left for him. Misty, beautiful Misty, was a wonderful young lady who embodied purity and meekness. How could someone so young be taken away so tragically? It hurt Greg to his heart to know that he now had to live his life without his daughter.

At the end of the funeral, Greg was walking out of the white, cone-shaped church. He was with his twenty-five year old son, whom he told to go pull the car around. Greg had spotted someone he knew, and wanted to talk.

The person he saw was a thin, middle-aged woman, with long wavy brown hair. The sun was shining intensely, but the crisp, cold air had filled this heartbreaking day. Greg moved gradually faster and faster towards this woman, who he had spotted standing a good distance away.

As Greg got closer, he waved the woman down, yelling, "Hey, Kathy! Kathy wait!"

The woman stood frozen solid, trying to see who it was calling her name. She took off her sunglasses and stared dangerously close at Greg as he approached her. Now that she had seen who it was, she produced a smile on her face. Greg did the same thing.

"Hello, Gregory," Kathy said.

"Hi Kat," Greg replied.

They both reached in and gave each other a comforting hug.

"I didn't think you were going to make it. I didn't know how to find you," Greg stated.

"I got word from your sister, Cheryl. She knows my brother-in-law, Tony. He called me and told me what happened. I tried to get here sooner, but I was strapped for cash and had to get some extra money," Kathy explained.

"I can't believe she's gone," Greg cried.

"At least you got to raise her," Kathy replied.

"Don't feel sorry for yourself, Kathy, you chose to leave us," Greg said.

"We've been through this same old song and dance before. I wasn't cut out to be a mother," Kathy said.

"That's still no reason to abandon your daughter! She stopped asking about you at an early age. She knew you weren't coming back," said Greg.

"I know you did a good job raising her. I know she turned out to be your pride and joy."

"It was easy to love Misty, because she was a loveable person. I just hope she forgave you for leaving her," Greg proclaimed.

"I know I messed-up, but I never stopped thinking about her. My life was just spinning out of control so fast. I couldn't breathe," Kathy justified herself.

"You missed out on her growing-up for no reason. I'll never understand why you left. I bet you have had more kids since Misty?"

"You would be right, Greg," Kathy answered.

"How many?" Greg asked.

"Two sons," said Kathy. "I have to live with this guilt until the day I die. I never should have left you and Misty. I regret it every day."

"There's nothing either one of us can do now, we can't change the past," Greg proclaimed.

"I'm not going to lie Greg, my connection to Misty isn't as strong as yours is, and my love for her isn't as deep as yours. I still feel grief though. I feel as if a part of me is gone," Kathy stated.

"You'll always be her mother, even though she's gone," Greg explained. "Life doesn't prepare you for these kinds of things. If someone would've told me that my daughter was going to die a teenager, I never would have believed them," Greg murmured.

"How do we move on without our daughter?" Kathy inquired.

"That's a question I've been struggling with ever since I saw Misty lying on that silver colored, cold table," said Greg.

Kathy and Greg ended their conversation with a hug, and a phone number exchange. For the first time he gained respect for Kathy as a woman, but now, as a mother also.

When Kathy first left, Greg hated her and didn't understand how their relationship of six years could be torn apart because of their daughter. It didn't make sense to him, but he had truly seen a change in Kathy. Only it was too late. The change needed to have happened when Misty was a little girl, when she needed her mother. But Misty was gone now.

That night as Greg sat in his daughter's room playing that tragic night over and over in his head, he tried to convince himself that maybe Misty didn't feel any pain or hurt. He tried to convince himself that she was unaware of what had taken place. He tried to bring forth a number of scenarios to help ease the guilt and grief that he felt. He was unsuccessful. He knew Misty had to have been terrified.

The way in which she died was too awful to even comprehend. Why did such a lovely and gracious girl have to die such a horrible death? That wasn't Misty in that car that night. Those cuts and scrapes, and loads of blood, was not who Misty was at all. Her lifeless damaged body in the casket wasn't her either. Greg didn't want those images of Misty in his head, but he knew that would be the last image he would ever see of her physically. He didn't want to just remember her the way she was. He needed to see her for himself, one last time.

Her room was empty and unwelcoming, but that hadn't stopped Greg from going in there. Greg decided to leave it as it was. He only cleared a few things out, because he wanted the memory of his daughter to still be omnipresent within the house. He didn't want to throw everything away because she was gone. He wanted to adapt to life without Misty the best he could.

Misty's killer, twenty year-old Justin Mitch Bragg, was arrested a week after the fatal crash when he was released from the hospital. He was immediately placed in handcuffs while leaving the hospital building. He would be charged with intoxication manslaughter, a second-degree felony. Greg was hoping for first-degree murder. The prosecution decided to charge him with this less serious offense, for some unknown reason.

Greg was present when the young boy was sentenced to ten to twenty years in prison. Greg felt cheated. He didn't think the justice system would let him down. How could the court only give him ten years after he took someone else's life? The only other recourse Greg had was to sue Justin for everything he and his parent's had. Ten years didn't seem quite long enough for someone who had actually killed his daughter. He would only be thirty years old when he gets released, Greg thought. He would be free to roam the streets again.

Even though Greg wanted the harshest punishment possible, he ultimately knew it wouldn't ever bring Misty back. Life in prison for this young man wouldn't bring his daughter back. Additionally, Greg saw Justin's sorrowful face; Greg could tell Justin was not only ashamed, but also remorseful. During his days in court, Justin cried and cried. He kept looking over his shoulders at his parents, hoping they could get him out of this mess that he had caused for himself.

The words at Justin's sentencing hearing still remain embedded in Greg's mind.

"I can't express how truly, and deeply sorry I am that I caused this accident that hurt someone else. My actions have caused so many people pain, and I just want to say that I am sorry," Justin read.

During this time, Greg would try to make eye contact with Justin, hoping to stir even more emotion within him, hoping Justin would be able to witness the devastation he had caused. However, Justin kept his head down while he was reading from his paper, while crying his heart out.

"My mom and dad raised me better, and I know I let them down. I let myself down. I was just having some fun that night, but instead, I hurt someone. I am sorry. To everyone, and especially to Misty's family, I am truly sorry," Justin stated.

After the sentence was handed down, Justin was ready to be taken away, but before he was taken away, Greg signaled for the officers to hold on for a second. He waved them back over to where he was standing. As the two officers were holding each of Justin's arms, Greg rapidly made his way to meet the officers and Justin.

"I know you're sorry, son," Greg said to Justin. "I need you to know that I forgive you. I was angry when I learned you only got ten years, but I don't feel that way anymore," Greg said. "If I carry hatred in my heart for you, I'll never be able to move on, and that gives you power over me," Greg finished.

As Greg was forgiving Justin, Justin began to cry again. Greg motioned to the officers to let him hug Justin. They didn't allow Greg to hug Justin.

"I'm sorry, sir," Justin cried.

"When you get out son, don't be that driver unaware again. If you make it, you're getting a second chance," Greg exclaimed.

"Yes, sir," said Justin.

Justin is currently serving his ten-year sentence in a maximum-security prison. Greg decided against his civil lawsuit, and instead moved on with his life the best way he knew how. His son came to live with him, and they spent months developing their relationship. Greg visits Misty's grave every chance he gets. He didn't listen to others who told him to not spend so much time visiting the cemetery. Greg felt differently.

He felt that her last earthly resting place was one of the few places where he still had a strong connection to Misty.

CHAPTER FIVE
Beloved Adeline

I moved away from home when I was twenty years old. I had gotten married, and was expecting my first child six months after our wedding. I tried to be the best daughter I could, but living in my childhood house, now that I was a grown woman, with my mother and stepfather, was not appealing to me any longer. I couldn't do it.

My mother begged me not to get married, and to go to college instead, or learn some kind of trade, but I ignored her. I wanted to get out of that small town, and out of the house.

Spending twenty years in one spot wasn't healthy anyway. I needed to grow up mentally, and experience life on my own. If that meant getting married and having children, then that's what I was going to do. At the time I couldn't see the sense in all the things my mother was telling me. I didn't want to grasp the fact that she knew what was best for me at that time. Instead, I outright ignored her and tried to take on the role of seemingly knowing it all.

It wasn't until I had my third child that I realized all that my mother had been trying to tell me was correct. I spent many days regretting some of the decisions I had made for myself. I looked at some of my other siblings who had perfect spouses, good kids, the best homes, and blessed lives. I wanted that. I wanted a good life. I felt I was entitled to a good life after the traumatic childhood I had experienced. I witnessed heart-wrenching, traumatizing events throughout my life. I deserved to be happy.

By getting married and moving away so young, I thought that life would bring happiness and an immeasurable amount of content. I was wrong. One of the lowest points in my life came when I was stuck with three children under the age of six, no husband, and barely enough money to survive on. My husband had died, and there I was trying to make it at a factory for minimum wage, with the assistance of the Government.

I often reflect and wonder if I endured these problems because of my rebelliousness, and not listening to my mother. 'Payback' is what people call it. Maybe it *was* in some weird way. Life was undoubtedly tough for me, but the teachings that my mother had instilled in me from when I was a little girl, and as a teenager, had stuck with me. Even though I didn't have the perfect life, or the finer things in life, one thing that my mother told me when I first moved out has always stuck with me. She said out of all of her children, I was the strong one.

My mother Adeline was the kind of woman who could turn enemies into friends. Because she was such a sweet, loving and caring person, she didn't have any enemies. Just people who were jealous of her, but she lived her life aligned with moral values, and a love for God. I watched her struggle through some dark days. At times it seemed easier for her to quit rather than push forward, but she didn't quit.

I grew up in a house with two older brothers, and two other sisters. All five of us knew that we only had one true parent, and that was our mother, Adeline Jamison. My father was an alcoholic man who didn't know the true meaning of love, fidelity, and what it meant to be a father. If he wasn't beating my mother senseless, or picking fights with us kids, then he was drinking for hours until he would pass out.

Life was hard for us. We grew up in a one story, cream-colored home, with two bedrooms and one bathroom. I can remember from a very early age being disgusted at how bad our living situation was.

Three girls crowded in one room, my two brothers sleeping in the living room on a pull out couch. I grew up resenting my father. I thought he should have done a better job of providing for us.

My mother was a registered nurse, and spent many hours away from home while doing her best to be a good mother. My father worked as a yardman. To me, he was a lazy man who wanted nothing more than to drink, fool around with other women, and watch his wife bring home a good majority of the money.

My father passed away when I was ten years old. I didn't care too much; it wasn't like he showed me a lot of love and affection. I may have shed a tear or two, but there was no need to cry myself to sleep, or sprawl on the floor holding his shirts and wishing he were here. Oddly enough, it wasn't alcohol that killed him. According to his doctor, my father had some kind of problem with his heart, and the surgery he needed to replace the faulty valve, he didn't get it. My mother, on the other hand, couldn't collect herself for months. She must have seen him in a different light, because I couldn't figure out what was so special about an adulterous, drunken husband.

Life was calm after my father passed. My mother was a godly woman. Come rain or shine, all of us would be in Sunday school at nine-thirty in the morning, and not a minute over. It was easy to love my mother, because she didn't just say she loved us, she proved it to us. Instead of remaining in the room she and my dad shared together, she moved out into the living room and gave the room to us girls, and let my brothers have our old room. For years my mother slept on a pull out couch in the living room. My mother demonstrated the true essence of selflessness, what it means to be courageous, and taught us how to be a child of God.

Growing up, I was ashamed of church and having to spend my Sunday mornings listening to long, drawn out sermons about getting right, or else we were going to hell. I knew by age six what adultery, fornication, and blasphemy were. My mother always made sure that we lived our lives in a Christian way. She tried her best to shape us to be good church-going young adults as we got older. However, things didn't quite work out that way.

I was a disappointment because I didn't get a college education, and I married early. My oldest brother, Earl, forgot everything he knew about the church and turned to drugs. Ken led a hard life, and spent a good majority of his young adult life in jail. My other two sisters turned out the best. They had good husbands, good jobs, beautiful kids, and would have made my mother proud. They were the two good Christians in the family.

For some reason when my mother died, the family fell apart right under our noses. I soon learned that our mother, Adeline was the only person who kept this family together. She was the reason why we, as siblings, grew up close, and why we had a moral compass. The foundation of our beliefs, and supposed bravery, came from our mother. I listened to my mother's teachings, and I benefited a great deal through some of the things she taught me.

After my father died, three years passed before my mother would marry again. The remaining children in the house didn't want her to get married again. One bad father was enough. We didn't want some man coming into our lives, pretending to care about us, and trying to be a father figure to us. Life with our mom was just fine. Conversely, our mother didn't see it that way. She would often confess to us how lonely she was. She wanted to be with someone who could satisfy her emotionally, and otherwise. I knew what she meant, and so did my brothers and sisters.

Against our protests and demands, our mother remarried. What a mistake her second marriage turned out to be. If ever there were a time to go through life, sexually frustrated, and alone, that was the time. My mother thought she knew what she was doing when she married a former co-worker named Ridge.

Even though he was not a drunk like my biological father, or lazy, he still was a monster. He was evil, and we could all see right through him. I don't know if my mother chose not to see him for who he was, or knew it, and didn't care, but she didn't leave him. She actually loved him, I think. One thing was for sure, he wasn't going to be any kind of father to me. Furthermore, if he even thought about trying to molest one of my sisters or me, I was going to make him regret the day he married my mother. I had two uncles who carried guns, and one of my uncles was a hunter. I knew he had rifles.

I did my best to try to get along with my stepfather, Ridge, but he was the kind of man who pushed other people's buttons just to get a reaction. He was a psychotic. He claimed to be a strong deacon in the church, but if you looked in the back seat of his old, beat-up, rusty, Ford pickup truck, there were tons and tons of sex magazines, and empty beer cans. Moreover, he was a smoker. Deacon? My foot! Our neighbor Eddie, who we made fun of, and who we thought was supposedly a pimp, was more of a deacon than my stepfather.

Life with him was hard, because we didn't want to upset our mother. At least he wasn't abusive like our father. Still, Ridge's redeeming qualities weren't enough for us to stop disliking him. In a way, I actually kind of felt sorry for Ridge. The only family he had in town was his half-sister, Beatrice. All of his relatives lived hours away from Kentucky. None of his family came to visit him. All he had was my mother. She loved him unconditionally. She loved him in spite of his faults. The same way she loved us.

We wouldn't ever know another love like our mothers . . . ever again, and when she announced to us that she was dying, we knew that day standing in the kitchen, that she was going to be taken from us.

It was on a Wednesday afternoon in July, when my mother gathered us in the kitchen and broke the news to us that she had breast cancer. She wasn't one of the lucky ones. They didn't catch my mother's breast cancer in time. By the time they tested her, it was too late, and the cancer had spread. She called herself the ticking time bomb. We used to tell her to stop joking like that. She would always tell us to have a sense of humor. I don't think any of us had hope in our hearts. It's sad to say, but I believe it to be true, there was no hope to have. My mother didn't get an early detection of her breast cancer. I wasn't stupid; I knew what the chances of her surviving were.

That was one of the hardest things to deal with. Knowing that someone you love is going to die, and there's nothing you can do about it. It was torture, day after day, going about my daily life, raising my children, and waiting for that phone call to let me know my mother had died. It was sickening. I was living my life, waiting for my mother to die. She sought her treatments, and medication, but it was just a smokescreen to delay the inevitable. It was going to happen one day. The only concern was when, and where. There was nothing any of us could do.

Our second oldest brother wasn't even allowed to see our mother. He never got the chance to visit her because he was incarcerated. He would call and talk to my mom when he could, but I knew it was a hard mental and emotional battle for him not to see his dying mother. My mother warned my brother to change his ways, and she told him there was nothing good that could come from a life dedicated to stealing. He didn't listen to her. It was as if some kind of spell had overtaken Ken. There he was, almost in his mid-twenties, robbing, and vandalizing. My two brothers had to be the densest men on the planet. With the kind of mother we had, they should have been the definition of perfect. They were just the opposite!

I suppose all my criticism, and holier-than-thou routine, came at a price. My brothers and sisters always thought I was trying to be better than them. They thought I was trying to be their second mother. True, when they stepped out of line, there I was trying to help them and give them advice. I was doing it from my heart though. They didn't, and couldn't, see that. How was I going to try to lecture someone on morality, and trying to be the perfect Christian? I was trying to be a loving sister. I was simply fulfilling the role my mother told me I was supposed to.

One night in the hospital when my mother was in the final stages of her cancer, she talked to me about the family, and how she wanted me to keep the family together. A lot of tension and negativity had transpired between the time my mother was diagnosed with cancer, up until her final days. We were arguing about who was going to get what, after momma died. How we were going to split the money. Completely stupid and senseless stuff in my book. There were so many times when I wanted to walk out of the hospital and just leave them arguing. My oldest brother and my sisters would stand right in front of my mother, and argue over money and personal possessions.

I can't blame them for their behavior at times, maybe for some of them it was a good distraction from having to deal with the fact that our mother was dying. Or, maybe we were just trying to make sure there weren't any loose ends when our mother died. One thing we all knew for sure was, that the inevitable was going to happen. If we had never been sure of anything before in our lives, this one thing we were sure of.

The bickering was just too much for me to handle, and my mother knew it was. As I was sitting by her side that night in the hospital, she touched my hand and told me what she wanted from me.

"I need you to be the backbone when I'm gone," my mother said weakly.

"I don't understand," I answered.

"If you don't help your brothers and sisters, this family is going to fall apart. I know it will," she explained.

"What am I going to do?" I questioned.

"Be me!" my mother proclaimed.

"Be you? Please mamma, no one could ever be you," I told her.

"If you have courage, a good heart, a love for God, and love your siblings, that's all you need," she replied. "You have all of that," my mother said.

"Why me, mamma? Why do you want me?" I asked.

"You're strong. I could always count on you. Your sisters may seem to have it all, but you have a pureness that shines through. I love all my children, but it's you . . . you have to keep them together."

After my mother laid this heavy task on me, I knew right away I was going to disappoint her. I couldn't stand to be in the same room with Earl for more than five minutes. My sisters, they were good women, but they were controlling and demanding. I didn't want to have to deal with all of these different personalities. I didn't want this task.

Sometimes I wonder if my mother just told me what I wanted to hear. I pondered if she gave me that long Spirit-filled speech, because I was the only one in the room with her that night. Could it be possible that she would've told the same thing to one of my sisters, had I not been with her that night? No matter what my mother intentions for delivering that news to me, I'm still grateful that she told it to me. She entrusted me to carry on guiding the family.

One thing I put an end to, was the fighting in the hospital. I told my brother and sisters that mom didn't need to be bothered with the chaos and commotion about money, and property. I limited all financial talk to be taken care of out of the presence of our mother. I worked hard to make my mother proud. I wanted to do something for her, because I felt ever since I was nineteen I was a disappointment to her. Yet she still loved me in spite of my choices, but by me honoring her request, I felt as if I had finally done right by her.

I came in the hospital one day, and as I entered my mother's room, it smelled like death. I knew she was on her way out. I was selfish that day. I didn't call any of my siblings; I wanted that one-on-one time with mom. I knew I would never get it again. The doctors had been in and out of her room that day, telling me that they didn't expect her to make it through the week. I held on to some hope that she would at least live a couple of more months.

Those days that I was visiting in the hospital, I wasn't praying so much for my mother's recovery, I was taking that time to prepare myself mentally for her death. I was spending time with her to help me to accept the fact that my mother was dying. I needed that time. My mom would get an occasional visitor here and there, but most of her family stopped visiting after a period of time. I'm not sure if they got caught up in their own personal lives, but I wasn't going to let other people stop me from spending the time I needed with my mother. It wasn't a waste of time. I was collecting all the memories and moments I could with my mother.

My siblings didn't understand. Not to say they were less concerned, or loved my mother any less, but it was important for me to make sure that I was always at the hospital every day, visiting and taking care of my mother. I didn't want to look back and wonder what more I could have done, or what if I had spent just a little bit more time with her. I didn't want any regrets.

When my mother was first diagnosed with breast cancer, she didn't sulk and wallow in self-pity! She told us that this had to happen to her, because this was her exit from the world.

"We all have to die one day," she told us, "in order for me to get to Heaven and see Jesus, I have to come out of this body and leave it behind," my mother explained.

Even though she went through her treatments and took medication, in the back of her mind, I think my mother was ready to die. It was hard for me to accept the fact that my mother could possibly *want* to leave her children. She had done her job though. She raised five children and maintained a Holy lifestyle.

Through her sickness, Adeline continued to attend church, and she would encourage others who were going through hardships of their own. That's one of the reasons why she was loved so much, she was selfless; a rare quality to find in people today. Her mission was to get to Heaven, and see Jesus.

Eight months after my mother was initially diagnosed with breast cancer, she passed away in the hospital, with me by her side. I had gotten up early that morning and found myself trying to get to the hospital as quickly as possible. The night before I had left my mother and wanted to get back to her soon. It was a bad day for her that day. I hardly recognized my mother. She was frail, and looked sick in her face. I understood though. She barely spoke that day I came to visit her. I called my sisters and oldest brother to come and see mom, because I felt it was going to be the last time we would see her alive.

They all arrived, and for once, we were able to come together and pray, and be civilized for the sake of my mother. It was hard for me to see my mother in so much pain. In a way I wanted her to be released from all the pain in her body, but I also didn't want to lose her. I didn't want my mother to die and leave me here. She was the only brave woman I knew. I didn't want my mother to die. How could I possible live my life without my mother?

I came in the hospital a little before ten in the morning, and I just sat by my mother's bedside. I kept waiting for her to speak to me, and look at me, but she was in a coma the doctor said. She had slipped into a coma that night and was unresponsive. I was immediately scared.

"Doctor, what does that mean?" I asked.

"At this point, your mother probably won't make it through the day," the doctor replied.

"How long does a coma last?" I inquired.

"There's no way for us to know that. All we can do is monitor her closely and continue to wait for her to come out of the coma."

"Should I prepare for the worst doctor?" I asked.

"Ms. Adeline might not make it through the day," the doctor repeated.

As soon as the doctor informed me about my mothers' condition, I called everyone. I rushed to the phone, and began dialing franticly all the numbers I could think of off the top of my head.

By the time I got back to the room, I took a seat right next to my mother and watched her peacefully. It was as if she was sleeping. I grabbed her hand, kissed her forehead, and began to weep. The one person in the world who loved me unconditionally, who labored for me, and suffered for us, was about to die. I rested my head on her shoulders' as she lay stretched out on the elevated bed. She was slipping away that very second.

When I finally looked up one last time to see her face, she opened her eyes, looked up at the ceiling, smiled . . . then her machine stopped. She closed her eyes for the last time, and peacefully passed away. I began to cry. I had just witnessed seeing my mother die. I felt a mixture of emotions. I was upset, scared, joyful, and confused. I was upset at mother for leaving us here to face the world on our own. I was scared because I had never seen anyone die right before my very eyes. But I was joyful because my mother was no longer in pain. Lastly, I was confused because I thought she would have at least made it through the day.

It took the nurses a few seconds to come in and explain to the doctor what happened. A skinny, pale, older, white nurse, told me to step outside, and let them remove the body. That's all my mother was now, just a body.

"I know what you're going through," the nurse whispered to me.

"Did your mother die of breast cancer?" I asked.

"Colon cancer," she replied. "Why don't you step outside and let us take care of everything in here. You don't need to be seeing this. Remember your mama in a good light," the nurse said.

"Can I stand outside of the door?" I inquired.

"If you wish," the nurse said.

I sat on the floor outside of my mother's hospital room. All I could do was wait. I was waiting for my siblings and other family members to arrive. When I called them, I didn't mention how critical it was for them to be here. I didn't believe mama was going to die today. I should've listened to the Oncologist.

It seemed like it took forever for them to get mama out of the room. As soon as the door burst open, I stood up ready to see my mother. However, I didn't get that chance. Her body was covered in a white sheet. They were taking her somewhere in the hospital where dead bodies are held until being released to the funeral home. I was holding off on calling the funeral home until my sisters and brother got here.

When they arrived, both of my sisters fell to the ground with tears flowing. They didn't expect the worse so soon.

"What happened," Earl asked.

"Her body gave out," I replied.

"When did it happen?" he questioned.

"About an hour ago," I answered.

"I wish I could've gotten here earlier," Earl stammered.

"Well, we can't go back. What's done is done. Mom is gone," I said.

"Sounds like you've already accepted mom's death?" Earl said.

"You'd be right," I answered.

We all came together, and I called the funeral home. They came about twenty minutes later, a man and a woman. They prayed with us, and loaded up our mother's body. That night was like none other. We had lost our mother, but in a way we connected. The only person missing was Ken. That night, I wrote Ken a letter, and mailed it the next day. Yet, I knew he would be calling from jail to get an update on mom's condition. We didn't know how to break the news to him. We figured writing a letter would be most appropriate until he called one of us.

No one really ever prepares someone for the death of a parent. My mother's death wasn't like my father's death. I wasn't sad then. I was almost borderline glad that he had passed away. He wasn't any good to us anyhow. I didn't care for him, and maybe since we didn't have a connection that's why I didn't feel anything. With my mother, it was completely different. I loved her, and the fact that she was gone, made me hurt inside. I'm glad I spent all the time I could with her. It was supposed to be my acceptance period, but I truly didn't accept the fact she was going to die until I witnessed it.

My stepfather didn't come around us too much until the funeral. He tried his best to muster up a few tears here and there, but I knew his MO. I knew exactly who he was. He couldn't wait to get his disgusting hands on money he thought was coming to him. He didn't want to dare mess with me; I made sure my mom left him as little as possible. I was the one who made sure she had a current will. Those problems however would come later.

After the funeral, I went home to get my kids. I wanted them to see the image of her, and explain to them what happened to grandma. I knew they wouldn't understand if I didn't show them. I got flack for it from my sisters. They didn't think it was appropriate for me to bring my children to a cemetery. Nonetheless, Adeline was my mother, and if I wanted my children to see her like that, that's my right as a parent. I didn't care what anyone else thought.

As I laid in bed that night, I kept reflecting on what the preacher said about my mother during the eulogy, and how she touched the lives of people in her community, on her job, and in the church.

"You can't find a holy, virtuous woman like Mrs. Adeline anymore. God don't make those kind of women these days. She was a special woman, who helped people she didn't even know she was helping," the preacher said.

He said she, in effect, preached her own funeral. The braveness and humbleness she displayed wasn't comparable, and can't even be touched. My mother was a true saint. Perfect, no, godly, yes! During my mother's sickness, she spent day and night praying and continuously working in the church. She didn't let her illness slow her down. She didn't focus on her situation, or trying to gain sympathy from others. She carried her cross, as her pastor would say. My mother, Adeline, found a way to comfort and listen to others, even though she was the one dying of cancer. I admired her because she was ready to die. My mother understood death, and what it meant to be Heaven bound. Death didn't scare her. It scared my siblings and I. We feared the unknown. We were afraid of living our lives without our mother's guidance. Most importantly, death was final. Where does one really go when they die?

I had questions. I didn't understand death and the whole afterlife concept. I was bewildered and livid. I wasn't ready for my mother to go yet. I had convinced myself that all the time I had spent with her, was all the time I needed in order to adjust to her leaving me. However, I was mistaken. I cried for weeks on end, and visited her grave everyday for months. How can anyone ever be truly prepared to say good-bye to someone they genuinely love and care about? In my book, it's impossible.

About a week after the funeral, my two sisters and I came together and went through mom's things. This was daunting and too painful, all at the same time. We could barely contain ourselves from the emotion that had taken control over us. We had snuck in one weekday morning while our stepfather was at work. Since he worked construction, we knew he wouldn't be home at least until the evening. He had the audacity to tell us that he wanted to go through mom's things first, and that he would call us to come and pick-up whatever items he had boxed up. I told him, "Over my dead body!"

I can remember Ridge calling me three days after the funeral, trying to discuss my mother's personal belongings.

"I need to go through a couple of items first, and then you girls can come on over and get what's left," Ridge said.

"Um, I don't think so Ridge. That's not how this is going to work," I replied.

"I was married to Adeline, I have legal rights to her property first," Ridge justified.

"Do you think I care about your rights Ridge? I was her daughter before you were her husband. Besides, why do you want her stuff anyway?" I asked.

"Sentimental value," Ridge said.

"No, Ridge. My sisters and I will be over there tomorrow morning to retrieve our mother's property!" I exclaimed.

"You better not show up here tomorrow. Adeline's gone, this is my house now, and you little streetwalkers better not come by here ransacking my home. I'll call the law," Ridge proclaimed.

"What!" I said in disbelief.

"You heard what I said."

He hung up the phone in my face that night. I needed the night to cool down and collect myself. I called my sisters early the next morning, and we plotted to go to our house, and get our mother's property. Who was Ridge to keep us out of our childhood home? We wouldn't be breaking and entering, because all the way up until our mother died, we had a key to the house that Ridge didn't know about.

We got up early the next morning, waited for Ridge to go to work, and let ourselves into the house. We were embarrassed and upset that we had to sneak around in our home that we grew up in, because of our stepfather. I always knew he was evil. My oldest sister unloaded empty, large plastic storage containers from her van, and began throwing all of mom's nightclothes, dresses, and shoes into the containers.

I carefully wrapped all of her dishes, silverware, and jewelry. My other sister discreetly threw out my mother's undergarments, and packed all of her collectibles and knick-knacks. My mother had a will, and none of her personal material possessions were going to Ridge. My mother did leave him the house and her car. As far as her money and personal possessions, she gave them to each of her five kids.

We worked feverishly until the middle of the afternoon, trying to get everything that was my mothers. My mother had indicated that she wanted her sister to have some kind of special piece of jewelry, along with a poem my mother had wrote for her. I didn't have time to sort through who was getting what. My mission was to just get everything out of the house that was my mother's personal property.

My sisters and I loaded up containers filled with pictures, dishes, clothes, personal writings, and her collectibles. We took it all. Frankly, I really didn't care if any of our aunts and uncles got anything. I was selfish when it came to my mother. In my mind, we were first. We were her children, and we were entitled to what was hers.

That night after we had divided up who got what, the only thing we were afraid of was the fall out. We didn't know how Ridge was going to react. By no means did we leave the house a mess, but we inadvertently emptied almost the entire house. I was ready for Ridge though. My mother had only been dead a week; I was fuming mad, and wanted a fight. I was angry anyway. I was just waiting for Ridge to approach me.

All my mother's teachings about being slow to anger, and reaping what you sow, went out the window. If Ridge wanted a fight, he was going to get one.

I spent that night crying over old photographs. I missed my mother greatly. With all her problems, she was one, strong woman. I needed comfort, and for someone to tell me they knew what I was going through and to tell me that my mother is smiling down on me. I was already feeling alone and depressed.

Is it true what they say, that time heals all wounds? I didn't really know what to believe. If I was going to believe this statement I was going to have to live it. How much time though? When is someone able to move forward and not be emotionally affected by the death of a loved one? I don't believe it's ever really possible to be so removed that a single individual can block out someone in their life significant who has passed on. It's not possible. There always has to be some sort of connection and emotional tie to that person.

I personally don't find death beautiful like my mother claimed. I also understand that she was at a different stage in her life where she could understand the hereafter and the spiritual body. I hate death, and the fact that people we love have to die. I loved my mother just like my other siblings. I continue to visit my mother's grave every day. It gives me a lasting connection to her.

The fallout with Ridge turned out to be nothing more than an old man trying to have some power. He didn't call the police because once the will was read, and he found out he had the house and her car, he didn't care about anything else. I guess he didn't know what our mother had left him, and he was trying to hold on to anything he could.

Ridge eventually sold our house and collected the money. That was his intention. We truly thought we would be heartbroken, but we weren't in the slightest. What he didn't know is that our mother offered the house to us first, but we turned it down. All of us with the exception of Ken didn't want to be reminded of our father's drunken, abusive fits, or how Ridge used to purposefully terrorize us. We didn't want that house. The only good thing that came out of that house was our mother. She was gone now, and there was no need to keep the house.

Ken was released from jail four months after our mother died. The first thing he did was to have us take him to her grave. He brought flowers and a card. We let him have all the time he needed. He cried like a baby. Our mother warned him about his lifestyle. I think actually seeing our mother in the ground, gave him the motivation to *want* to change. He, in fact, *did* change. He even married and had a daughter.

Its amazing how one person can have such an impact on someone else's life! Aside from the fact that Adeline was our mother, it was more than that. It what as if she was some sort of Angel sent from Heaven. We can all try to be her, and try to bring forth her qualities, but the truth remains no one can ever be Adeline, our mother. Her pastor always called her, "Beloved Adeline." I knew what he meant by that. He cherished her, and adored her.

One of the most humble, loving, and compassionate woman, any of us have ever known. At times our family deviated from the love and respect our mother had instilled in us, but there I was, trying to keep everything and everyone intact. There was no way I was going to break my promise to my mother. She was depending on me to carry the family. I had to obey her dying wish.

In honor of my mother, all five of us gather at her grave on her birthday, and at Christmas. We think about all the loving things she gave us. Most importantly, she taught us about being a good Christian. What I learned from my mother, was how to be valiant, but also caring and loving. Each one of us took away something different from our mother's death. For some of us it was a wake-up call, that death is *real*, or that it's time to change our lives, and for some of us, it was a way to see the power of God.

I understand now, why my mother wasn't afraid of death. I didn't understand how someone could be so accepting of embracing a deadly sickness. My mother understood death, and she tried her hardest to explain to us why it was important for her to pass on. Heaven was waiting for her, she said. She told us that if death met her, she would be ready. She knew she wasn't going to be healed from cancer, and that was fine with her. Death didn't scare her.

Not many people are able to peacefully accept the fact that they are staring death right in the face. However, she was one of them.

If someone were to ask me if time heals all wounds, the question I wanted an answer to, I would have to say no. Time doesn't make the death of a loved one easier. What it does is allow time for someone to accept the fact, that person isn't ever coming back. Once time passes, and you have accepted it, that's when life is manageable again.

The death of a parent was one of the hardest things I ever had to endure. There isn't a day that goes by that I don't think about my mother. I lived up to the promise I made to her. All five of us are closer than ever before, and I make sure to foster the loving relationship my mother established.

My mother remains in my heart, and I only hope that I have her spirit of readiness and acceptance, when I meet death.

CHAPTER SIX
A Night of Fallen Tears

I can remember all too well, the night that not only changed my life, but the life of my family as well. It was my senior year in high school, a time when I was supposed to be immeasurably happy. It was also a time when my life was supposed to be problem-free. It was a cold, crisp November night, a night just like any other night. I had just turned off my television and slipped into bed. I hadn't even been asleep for ten minutes, when I heard a noise.

I was slightly awakened by a voice. It wasn't a loud talking voice; it was a crying voice. At first I thought my parents were laughing and joking around, but why would they be up laughing at midnight on a school night? I convinced myself it was my mother laughing, but the tone in her voice became so terrifying, I had to get up and see what was going on.

When I entered the hallway, I quietly peeked into my parent's room, hoping they were laughing. However, they weren't. When I entered their room, there was my mother sitting up in the bed, holding the phone and crying. I didn't know what was going on. I was angry at whoever was on the other end of the phone making my mother cry.

There was my father with an enraged look on his face. What was going on? My mother suddenly hung up the phone, and told my father and I, that Jacob, my older brother, had just been rushed to the hospital. He was in a car accident.

My father threw a rocking chair over, and wasn't sure how to process what my mother had just told us. My older and youngest sister, hadn't heard anything yet, and remained sound asleep.

My parents were rushing about trying to find some clothes to throw on, and get to the hospital. My brother had been taken to a hospital in the next town, and it would be at least an hour to drive there. By this time my older sister came out of her room, looking dismayed, trying to figure out what the commotion was about, I carefully explained to her that Jacob had just been taken to the hospital due to a car wreck.

She was confused, and didn't know what to say. We were all stunned thus far, about what we had just heard. Nothing like this had ever happened to our family before. Getting a call in the middle of the night, to tell us that someone we loved was just airlifted to the hospital because of a car wreck, was unbelievable.

My first reaction was positive. I told myself my brother was just being treated for minor scrapes and cuts, and that he was just involved in a little fender bender.

Stupid me; I was eighteen years old, a senior in high school, and I didn't know what being airlifted to the hospital meant. Anyone knows that being airlifted to the hospital isn't good. So I told myself my brother was okay. I told myself nothing was wrong. I had quietly walked down the stairs after speaking with my sister, because I heard more crying. It was my mother crying uncontrollably on the phone. She had called my uncle to tell him what happened. I had never been so scared in my life. The way my mother sounded on the phone, I had never heard her cry out like that before. It was at that moment that I realized everything *wasn't* okay.

As my parents gathered themselves together to head out, and get on the road, they told me to stay by the phone in case they needed to communicate with me. I felt sorry for my parents that night. There was dad trying to be strong, but hurting on the inside. He was trying to rush, and get himself together with his hurt foot, barely able to hold himself up. There was my mom, full of tears. There was nothing I could do for either one of them. I felt so helpless!

After my parents left the house, my older sister and I met in the kitchen and decided that we needed to pray, and tell some of the family what had happened. The seriousness of what was going on hadn't fully registered in my brain. I knew my brother was in the hospital, but I wasn't aware of just how critical the situation was.

The first thing we did was call our grandmother, and explain to her what had happened. We felt bad calling her in the middle of the night, but we wanted everyone in the family to be praying for our brother. She began to weep, and told us she would be praying. We called one of my aunts and told her also to start praying, and she informed us that she would definitely do so.

After we made our phone calls, it was time for us to start to pray ourselves. I was stuck. I didn't know where to begin . . . I didn't know what to ask for. I had never been in this situation before. Yet, I remember my mother telling me that a prayer is just from the heart. It is your own personal connection with God. So speak from the heart. My sister and I went into the dark living room, turned on a dim light, and got on our knees. There was no time to be introverted.

"Lord Jesus, you know the situation, you know what Jacob is going through," I began. "Please heal him right now, in the name of Jesus. We don't know how serious this is, but help him.

Please bless my mom and dad on the dangerous highways that they get to the hospital safely without any danger arising upon them. Touch Jacob's body right now, in your mighty name. In Jesus name I pray, amen," I finished.

When I finished saying my prayer, my sister said her own prayer.

"Oh, Lord Jesus, we're asking you to let Jacob be okay. We know you are the Almighty, a healer and deliverer, touch him right now," she said. "We don't know his condition, but you know, and you know how to help him. In Jesus name I pray, amen," she said.

We both got up and walked out of the living room, and I turned out the light behind me. I didn't know what was going through my sister's head, but I felt as if our brother was going to be okay. At this point in my life it wasn't even possible for me to stretch my mind to fathom that anything could go wrong. What possibly could go wrong with my brother? I honestly believed my brother was in the hospital for minor injuries. I wanted more information, I wanted to know what caused the accident, and I wanted more answers. If I was given more answers I could assess the situation myself, and piece together just how *bad* this accident was.

I was so confident that my brother was alright, I caught myself holding a smile a couple times throughout the night. There was no need to shield my current state of mind. I knew he was okay. My sister and I spent the early morning hours sleeping in our parent's room. I slept on the couch, and my sister slept on a chair. We couldn't go back to our own beds, because there was no word from mom and dad yet. We didn't know what was going on. As the clouds filled the sky, my youngest sister was still asleep, unaware of what had taken place a few hours before.

I remember being awakened by a call from my mom, stating that everything was okay so far. She told me that my brother was a little banged-up, but that the doctor said he was going to be okay. I felt warmth of relief rush through my body as I relayed the news to my sister. We felt that God had answered our prayers that night.

Come the six o'clock hour, I was unprepared for the news that was coming my way. I already knew going to school was out of the question, but I never expected that I would be taking a trip to Trenton University Hospital. As my youngest sister quietly opened her door, the phone rang. I knew it was an update.

"Hello," I answered.

"Who's this, Tyler?" a woman asked.

"Yes," I replied.

"Listen Tyler, this is your aunt Joy, your mom and dad told me to tell you and Kim to get dressed, and I'm coming to pick you all up," she stated.

"What . . . why? What's wrong?" I asked frantically.

"They want you all here at the hospital."

"What's wrong?" I asked again.

"There's something wrong with Jacob's brain," My aunt exclaimed.

"Something wrong with his brain!" I shouted.

My heart skipped a beat, and I was now officially terrified. I began to feel the tears swiftly fall from my eyes.

My younger sister, Kim, was standing in the doorway as I shouted what my aunt had just told me.

"But don't tell Kim, your parents don't want to scare her," My aunt stated.

It was too late; I had already yelled it out loud.

My sister instantly asked what was going on. Trinity, my oldest sister, felt compelled to tell her. My aunt released me off the phone, and Trinity and I started to explain what happened last night. Kim immediately began screaming at the top of her lungs. She ran into her room and then back into our parent's room yelling, "Noooo . . . noooo . . . no!" Trying to comprehend what she was saying through her breakdown, she informed Trinity and I, that she had a dream in August that Jacob had died. I thought to myself, at a time like this, my sister is carrying on with her hysterics, now she's making up dreams about death. I didn't dare tell her this to her face, but I didn't give her confession a second thought.

Kim was determined to get someone to understand what she had dreamed, and she wouldn't move away from the topic. She kept trying to get Trinity to admit that she had told her this once before, back one morning in August. Trinity stalled for a moment, trying to recollect. Shortly thereafter, she confirmed my sister's dream, and told me that she did remember Kim telling her that she had a dream that Jacob died. Either way, I still refused to believe that a thirteen year old could have a premonition, especially about something as serious as death.

The morning dragged on from that point. Everything seemed to be happening in slow motion. When my aunt arrived at our house, she told us that our dad didn't want Trinity to come just yet to the hospital. He only wanted Kim and I there. I didn't know why my father was making such a strange request. However, we obeyed, and Trinity waited for dad to come back home. During the car ride to the hospital, I tried to get more information from my aunt, but she proved to be useless. She didn't know any more than what she had told me earlier on the phone. Or could it be that she was hiding something else?

During that car ride my mind and heart switched gears. Something had taken over my current state of mind, which had been built on hope, and a blissful outcome. I no longer felt confident in my prayer, that my brother was going to be okay. Every time my aunt's cell phone rang, I thought she was going to hang up, turn around, and tell my sister and I, that our brother died. That's not normal. No one is supposed to sit and wait and be anxious to hear the news that his or her sibling had just died. That's when I knew this was severe.

What could possibly be wrong with my brother's brain? I wasn't processing what was going on just yet. Too much had been coming my way. I wasn't finding the right time to catch my breath. Even though I had rescinded the idea of hoping for the best, my mind wasn't fully wrapped around the idea that Jacob was going to die. Nothing in the world could let me reach that place quite yet. All this bad news produced fear and worry, but death wouldn't touch my family. Not *my* family. It couldn't be possible.

When we reached the hospital, the day began to speed up. Everything was happening all at once. My family was crowding the ICU waiting room, aunts, uncles, and cousins. As Kim and I stepped off the elevator, the floor we were on felt cold and isolated. It looked like a death floor. I don't know if it was from the rain and the thunder storm, but the whole intensive care unit was barely lit, and every face I saw leading up to the waiting room had a look of despair.

I spotted my dad, and quickly gave him a hug. I saw the terror in his eyes. I saw the fear of not knowing. I still hadn't received the answers I desperately wanted. If I critically thought about the situation, and assessed the conditions, I could've come up with my own conclusions. I'm in the intensive care unit, my aunt told me there's something wrong with my brothers' brain, and my sister had a dream about our brother dying. The answers to my questions were right in front of me. I chose not to see the obvious.

I walked angrily around the corner into the waiting room. I stared at my brother's friend. There he was, able to sit, and didn't look like he had a hair out of place. My brother was the one in the hospital bed. If looks could kill, his friend would've suffered a terrible death. That's how angry I was.

There was my mother, crying her eyes out. I had never seen her like that before. She was rocking back and forth, letting her tears fall from her eyes. There was a woman holding her hand, as if she was trying to pray for my mother. Then, another woman came over. They were both trying to comfort my mother. Two perfect strangers taking the time to comfort someone else. I wish there were a lot more kind-hearted people like that in the world.

My cousin Angela sat right next to me and reached out for my hand. I grabbed her hand and began to cry. I tried to hold it in, but seeing my mother break down, having looked at my father being horrified, and imaging my brother with brain damage, was too much for me to keep in. There wasn't a period of trying to cope, and trying to deal with what was going on. Everything was happening so fast, there was only time to accept the devastation that had plagued my family.

After about forty-five minutes had passed, visiting hours had started. The doctors were allowing one person at a time to go in and see Jacob. My mother rushed up and moved hastily to get to Jacob's bed. Kim was crying and wanted to go with my mom, but my mom's main focus was getting in the room to see Jacob. My mother ran past my sister unconsciously ignoring her. My sister threw a mini fit right in the ICU hallway. I thought to myself, this is not the time. I felt sorry for my mother, there she was crying and afraid, and my sister was being unreasonable.

After an assortment of promises to see Jacob, my sister relinquished her appalling behavior. I stood right outside the door waiting for my chance to see my older brother. I didn't know what to expect. I was terrified. My mother and father were the first ones to see Jacob. When my dad came out, he signaled for me to go in. I opened the door painstakingly slow, looked around at each of the curtained off sections, and found my mother standing next to my brother's bed. I released the heavy door from my hand, and walked over.

Jacob didn't look good. It took me a minute to gather myself. I couldn't believe what I was seeing. I knew him as a strong, twenty year old athletic male. Now, he was lying in a rotating bed. My brother was so badly injured he couldn't be put in a regular hospital bed. He had his gown on, a tube down in his mouth, and his bed was rotating feverishly slow side to side, and front to back. I had never seen anything like this before. I gazed all around the intensive care unit. It was a big room with several sections, and the doctors had a work station in the middle. Basically, it was one large hospital room with no doors, and only a curtain to separate each patient.

I looked all around at the machines, and then at my brother. I knew where to find the machine that was keeping track of his heart rate and all that, but there were a couple more machines that I didn't know what they were for. It was hard to look at my brother in this setting. I looked at his hands, they were scratched up and bloody, and I began to shed tears. I held my head down and began to imagine what it must have been like for my brother, having to suffer through a car accident. At this point, I still didn't have the details about what *actually* happened.

My mother was trying to compose herself for some reason, but I could see the sad look plastered across her face. She told me to go out and let the next person come in. The doctors only wanted one person at a time in the room, but my mother flat out told the ICU team she wasn't going anywhere. They ultimately allowed her to stay as long as she wanted. I left, and allowed one of my aunts to go in. I stood outside the door trying to remember the image of my brother. It wasn't the best image to hold, but it was the most recent thing I had to hold on to.

My brother had been away at college, and I hadn't seen him in over two months. The first contact with him now consisted of him lying in the Intensive Care Unit. Some kind of way my brothers' best friend was linked to this accident. I wasn't quite sure what it was. His friend had a wrapped up foot and one crutch to help him. I wanted to walk over there and take his crutch, and beat him over the head with it, and then punch him right in his disgusting face. My brother had been warned by our parents to never travel at night. For my brother to be traveling at night there was an underlying reason for him to make a trip home just two weeks before Thanksgiving. College students don't come home two weeks early for any holiday.

After two full hours had passed that day in the hospital, an abundance of family had showed up. I had retreated to the Chapel downstairs. I didn't have some big miraculous prayer to pray, but I needed the stillness, even just for a moment or two. I needed time to mull over the day thus far. Nothing seemed to be making sense to me. A few hours ago I was in bed, now I'm in the hospital visiting my brother. This is a perfect example of how *life* can be so unexpected! We, as a family, were unprepared. In an instant, things can go from good to bad.

I spent most of the day down in the Chapel, trying to piece together a seemingly sincere prayer. My heart wasn't in it, because I was confused, and didn't know what I should be praying for. I knew I wanted my brother to get better, so praying for his healing was a given fact. However, I was so desperate for Jacob to live, that I didn't know if I should have prayed for him to just live, no matter what condition he was in. Furthermore, I was spiritually drained. All I could do the rest of the day was just sit in the Chapel, reflecting.

When Trinity arrived later that night, she met me in the Chapel. She had more details about what happened to Jacob. She found me sitting on the front row by myself.

"Jacob's SUV flipped over," Trinity informed me.

"Flipped? How?" I asked.

"From what I understand, he was trying to avoid hitting a deer in the road," Trinity explained.

"He wasn't alone," I stated.

"His friend Brandon was in the car with him," Trinity said.

"But nothing happened to *him*. Our brother was the one who got hurt. I don't understand, he didn't want to hit the deer?" I asked.

"I guess he didn't, he tried to avoid hitting it, and when he did, he flipped on the pavement into a ditch," Trinity stated.

"It happened at night?" I inquired.

"Yes," Trinity replied.

"I don't understand why he was coming home at night. It doesn't make sense to me!" I closed my eyes, and a vision flashed before me. I put myself in my brother's position. I felt as if I was right there, where he had been. Instantaneously, I was scared. I could only image what it must have been like for him to flip off the pavement into a ditch. He must have been so scared. The situation my sister had described to me sounded like something out of an action movie. I could barely stand the image she had just given me. I know if I felt that way, my parents were suffering ten times worse.

The night seemed to progress rather quickly, and the morning light was shining brightly. Everyone had stayed the night in the hospital fearful that Jacob might take a turn for the worse. The doctor informed us that things weren't better, but he told us they weren't worse. There had been no change in my brother's condition. The latest test results showed that my brother was in a coma. At that moment I had gathered a small portion of hope. A coma meant he was just sleeping. I didn't believe things could get worse if he was asleep.

I spent the entire second day in the Chapel, like I had done the first day. If there was a time for prayer, this was the time. I spent endless hours praying, hoping to get a miracle. Even though my brother needed a miracle, I didn't fear the worse. Jacob was in a coma. A coma meant he was still alive. That's all I wanted. All I wanted was for him to be alive. Nonetheless, I kept thinking the worse would happen at any moment.

One particular incident comes to mind. It was after the weekend had passed and Kim, my father and I, had returned home, to try to seemingly have a normal home life again, while Jacob was still comatose. My mother refused to leave the hospital. There was no way she was leaving his side. The only reason we left was because through Jacob's coma stage, my mom wanted my sister and I to go to school, and *try* to have a home life. Jacob's condition hadn't changed, there was no need to stay at the hospital for hours, waiting and waiting.

One rainy day, Jacob's heart stopped. A team of maybe three or four doctors told my mother and I to step out. I was scared. I didn't know what was going on. I had never witnessed anything like that before in my entire life. As soon as my brother's heart machine stopped, the nurse jumped out of her chair and rushed over to Jacob's bed. We stepped out, and while my mother was frantic, I began to say a silent prayer within. That moment had to be the most terrifying moment of my life. I was so afraid, my heart literally hurt. I couldn't believe what was going on. Jacob was supposed to be okay. He was in a coma, how did his heart stop?

After about fifteen minutes had passed, one of the nurses came out and told us that Jacob was stabilized. I grabbed the nurse and hugged her. I was relieved that Jacob was okay. Word soon began to spread about Jacob and his accident. The next couple of days were flooded with his friends who came to see him. I still resided, and found comfort, in the Chapel. I was in school during the day, and at the hospital at night. Trinity joined me a couple of nights in the Chapel and prayed with me. I believed in her prayers, and I knew she was sincere. We prayed together for Jacob's recovery. During our time together in the Chapel, I never asked her if she thought Jacob was going to die. I believed she wanted the same thing we all did. There was no reason to question what she was thinking, or feeling.

It was after my father had received a call from my aunt telling him to bring Kim and I back to the hospital that things would never be the same again. Trinity hadn't received the message that night, and as a result, we had to leave her behind. My aunt had declared an emergency. It was serious. We traveled that night with my aunt back to the hospital, and didn't leave again.

Everything at this point seemed so unreal. I kept seeing my mother faint and fall to her knees. Nothing made sense. How was this happening to my family? I never understood why Jacob was going through this, why he had to suffer like this. Every time the doctors would give us an update on his condition, it was terrible news! Jacob didn't have good days any more. The doctor kept telling us all the heart attacks my brother had, and how his brain was severely damaged. I saw the dent in my brother's head. I wanted to cry.

The doctor pulled us aside and told us that after Jacob's exploratory surgery in his stomach, they couldn't move him anymore, or he would die. I wanted to collapse. I didn't understand why they needed to do surgery in his stomach, if the problem was his brain. It was too much to handle. There was nothing else they could do for Jacob. It seemed like every time someone would go visit Jacob, they would be told to leave the room, because Jacob's heart had stopped. It didn't matter to me though. When the physicians would tell us that they got him stabilized again, I was hopeful. Nevertheless, I knew in my heart it wasn't good. Someone's heart can't stop that often. It isn't a good sign. On Thursday night I came to the realization that Jacob might die, but I was holding on to hope still.

I remember one of my great aunts, taking my mother's hand, and telling her to just let Jacob go.

"You have to let Jacob go," my aunt said.

"No!" my mother replied. "I'm not going to give-up."

I was sitting a few feet away when I heard my great aunt tell my mother that. I grew disdain for my aunt in that moment. Who was she, to tell my mother to let one of her children go. She wouldn't let someone dictate to her to let one of her children go. I thought to myself how unsympathetic that was. My father later told me that one of my uncles told him to pull the plug. This was the kind of sick family I had. At our lowest point, my great aunt and uncle were basically telling my parents to kill their own son.

That night, I stayed up late with Jacob. I stayed by his side until the early morning hours. Something in me wouldn't let me leave his side. I didn't leave his side until I was too tired to stand. I'll never forget the love my aunt Gina showed for my brother that night. She stayed up with me and didn't leave me until I was ready. Everyone else had left, but she stayed that night.

"Your brother is fighting. He got the worse end of the accident," my aunt Gina said.

"How?" I asked.

"Think about it, when his SUV flipped, the impact was on his side. His friend landed on top of him. All that weight was on your brother. Plus, his head was the one that hit the roof of the car all those times," she informed me.

"I didn't think about that. That's true," I cried.

"That's why we're here. We're here for your family. We're supposed to bear the infirmities of the weak," my aunt proclaimed.

"Do you think he's going to be alright?" I asked.

"I pray he will," she replied.

Around two thirty in the morning, I finally left my brother, and went to the waiting room to sleep where the rest of my family was. I felt good that I had stayed up with him, because I thought he was going to be okay. I didn't rest easy, but I was able to ease my mind that night.

Around eight in the morning on Friday, as the doctors were making their rounds, they informed us, Jacob had a heart attack at five o'clock in the morning. My heart dropped. I didn't understand. I was just with him less than six hours ago, how in the world did he have a heart attack. The doctor lied. I believed in my heart the doctor was lying.

Jacob's doctor told us his condition was so severe, Jacob really couldn't be treated anymore. Scared isn't even the word to describe how I felt that day. I believe they saw him as a lost cause. Prayer didn't seem like it was working, and all the good thoughts, cards, heartfelt sympathies, gathering of family and friends, didn't minimize the pain at all. Other people could pray; I was done. Now, I was operating on fear, mystification, and rage.

The day seemed to move faster than normal. I hadn't eaten all day, and my great aunt was trying to get me to go with her to go eat. I wasn't concerned about feeding my face when my brother was on his last legs. I knew in that instant where my great aunt's mind was. She was a phony, and she didn't care about Jacob. I wasn't jumping to the extreme, her actions prior had let me know where her mind and heart were. Additionally, she had further upset me and it was best for her to remove herself from my sight. First, she tells my mother to let Jacob go, then, she wants me to go out to eat with her like it was dinner and a movie night.

As the evening approached, something wasn't right. My father and I were standing next to Jacob during visiting hours, and even though there was calmness and things seemed peaceful, I felt uneasy. I gently glided my hand down the sole of Jacob's left foot, it was as cold as ice, something wasn't right. I studied all the machines Jacob was hooked up to, trying to act like I knew what I was reading. However, I knew enough to keep my eyes focused on the heart machine. As long as I saw those lines moving up and down, I knew he was okay.

Abruptly, one of the nurses rushes up and tells my father and I to step out of the room. The manner in which she asked didn't alarm me, or indicate there was something wrong. We both stepped out and I took a seat right on the floor outside of the door. I leaned up against the wall and didn't think anything was wrong. I simply thought she was going to run a test, or clean him. As I sat, Trinity strolls off the elevator carrying a bag as if she was prepared to stay the night.

I immediately got up, and embraced her. There was a connection between us right then and there that I couldn't explain. I didn't understand why I was growing emotional. I had been overtaken in trepidation. The red-headed nurse walks out of the ICU and tells all of us to come and gather in the room straight down the hall. I walked down the hall with Trinity, and entered the small rectangular room. I sat on the couch trying to think about what she was going to tell us. The room became overcrowded with my parents, aunts, uncles, and Trinity. Kim wasn't with us, she had been in the actual waiting room with some of Jacob's friends.

When the nurse walked in, she shut the door, and sat down off to the side, away from the rest of us, as if we were her enemies. I didn't brace myself, because I thought she was coming to tell us more negative information about Jacob's condition. I was already mentally prepared for the news. I was used to hearing the upsetting news the doctors gave us each day. Still, I should have come to the conclusion that if she gathered us all in this room, something wasn't right. I held out on the little hope I still had left.

"I want you'll to know we did everything we could to save him," the nurse started off.

I wasn't prepared for what she said next.

"But, he passed away about fifteen minutes ago," she said.

The room was filled with silence. I didn't understand what she had just said. My mouth was dropped open and my mind was clouded. The way she said it, made me mad. How did my brother just pass, when I was just with him ten minutes ago?

"So he died," I asked.

"Yes," the nurse replied.

After she confirmed what I feared, my mind went back to my grandfather and his death. My aunt told my father that through God, if she would've touched her father on his dying bed, she would've brought him back to life. I immediately got up and ran for the door. My only thought was to get to Jacob.

However, before I could even get through the door, my mom yelled and told the family to grab me. I didn't understand why everyone was grabbing me. Maybe my mother thought I was going to hurt myself, or someone else. Whatever she thought she was preventing me from getting to Jacob, they were wasting precious minutes.

"Let me go please, please, please!" I begged.

No one would let me go. All I wanted to do was to go to Jacob's room and see him. I was unsure where all the hostile behavior was coming from. My family caused me to become furious, because they wouldn't turn me a loose. They were holding me as if I were a fugitive running from the law.

"Please, let me go, let me go, please!" I shouted.

Finally, my mother told them to let me go. My shoes were off and I ran as fast as I could to the intensive care unit. When I got there I had yet another stumbling block. Someone had locked the door. There I was banging on the door, wanting the gray-headed man standing there to let me in. He stood right at the door and wouldn't even let me in. I'm not sure if my actions scared him, but he left me outside and didn't even budge.

After these two incidences I was infuriated. No matter how hard I tried, I couldn't get to Jacob. To this day, I'll never know if God would have brought him back. Aside from that, I wasn't even able to say good-bye. The last conversation I had with Jacob was over the phone on his birthday, a month prior. Never would I have thought a few weeks later he would be dead. It's true what they say, that life is short.

I felt a hand from behind grab me, and remove me from the door. I began to lash out. I was upset, and nothing I did brought me to Jacob. I saw the redheaded nurse standing right before me.

"You killed him!" I yelled. "That blood is on your hands, and God will get you!" I told her.

In my heart I honestly felt as if she had walked in and shut off Jacob's machine that night, because she didn't want to deal with him anymore. No one could convince me otherwise at that particular time. It didn't make sense to me, that all day Jacob was fine, and then we she shows up, he dies fifteen minutes later.

My great aunt had placed herself in my view, and she was trying to signal to tell me something, and all of her actions that she had displayed prior, enraged me even more. Before I knew it, I was lashing out at her as well.

"Shut up, you're crying those crocodile tears, but you didn't care about him!" I screamed. She looked behind her in disbelief, as if she couldn't believe that I was talking to her. She was hoping there was someone behind her, but she soon learned it *was* her I was talking to. My face was covered in tears, and I could feel the veins in my head come forth. Someone was holding me back, thinking I was going to physically attack someone, but I knew in my mind I wasn't going to hurt anyone. I was just upset, and the only reason I became hostile was because no one would let me see Jacob. I had been stopped on two different occasions, and held like I was a prisoner.

One of the nurses was so frightened by my behavior, she threatened to call security. I told her to shut up and get out of my face. My mother even told the nurse to leave me alone. Nonetheless, the nurse called security anyway. I remember seeing security rush off the elevator as if they were running in a track meet. Once they saw a hallway full of grieving family members, they quietly excused themselves.

When I approached the Intensive Care Unit door again, thinking I might be able to see Jacob, someone else grabbed me, and in the struggle, I fell to the ground.

"He wasn't saved," I cried.

Through the tears, I remember my father saying, "Yes he was."

"Daddy!" I cried. "Daddy!"

My father rushed to me and I hugged him. I had never been so scared in my life. It had gotten out that some of the family members thought my mind had been negatively affected by different spirits, because of my time in the chapel. I didn't understand how they came to that conclusion, being that they were the ones who forced me to react in such an angry manner. After I received the most devastating news of my life, I simply wanted to see my brother, and say good bye! They were the ones who grabbed my hands and tried to prevent me from leaving the room.

When we were all brought back into the room, and everyone learned about Jacob, I could hear everyone crying. I had been so angry that my heart literally hurt. I clutched my chest, wanting the pain to go away. Someone ran to get a doctor and I was taken in a wheelchair to the Emergency Room.

I can recall lying on the table in one of the examination rooms, and looking up at the ceiling. I saw Jacob waving at me in the midst of white clouds. I knew he was gone, and there was nothing that was going to bring him back. It was difficult for me to momentarily try to wrap my head around the fact that my older brother had just died. I couldn't believe it.

Death was something that happened to other families. Not to mine! How in the world could someone in my family be taken, especially at such a young age? I had lots of questions that I needed answers to, but there wasn't anyone I could talk to. My mother was trying to be strong for the sake of my sisters and I, but I knew it was a matter of time before she completely broke down.

After I was released from the doctor and taken back up to the ICU, where the rest of my family-members were, before I could leave the hospital I had to ask the nurse a question. When I got off the elevator with my aunt and sister, I went back into the ICU and located the nurse who had worked with my brother for the entire week he was there. I glanced over to where Jacob's bed used to be, and now that corner was empty.

"What happened?" I asked.

"He fought as hard as he could, but his body just couldn't take anymore," she replied. "I'm sorry," she added.

I still wasn't satisfied with her answer, but I thanked her and walked out anyway. There was never going to be a good answer that I could accept, that would put my mind at ease. There wasn't anything that could be said to make me understand why my twenty-year old brother was taken away from me.

That night when my head hit the pillow I fell fast asleep. I didn't reflect on anything that happened that night, or try to envision Jacob. I wanted to forget what happened, and the best way for me to do that was to fall sleep. My mind had been put to rest, at least for the next five hours.

When morning came, I remember looking out of the window and seeing the hospital where Jacob passed on. It was time to accept that I didn't have a brother anymore.

The next couple of days seem to run together. My mother and father tried to put on a brave face, but I knew they were hurting inside. It was scary to hear my aunts talk about funeral arrangements, and seeing my dad pick out what Jacob was going to wear in his casket. The first funeral I would ever attend would be my brother's. It was hard for me to picture Jacob lying in a casket, but the night of the wake, there he was, lying in a black suit with a stocking cap over his head to cover the dent he got when he was in the accident.

It didn't look like Jacob at all. The person in that casket wasn't the brother who I grew up with, laughed with, and shared the same room with. It wasn't him. I remember standing over his casket crying. I never thought I would be looking at my brother in a casket. If I hadn't come to terms with his death by now, I did in that moment. I knew it was final.

The day of the funeral was sad, but also a joyous occasion as well. Over one thousand and fifty-five people came to Jacob's funeral. Half of those people were his friends. My uncle, who is the pastor of his own church, preached Jacob's funeral. They called it a home-going celebration.

I had been consumed with the thought of not saying good-bye, and trying to seemingly perform a miracle to bring my brother back, that I forgot the true reality of the situation. That full week that my brother was left here was for a purpose. All those prayers weren't in vain. They meant something. I had to think about all the people who had loved-ones or friends, who had died in car accidents and never even got to see them because they died instantly. My family was blessed to have the chance to see Jacob one last time. At least he remained in the hospital for a week.

The state of mind that I was in soon turned from anger to being grateful. Losing a brother was the hardest thing I had ever dealt with in my life. Nothing in the world could have mentally and emotionally prepared me for the hurt and confusion caused by losing my brother. It wasn't until after we had left the hospital that I realized that death is all too real.

I always knew that people die, but it wasn't real to me until it happened in my family. That was my parent's greatest fear, to lose a child. I remember my father telling all of us that, when we were little. He told us he never wanted to lose any of his children, but his greatest fear came true.

It was a tough couple of years after Jacob had passed, before all of us found our way to being a family again. We were all lost. It didn't matter what we thought we knew about life and death, we have to live as a family knowing that someone will always be missing. As the years go by, it's easier to reflect on the good memories and happy times that we had.

I've only been to Jacob's grave twice since his death. It's been hard to think about what life would've been like if he was still here. If he were alive today he would've been twenty-seven years old. Another thing which plagues me is, the fact that it all happened to fast. One minute I'm getting ready for bed, the next I'm in the hospital with Jacob, and then a week later he's passed on. If there was a chance that Jacob was going to recover, we would have stayed in the hospital, no matter how long it would've taken. Things didn't work out the way we wanted them to.

I still can't say that there's any good, which came from this situation, or that I completely understand Jacob's death. I don't. Until the day I die, I'll never understand why my twenty year-old brother had to leave this earth so unexpectedly.

I think about Jacob every day, and what helps me is knowing that I will see him again one day. The death of a brother is painful to endure, but reflecting on the positive memories, and the love shared, will be enough to hold someone close until they are able to see them again.

CHAPTER SEVEN
Suffering Silently

It was after Christmas, and my grandparents had just left to go back home to Wyoming. They had spent the entire Christmas holiday with us, but told my mom and dad they wanted to go home for the New Year. I thought to myself, why not just stay here with the rest of us and go back home when the holidays are over, but my grandpa insisted that he get back home to be in his house by the turn of the New Year. My dad gave up trying to argue with his father, and eventually paid for my grandma and grandpa to go back home.

They arrived here two weeks before Christmas, and spent time buying my brother Kyle, my sister Lacey and I, all kinds of presents. Grandpa was a little bit of a liar. He would always pull us aside and tell us individually that we were his favorite, and not to tell anyone, because if we did, he would know about it. For years we each thought grandpa loved each one of us more than the other. Or at least I believed it. Plus, it showed in his gifts. I always seemed to get a little bit extra from him. To my brother and sister, they just thought he was giving me more because I was the youngest, and I wasn't the favorite.

Well, those days of getting almost every toy imaginable from grandpa was over. I was almost out of high school, a teenager who was more interested in getting a car, than wondering if I was grandpa's favorite. However, he and grandma never stopped the gifts, no matter how old we got. This Christmas was different though. No one could figure out why grandpa Frank wanted to get home after Christmas in such a hurry. Aside from the fact that he was almost ninety years old, and a little sickly, what possible reason could he have to want to leave us so swiftly?

After New Years, sometime in the middle of January, my dad got a call from grandma telling him he needed to come down to Wyoming as soon as he could.

"What's wrong, mom?" my dad inquired.

"You need to get down here as soon as you can," grandma said.

"Are you okay, is dad okay?" he asked.

"I need you here Franklin," grandma exclaimed.

"I'll be on the first flight I can get, mom," Dad said.

My dad spent the night trying to get a flight to Wyoming. He seemed frightened. I wish grandma would've told him what was wrong. I heard him talking to my mom, asking her what it could possibly be. My father wasn't clear-headed at the time, and he asked the rest of us to come with him. My brother Kyle was already back at college, so my sister and I, packed up, and went with our parents to find out exactly what was going on.

When we arrived at the house, grandma was sitting on the porch wrapped up in a long heavy white coat. She scared all of us to death, we didn't know what to expect. All we knew was that something was terribly wrong. Grandma greeted each of us with a kiss to the cheek, and invited us in. There was my dad, out of his mind worried.

"How are you doing, mom?" Dad asked.

"Not too good," she replied.

"Where's dad?" Dad said.

"He's in the bedroom."

"Mom, what's going on?" my dad demanded.

"I didn't want to tell you over the phone, but it's your father," she cried.

"What's going on with dad?"

"He might die this week," Grandma explained.

All of us stood in the living room stunned beyond belief. I couldn't believe what I was hearing. How could my grandpa only have a week to live? I dropped my bag and hugged Lacey. I could see my dad begin to cry.

"What are you talking about mom?" My dad asked.

"Your father has a terminal illness, and the doctors don't think he'll make it through the week," she replied.

"When did he find this out?"

"Months ago!" Grandma answered.

"It's been months since he's known, why didn't he tell us? Mom, why didn't *you* tell us?" Dad yelled.

"Don't yell at me Fanklin," grandma proclaimed. "Your father didn't want anyone to know about it. He didn't want to spoil the holidays for anyone."

"I can't believe this mom, you should have told us," dad cried. "Where is he?"

"I told you, in the bedroom!"

Dad dropped his things, and ran hastily to the bedroom. I followed right behind him. When dad slowly opened the door, there was grandpa hooked up to some kind of machine with a nurse at his feet. She smiled at us, and told us to come in. My dad held the door open for me to come in and pointed for me to go sit by the window. I obeyed, of course, and took off my coat and stared grandpa up and down. He didn't look too good. He had a long tube in his nose, his skin was as white as snow, and his body was much frailer than it had been at Christmas.

"Dad can you hear me, it's Frank," my dad whispered.

Grandpa didn't respond just yet. Dad touched grandpa's forehead, and kissed him. He stroked grandpa's hair. I guess he was trying to give him an incentive to wake up. I got up from the pink chair I had been sitting in, and walked closer to the bed. I touched grandpa's hand. His hand was surprisingly warm, but I could see all the veins in his hand, and the bruising he had. I looked over at dad and saw a single tear fall from his eye. I touched grandpa's hand again, and this time, he barely opened his eyes.

"Dad," my dad said.

"Grandpa Frank," I said.

Finally, Grandpa Frank looked up at my dad and smiled. He motioned his hand for dad to grab it. I was holding his other hand trying to figure out if he recognized who we were. With a little strength, grandpa told us to lean in towards him.

"I got my favorite son here, and my favorite grandson," grandpa whispered. Being that dad was an only child, and I had finally caught on to grandpa's little game, we at least knew grandpa wasn't losing his mind; he still had a sense of humor.

"I'm mad at you, dad," my dad said. "You didn't even tell us you were sick. Why would you do that to me?"

"Because there's no need to bother you with worry, I'm going to be just fine," Grandpa replied.

"Dad, all these machines, means you're *not* fine," dad exclaimed.

"Hey, I'm fine. Tell him, nurse," said grandpa.

I could tell the nurse felt uneasy, and didn't want to lie. She smiled and said, "We're taking one day at a time, Mr. Gillian, aren't we?"

I knew grandpa wasn't fine, he sure didn't look fine either. The nurse quietly excused herself, and went into the hall, and then my dad followed after her.

"Why isn't he in the hospital?" Dad asked.

"We're doing in-home care," the nurse replied.

"Shouldn't he be in a hospital though? I mean he looks terrible," dad stated.

"Mr. Gillian, you father wanted to be home, and we're trying to accommodate his wishes. Besides, according to his doctors, he could go any day," the nurse said.

My dad didn't want to argue with her, he went to the living room and told my mom and Lacey to come see grandpa immediately. They walked in not knowing what to expect. Instantly, Lacey began crying. I guess she wasn't used to seeing Grandpa Frank in such an awful way. He really was bad off. I just don't understand why he didn't say anything over the holidays. I also don't understand why grandma waited until the week grandpa is suppose to die, to call us and tell us. Maybe she is as optimistic as grandpa Frank is. Maybe she believes nothing is going to happen, and she just wanted us here just because. I didn't know what to think.

That night I called Kyle, and told him what was going on, he had made plans to come in the next two days. I just hoped grandpa was still going to be alive. I stayed up in the bed looking at old photos of Dad, Grandma, and Grandpa Frank. It was such a different time back then. Everything looked easier, and if it wasn't, people sure made it seem that way.

"Ben, are you going to bed?" my mom asked.

"I am, I'm just looking at this old photo album," I answered.

"I'm not going to lie to you Ben, your grandfather is in real bad shape, and the doctors think he might not . . ."

"I know, Mom," I interrupted.

"I don't want you to be shocked if something happens to him. I want you to know that death is a part of life, and it may be your grandfather's time to go," my mom said.

"Mom, please, I'm just trying to look at these photos," I said.

"Alright, goodnight," she replied. I didn't answer, and she shut the door. I wasn't trying to be mean, but I didn't want to hear the death talk. I didn't want to hear the whole life is precious, and short, and we have to cherish each other. That night all I wanted to do was look at old photographs of my grandpa. I spent over two hours just looking at how young and handsome grandpa was. I couldn't believe it, dad looks just like grandpa. They could've been twins. Into the early morning hours, I finally closed the book, and went to sleep.

The next morning, I got dressed, and went to see Grandpa Frank. I went into his room, and there was his nurse adjusting something on the machines.

"Good morning," I said.

"Good morning, young man," the nurse replied.

"How is he this morning?" I inquired.

"He's still the same," the nurse answered.

"Can I stay with him for a while?" I asked.

"Yes, but if he wants to rest, or doesn't respond to you, let him be, okay? He could use the rest," the nurse ordered.

I nodded my head that I understood. The nurse left the room, and I sat in the same place I had yesterday, waiting for grandpa to respond. He just wouldn't wake-up. After about an hour, I was ready to leave. When I opened the door, grandpa saw me and told me to come back in, and sit on the bed. I did what he asked.

"I didn't mean to wake you up," I said.

"No, no, Benjamin, you didn't wake me up," grandpa replied.

He told me to put my hand on his chest and feel his heart. I thought to myself how weird was that, but I did it anyway. There wasn't anything abnormal about his heartbeat. As a matter of fact, I couldn't really feel the beat of his heart, but if it wasn't beating, he wouldn't be alive.

"This is an old war heart," grandpa said.

"War heart," I said baffled.

"Your father never told you about my time in World War II?" Grandpa asked.

"He just told me you served," I answered.

"Your Grandpa, Franklin Gillian, served for two years."

For the next three hours, grandpa told me about his time in World War II, from 1943 to 1945. He told me that he had got caught when Congress approved the military draft, and he had to register. In the heat of the battle, he was drafted to go. Grandpa lasted until the war was over, and he then was brought back home. He told me he was one of the lucky ones who had survived. He told me he had never seen so many dead bodies in one place in all his life. I felt sorry for him, he barely had his eyesight when he came back from the war, and he had to live the remainder of his life partially blind in one eye. I couldn't really imagine what it was he had experienced, but I become intrigued.

Grandpa Frank also told me the story about how he met Grandma. It was after the war, and grandpa had returned home to live with his parents. He said Grandma Lynn, was working with her mother at his house, when they would come to clean. He was much older than Grandma Lynn, she was only sixteen or seventeen, and Grandpa

Frank was almost twenty-six. Her mother didn't want Grandma Lynn hanging around Grandpa Frank. Her mother did everything in her power to stop them from getting together, but when Grandma Lynn turned eighteen, she married Grandpa Frank.

The road ahead for my grandparent's wasn't easy. Grandpa told me they endured one tragedy after the other. First, the twin's Grandma Lynn was pregnant with, died. Then, their house burned down and they had to move in with Grandpa Frank's parents. After about five years had passed, Grandma had a little girl, but when she was three years old, she died from a brain condition that no one knew she had. Grandpa blamed himself, because he felt by marrying Grandma so young, their marriage was cursed.

Grandpa said it wasn't until 1961, when my dad was born, that he and Grandma Lynn became truly happy. Grandpa told me the vision in his right eye eventually gave out, and he could only use about thirty to forty percent of his right eye. He said he also developed a heart condition, in which he would be required to take a certain kind of medication for the rest of his life. He also told me the limp he has, was because of the war. He had been shot in the leg.

Grandma Lynn lived in fear the first five years of my dad's life, grandpa said. She didn't know if he was going to die, like all their other children had. Grandpa said he made his relationship with my dad special. He wanted to be close to his son, and wanted dad to love him. It obviously came true. Ever sense I've known Grandpa, he and dad have been closer than any father and son I've ever known.

It was shocking to hear all of this stuff that Grandpa Frank was telling me. He said he lived through some of the worst times in this world, and he recounted to me the time when he had watched a black man get beaten senseless outside of a restaurant, that he and grandma were in, just because the man came into the restaurant through the front entrance.

"They beat that poor black man like he was nothing, like he was an animal. All he did was go through the wrong door," Grandpa said.

"Did you watch his beating?" I asked.

"I'm ashamed to say Benjamin, but I did," Grandpa answered.

"I can't believe people were that mean," I said.

"There are a lot of mean-spirited people in this world," Grandpa stated.

Grandpa eventually fell asleep, I think I had tired him out from all of the questions I had about his life. He didn't seem like he minded though.

I left the room and shut the door quietly, and let him sleep. I joined the rest of my family in the kitchen. Grandma Lynn was talking about moving.

"I won't stay in this house when he's gone," Grandma stated.

"Where are you going to go?" Dad asked.

"Anywhere, but I can't stay here."

"You're just going to give up this house, and all the memories and love you and Dad shared here?" Dad questioned.

"Franklin, I don't want to stay in this house when my husband dies. Why can't you understand that? It's too painful, son, surely you understand?" said Grandma.

"Why doesn't Grandma come live with us," I asked.

My dad turned and looked at me with a blank look on his face. I couldn't make out if he was mad or thrilled at the idea.

"Would you be willing to stay with us, Mom," Dad asked.

Grandma Lynn turned to my dad, and put her head on his shoulder. She began to weep. I didn't mean to upset her; I probably just should've kept my mouth shut.

"I just don't want to think about that right now. Maybe he'll pull through this," Grandma said.

"Mom, Dad's almost ninety, I don't think . . ."

"You want to go lay down, Lynn?" my mom interrupted.

My mom signaled for my dad to stop the conversation with the fierce shaking of her head from side to side. My mom took grandma by the hand, and helped her to her room. I felt sorry for my grandparents. Is this how their love was going to end? Is this how my grandpa's life was going to end? I guess this is what life holds for those who are up in age. It just didn't seem fair to me that my grandpa was going through so much pain he didn't deserve. Next to my dad, he was the best man I had ever known. He loved all of us and showed it. I didn't want to get used to life without Grandpa Frank.

The next day Kyle came, and he spent some time with Grandpa. Grandpa was telling Kyle, Lacey, and I, old war stories again, and how he never thought he would get home. I began to think about how brave my grandpa was. To be in the heat of one of the bloodiest wars in the world, was incomprehensible to me. I always knew grandpa was strong and courageous, but I came away with a deeper respect for Grandpa Frank.

It was now three days since we all had come to be with Grandpa Frank, and things didn't get worse, but they weren't better either. He now had two nurses to care for him. In my mind I'm thinking nothing bad is going to come Grandpa's way, how could my grandpa leave me? I loved him so much that I refused to think about anything negative. Whenever my dad wanted to talk about Grandpa's death, I left the room. There was no way my mind was prepared to handle death. I was only seventeen. I didn't understand anything about dying and the impact it can have on someone.

One night Grandma Lynn called us into the living room. She had us all take a seat, and she played some old records for us to listen to. They were from the fifties. I thought the music was pretty soothing, but Lacey didn't think so. We all wondered why in the world Grandma was playing this music. She said she wanted to remember her Frank through music. As the music played quietly in the background, Grandma Lynn began to talk to us about her life, and her life with Grandpa.

She pretty much told us the same story that Grandpa had told me, but I already knew the story. It wasn't a shock to hear how they were not supposed to be together.

"When you love someone," Grandma said, "there's nothing in the world that can stop you from being with that person. Whatever happens in the next two days, I don't want you all to be sad," Grandma told us.

I think Grandma Lynn was preparing herself for the worst, and she needed us to help her. She hurt me that night because any hope that I had, I didn't have it anymore, after I saw the way Grandma just gave up. I know Grandpa Frank was old, but why did he have to die? Why do people have to die? That was a question I mulled over in my head for the next couple of days. Then the question became, why do good people have to die?

I couldn't sleep that night Grandma had played those old records. She was giving up, which meant I had to. I quietly went into Grandpa Frank's room, he was resting peacefully, and I watched his chest going up and down slowly. I closed the door and went over to his bed. I took his hand and tried to say a little silent prayer. I wasn't good at praying, besides, why would God even care to listen to what I have to say, I thought. I didn't leave his side that night, and I stayed with him until the morning.

When I awoke, I put my hand across Grandpa's chest to make sure his heart was still beating. I felt what he called his War Heart. It was still beating. I left the room and found Grandma Lynn sitting on the floor next to Grandpa's door.

"What's wrong Grandma?" I asked.

"I'm just here Benjamin . . . just thinking," she replied.

"Grandma why didn't Grandpa go to the hospital?" I questioned.

"Well, your grandfather said he wanted to die in his own bed," she answered.

"He said that?" I asked in disbelief.

"Yes, he said that."

What do you think about his condition?" I inquired.

"It could be any day now," she cried. "The nurse said they don't expect him to live no more than forty-eight hours," Grandma said.

I began to break down right in front of her. She comforted me, and told me she knew I had spent the night with Grandpa, and that she wasn't going to bother me because she knew I needed all the time I could get with him. She said, she already had spent a lifetime with him, and she had all the memories she needed. I hated the fact that we had found out about Grandpa's health so late. He didn't leave us much time to be with him. Two days to live, was stuck in the back of my mind. I had two days to tell my Grandpa I loved him, and to spend all the time I could with him.

That very night I caught Grandma cleaning out a drawer and packing things away in a box. She was getting herself prepared.

Nonetheless, I thought to myself, she was acting kind of hastily. What if things would turn out for the best? That hope I had however faded when I saw all the things my Grandma had done, up until this point. My mother told me probably the best way for her to deal with his death was to face reality, and not live in denial.

"It's a bad thing to live in denial, Ben," my mom said.

"What if someone's not ready to let go?" I asked.

"When you're almost ninety years old, you have to expect the worse. I'm sorry, but you do," she proclaimed.

My mom explained to me that she spent months not accepting *her* mother's death. She told me something that really stuck with me that night.

"We, as humans don't want the hurt that comes with life. The connections we make here on earth are truly only for a little while," she said.

Why I thought? Why do we have to let go of someone we love? I was trying to understand death, and the complexity of dying. Being gone forever wasn't something I knew how to come to terms with. Once my grandpa died, I would never see him again. I would get sad all over again. I had decided that night that I wasn't going to accept anything until Grandpa Frank actually died. Why put myself through the hurt.

I found my dad the next morning, I hadn't really talked to him that much since the first night we had arrived. I wanted to know where his head was at, and what he was thinking. After all, I would be losing a grandfather, but he was losing his father.

"Do you think Grandpa is going to pull through?" I asked.

"I don't think so, Ben," he said.

"I'm sorry you have to go through this, Dad, I know how close you and Grandpa are."

"Thanks son, but your grandfather is going to a much better place."

"You believe that?" I said.

He looked at me as if I didn't believe grandpa was a good person, or something.

"Where does someone really go when they die?" I asked.

"I know what you mean, Ben," he replied.

"Grandpa Frank is a good person, he's going to be free from the troubles, hate, and problems of this world."

"Yeah, but, where do people really go when they die?" I insisted.

"I believe to paradise."

"Paradise?" I said.

"Yes, son, Paradise."

That answer satisfied me for the time being, and when I looked at Grandpa Frank, I imagined him in some place my dad considered to be paradise. Exactly where that was, I didn't know. The thought of death scared me. How was Grandpa going to look, what was his body going to look like? Some things made me a little tense, but I knew it wasn't about me and my fears, it was about Grandpa Frank.

It was Sunday evening, and Grandpa Frank was still alive, despite what the doctors and nurses had been saying. Dad thought the only reason Grandpa was at home, was because the doctors knew he was going to die, and there wasn't a need to waste time and resources on an "old man." I thought Dad was wrong, he didn't know what he was talking about. Grandma told me why Grandpa was at home. He told her he wanted to leave this world in his own home, and in his own bed. To me it made sense. He had built a life for himself in this home, this is where he felt comfortable.

The whole family was packed up and ready to leave that night, except Dad. He was going to stay behind, and the rest of us were going back home. We didn't want to leave, but we had been there a week, and Grandma insisted that we leave to get back to our lives at home. Yet, Dad refused to leave Grandpa's side. He made it clear he wasn't going anywhere. Dad promised he would keep the rest of us informed if anything changed.

"You promise, Dad," I said.

"I will," he answered.

As we began to gather our things, I overheard Dad talking to Grandma. He was a little bothered.

"Were you just going to let him die, and then tell us?" Dad asked.

"I wasn't trying to keep anything away from you or the family," she said.

"I'm taking them to the airport, call me the minute his condition changes," Dad demanded.

"I will do that," Grandma said.

I couldn't believe we were leaving so soon. I was so scared, and I didn't want to leave, but my mom said we couldn't wait around forever. I thought she was being a little cold towards Grandpa Frank, but she was right. The doctors had said he was going to die within six months, but that was eight months ago. They said he had a week to live, however, that was two weeks ago, then it was forty-eight hours, and now it's been three days. No one knew! I just didn't want to go just yet, but it was time.

We packed up and headed out of the house to go to the airport. As Dad started up the car, Grandma came rushing out of the house, waving her hand for us to come back into the house. Something was wrong! Did Grandpa just die? We all swiftly got out of the car and ran as fast as we could back into house. Dad shoved his way through the front door, and headed into the Grandpa's bedroom.

There he was, white as a ghost, his machines had been turned off, and the cotton green sheet rested at the top of his chest. I looked at the nurse, she had a few tears in her eyes. He was gone. I felt myself release the confusion, pain, and hurt, I had bottled up inside. Grandpa Frank had died while we were packing up to go home. In a way I felt mad, because instead of packing up, we wasted precious moments that could have been spent with him. We wasted all that time waiting for something to happen, and it had already taken place.

Dad was right by Grandpa's side with his head on Grandpa's chest, and holding Grandpa's hand. I had never seen my dad cry before. I immediately went over to Dad and tried to hug him. My comforting wasn't doing any good . . . he had just lost his father. Grandma was talking to the nurse, trying to be strong. She knew about Grandpa' sickness, and maybe that's why she didn't react the way we did. She had already had time to prepare herself.

Kyle and Lacey were heartbroken as well, and we were all trying to find comfort in each other.

"It's okay, guys," my mom said to us, "your grandfather is not in pain anymore."

"She's right," Grandma said. "Your grandfather doesn't have to suffer."

Suffer, I didn't know he was suffering. When I talked to him every day, he didn't seem like he was in any pain. Maybe he was trying not to show it? He was still trying to be brave while he was suffering silently. I never would've guessed his body was suffering.

"He suffered for eight long months," my grandma said.

"Everyone, can I have a minute alone please," Dad requested.

He wanted all of us to leave the room, and so we did. The nurse informed him not to move the body or touch any of the machines. Someone was on their way to take the body away. Dad shook his head, complying with the nurse's orders.

I held Dad, and tried to give him a hug.

"I'm okay, buddy," he told me. He hugged me, and told me he would be out in just a second.

We all stepped out and gave our dad the time he needed alone with Grandpa. I stood outside the door and continued to cry. He was gone. It didn't really hit me until I saw Grandpa's lifeless body covered while he was being taken out of the house. The fact that he had his eyes closed didn't mean that much to me, because that's how I saw him throughout my time in his room. He always had his eyes closed. I didn't feel the hurt to my heart until he was removed from the house. Then, Grandma broke down. I knew it was coming.

She sobbed and sobbed while Dad held her in his arms. She was a mess. I didn't want her to be strong for us, I wanted her to feel what she was feeling, and not try to hold back for our sakes. She had just lost the great love of her life. They were married for over sixty years. To have someone drift out of your life after knowing them for sixty years, would be hard on anyone. I now understand why Grandma didn't want to live in the house anymore.

The rest of the night was quiet. Naturally we stayed, and canceled our flight back home. My mom and Lacey slept with Grandma, they didn't want her to be alone. I stayed in a room with Kyle, and Dad slept in the room where Grandpa had died. He wanted to be alone for the rest of the night. I couldn't blame him for that, I don't know what I would do if I lost *my* dad.

I spent the next day trying to understand death, and trying to accept that Grandpa Frank was gone. It was a rough couple of days, and I could feel the sadness throughout the house. As we prepared for the funeral, Dad kept insisting that Grandma come back with us, so that we could take care of her. She didn't want to leave! Now that Grandpa was actually gone, I don't think she wanted to leave. If she were to stay, she would still have that connection with him. She didn't want to lose that connection.

Grandpa's funeral was that Thursday. I remember the limo ride to the church, and how quiet everyone was. The drive seemed to take forever, and all it made me do was think about Grandpa even more.

I walked in, and as my feet began to hit each square tile on the floor, it was inevitable . . . I was going to have to see Grandpa in a casket. I was going to have to see him lying there. I wasn't ready to see that, but I needed to see it. I didn't want to regret years later and looking back, not knowing what he looked like, and coming up with my own picture in my head. Besides, this was going to be the final good-bye from me to my Grandpa Frank. This was going to be the last time I would see his natural body.

At first, when I took a seat, I didn't know what to expect. I didn't know who was going to speak, or what the procedures were. Soon, everything just sort of fell into place, beginning with a beautiful choir. I even shed a few tears because the song was so beautiful. Indeed, it was a sad time, but like Grandpa's program said, it was a time to rejoice and be glad that we were allowed to spend the years we did, with him.

I've never quite understood what people mean when they say, to be grateful and treasure the time we spent with the one's we loved, who are now passed away. To me, now that I know what it's like, I don't feel that way. Why should we have to be grateful? Is it wrong to have questions, and be upset, that we're never going to see them again? All this was going through my head as I was sitting in the church. I didn't know who was going to give me these answers, but at that particular time I didn't want to be grateful, I just wanted my Grandfather back.

The funeral was in some Baptist Church, even though my grandparents weren't Baptist. Dad always told me that Grandpa believed in being good, and doing well. His theory was, if you were good, and did good things all the time, there was no need to go to church, or to ask for forgiveness. Basically, Dad believed in the same philosophy, because I can't remember the last time I was in a church.

After the funeral, a good majority of friends and family came back to Grandma's and ate and talked for hours. Grandpa had a lot of friends who showed up, and they shared stories with us about Grandpa. There was one man in particular, by the name of Clemmons, who said he served with Grandpa Frank in World War II. He told us how they knew each other from school, and the neighborhood.

"Your grandfather was one of my best friends, growing-up," Clemmons said.

"What was the war like for you, sir?" I asked.

"Terrifying. See, I got called up first, and then Frank came after me. Boy was he scared to death," Clemmons proclaimed.

"Did you lose your arm because of the war?" I inquired.

"Ben, that's none of you business!" Mom shouted.

"It's quite alright, madam," Clemmons replied. "I tell this story everywhere I go."

"So you did lose it in the war?" I said.

"Yes son, I did. I also have a prosthetic leg, and I have no hearing in my left ear."

"You and my father were brave men," Dad said.

"I'm not any braver than the next man, I was just called to serve my country, and I did just that. I don't regret a second of my time there," Clemmons replied.

Clemmons had certainly come away with more injuries than grandpa did, but they were both heroes in my eyes. I couldn't imagine going to war and fighting . . . I just couldn't do it. Clemmons went on to tell us how he thought the war was going to last forever, but when he heard of the surrendering of Japan, he knew he was going back home again. Clemmons said a lot of friends didn't make it back, and some of his friends, he watched die right before his eyes. I liked Clemmons, he reminded me of Grandpa Frank in an odd way.

The next day we all went to Grandpa's grave. It was just a pile of dirt so far, but he was gone. We all stood around and watched grandma sit on the cold ground wrapped in one of grandpa's old jackets. She cried to no end. Dad tried to comfort her, but she just gently removed his hands and said, she just needed a few minutes to be alone with Frank. I think Grandma was trying to remember this day, because I don't think she was going to come back for a while.

As the day came to a close, and we were packing to leave the next morning, dad continued to beg Grandma to come back with us.

"Please come home with us, we don't want to leave you here alone," Dad said.

"I can't leave," Grandma Lynn replied.

"Why do you have to stay?" Dad asked.

"I need to grieve by myself for Franklin," she answered.

Dad didn't bother her anymore once she had told him that. Mom says people grieve in different ways, and for grandma, her way was being alone. She was accustomed to grief. She had a life filled with tragedy after tragedy, but I think what kept her going, and what kept her spirit alive, was the fact that she had Grandpa. Now, she didn't have him anymore, and neither did we.

Life when we returned home was sad, but when I reflect on the good things in Grandpa Frank's life, he truly lived the fullness of a life. Ninety incredible years, I only hope I can make it to ninety. What makes me love grandpa even more, was the fact that when he was here over Christmas, and he was suffering, he was still in good spirits, as if nothing was wrong. Like my dad said, he is, and will always be, a brave man whose war heart will never stop beating.

CHAPTER EIGHT
Dear Friend

Fifteen years had gone by since I last talked to LuAnn Billings. That girl just moved away from here and didn't even keep in contact with me. Last I heard she was married with two kids, and working in her mother-in-law's hair shop. I didn't understand why LuAnn had been so upset with me, the last time we talked, and I believe she skipped town to avoid me. I had a good idea of why she left, but I wasn't sure enough. I didn't care though. I was good to that girl. I was the one who was there for her when her own mama didn't even take care of her. LuAnn used to come over to my house all the time. She claimed she was trying to escape her father, who she says was touching her inappropriately. Please, that man wasn't touching her, he was trying to beat her butt.

LuAnn was a wild child, and no one could do anything with her. Her mama tried so many times to pawn her off on others, but no one wanted LuAnn. That heathen of a child was having sex by the time she was fourteen. She would come brag to me, and tell me how all the boys in the neighbor knew her. By the time she was seventeen she was a runabout.

However, I missed LuAnn. No matter how bad things got between us, I still considered her my best friend. I had a hard time growing-up in Louisiana. I felt I was ugly. I wasn't light-skinned like some of the other black girls, and I didn't speak like them either. LuAnn was the only girl who liked me, and wanted to hang around me. I could never understand why.

It was 1956, and my younger sister, my parent's and I, had just moved to Louisiana from Alabama. My father had moved back to Louisiana hoping to find more work. He said the people were racist, and there weren't many opportunities for a black man in the south. I didn't know what he meant, I saw him working hard every day. What was he talking about, *no opportunities*?

He worked for some man at a local store, fixing stuff around the place, and then he would work in some white man's yard, and fix stuff for him too. Mama washed other people's clothes and cleaned houses for her pay. Daddy would complain, because sometimes mama didn't always get paid. He would get mad, and there were many times when he would get his small gun, and try to go and get mama her pay. He never did anything, because mama wouldn't let him. We survived as best as we could.

I was ten years old at the time, and my school was in a little small red, shed-like building with about six big rooms. Most of the kids were black just like me, but no one really knew what grade they were in. We were pretty much just placed in a room with enough space, and an available teacher.

My little sister was only three years old, she would go with my mama on her jobs when she would clean homes, and when my mama stayed at home to wash clothes, my sister was right by her side.

It wasn't until I was entering high school in 1960, that I learned the true meaning of racial lines. I no longer had to go to an, 'all black school'. The way had been paved for me to go to school with the white kids, and my mama told me I was going to be getting a good education.

"You're going with the white kids now," mama told me.

"So," I said.

"So, don't you act like *that* girl. You gonna get the same education the white kids get, you understand me?" mama stated.

"I was getting a good education at my other school, mama. Them people aint going to be teaching me nothing different," I said stubbornly.

"Don't be back talking me girl, your father would lay you flat if he heard how you were talking to me."

"I'm sorry, mama," I cried.

"Get on in your room now, and get that material from behind your closet and I'll make you a dress for your first day of school," Mama demanded.

I don't know why my mama was so excited about me going to some white school. I don't know why she thought things were going to be so much better. Besides, even though that law was enacted, a lot of the schools didn't integrate immediately. I wasn't stupid, I knew they didn't want colored people at their school. I wasn't getting excited like mama was. In fact, I really didn't want to go. I didn't want to have to meet new people. I was angry! I guess it showed.

"Don't be acting up over there at Hillside, Mattie," daddy told me.

"I won't," I replied.

"Mattie, he's serious. You treat them people with respect, you understand?" Mama said.

"Yes, mama," I said.

I remember my first day, a hot muggy day in September. Before daddy went to work, he drove me to school and told me to wait outside the schoolyard, and that he would pick me up. He didn't want me to walk home or get on the bus. I told him I understood. I got out of the car, and before I could even walk up the steps, a teacher told me I needed to wait with him. Daddy saw what was happening, but he didn't move. He watched from the car.

When the bell rang, I was standing with a few other black kids, the teacher let all the white kids go in first, and he made us walk in the school last. We walked single file in front of the teacher. When we entered Hillside High School, I about fell over. Not only was the floor covered in clean light blue tiles, the walls were coated with the whitest paint I had ever seen. The freshness of the building smelled like a summer garden in France. The teacher held the door open for us, and told us to wait for him. I remember telling the lady in the office that my name was, Mattie James, and I was in the ninth grade. She was polite, and escorted me to my first class.

When the lady dropped me off and told me to go in, I was nervous. I entered the classroom and saw nothing but white girls and white boys. They didn't say anything to me. In fact, there weren't any seats left for me. The teacher acted like he didn't see me, and totally ignored me. No one was going to help me. I was not about to sit on the floor. I eased my way to the back of the classroom, and stood there for about fifteen minutes.

Finally, a pretty blonde-haired girl got up, walked to the front of the class, got a chair, and brought it back to her desk. She waved me over to her seat. I didn't move, I didn't know what she was doing. She motioned for me to come over once more. This time I moved. She put the chair right next to her desk, and pointed for me to have a seat in her desk. I tried to take a seat in the extra chair, but she physically moved me to have a seat in her desk. She took the chair, and allowed me to sit at *her* desk.

"Thank you," I whispered.

"You're welcome," she replied.

Throughout the class she was helping me with my notes, because I didn't understand what that man was talking about. He was going too fast, and he didn't stop for anyone's questions. When the class ended, the nice girl stuck out her hand and I did the same.

"I'm LuAnn Billings," she stated.

"I'm Mattie James," I replied.

"You scared?" LuAnn asked.

"Yes," I answered.

"Why don't you stick with me," LuAnn said calmly.

Ever since that first day in class we became friends, the best of friends. It wasn't until I brought LuAnn over to my house one day, that I realized some people didn't like our friendship. My mom and dad were among those people. My mama about threw a fit, because LuAnn was inside of her home.

"Why you go and bring that white girl over here, Mattie?" Mama asked.

"Why not?" I asked.

"Her parents don't want her hanging around some little black girl," Mama said.

"You don't even know her parents," I said.

"You can't be doing stuff like that Mattie, you gonna get in some trouble."

That night my dad had a long talk with me about racial boundaries, and how doves stick with doves, and how black birds stick with black birds. I didn't quite understand all of this until I was much older. I soon learned that mama and daddy were just trying to protect me. What they didn't realize, or failed to realize, LuAnn and I were friends. She wasn't afraid to talk to me in the hallways at school, or ashamed to eat with me at lunch. She introduced me to her friends, and she brought me around to her family.

Nevertheless, there was something about LuAnn that didn't make sense to me. She seemed to have a loving home, but I could always count on her coming to my window in the dead of night to let her in. She always spent the night at my house, and she never wanted to go home. From the outside it seemed as if LuAnn had everything she could want. Not only was her house bigger than mine, she had all the clothes in the world, what could possibly be missing from her life?

Our friendship grew year after year, there was no one like LuAnn. She taught me things my mother would have had a flat out conniption over. I also learned more things than I ever cared to know about. The years just seemed to sort of pass us by. Before we knew it, it was time to graduate. There weren't many educational opportunities for me as far as college, so I ended up taking a job at a local grocery store until I decided what I wanted to do, or could afford to do.

LuAnn left me, and went to some college in Texas. She wanted to be a journalist. I didn't know why she wanted to do that; I thought she would've chosen something like fashion, or interior design. She was better at it than I was. The first year apart from my best friend was rough. I didn't have anyone else to hang around. A good majority of the girls weren't like LuAnn. They didn't want to be seen around town with some dark-skinned girl. I understood that, but still showed myself friendly towards them.

A few months into the spring, LuAnn came back home, and told me her parents were getting a divorce, and that her father might be going to jail. I didn't want to poke my nose in her business, but I just had to know why her father would be going to jail.

"What did he do, LuAnn?" I inquired.

"The cops say he's a prime suspect in a rape," LuAnn said.

"Oh, Lord, are you serious?" I stated.

"He's already been arrested!" LuAnn told me.

I thought about all the times LuAnn had told me about her father, and how he would try to touch her. I didn't believe LuAnn, but now I was tending to believe her. It wasn't that I thought she was just a liar, I just couldn't imagine a man doing that to his own daughter.

"I want you to be honest with me, LuAnn," I stated. "Did your father really try to molest you?" The words just sort of came out of my mouth all at once. Before I knew it, what I was thinking, came out. She hesitated for a moment.

"He had sex with me," she blurted out.

My heart fell, and I didn't know what to say.

"My mother didn't believe me, she didn't want me in her house. She didn't want me saying those things about my father. Whenever I would bring it up, we would get in a huge fight, and I would leave."

"And you would come to my house," I said.

"Every chance I got, I tried to get away from that house," LuAnn professed.

LuAnn didn't go back to college the next year. She stayed in Louisiana and went to go and live with one of her aunts. Things got bad for LuAnn and I. The beautiful friendship we once shared would be turned upside down. For the sake of our friendship I wished LuAnn would have stayed in Texas and finished college. It was because of her staying in Louisiana, which caused us to grow apart.

Our friendship was rocked to the core because of Buddy Hicks. Buddy Hicks was the kind of guy who all the girls in town wanted. He was tall, he had clear blue eyes, and slicked back brown hair. He worked over on a ranch about five or ten miles from where LuAnn and I lived. He first caught my eye one day while he was in the store that I was working at. He glanced over at me and smiled at me, as if I was the prettiest girl he had ever seen. I didn't pay that boy any mind, he did that with all the girls, but it sure did feel good to be noticed by a male.

I remember telling LuAnn about what happened between Buddy and I. She didn't seem too excited about what I was telling her. I didn't understand. I knew it was never going to go anywhere.

"Don't be trying to fall for Buddy, Mattie, people would run you out of town," LuAnn said.

"Why?" I asked.

"Mattie, a black girl and a white boy getting together, please, that's like an abomination. Folks don't take that kind of stuff around these parts. They'll kick your butt," LuAnn proclaimed.

"I was just telling you what happened today, that's all," I muttered.

It was funny how things turned out for LuAnn and I. I didn't listen to her, or take her advice. I grew to like Buddy, and eventually, I loved him. He would always come to see me, and he would walk me home. Sure we got deadly looks, but I didn't care, and neither did Buddy. Not only did I have to worry about the folks around town, I also had my parent's to worry about. My mom beat me good, when she saw that I brought a white boy home. I was almost a fully-grown woman, and there my mama was, whipping me with a switch. Her and daddy scolded me all night long.

It didn't matter what anyone said, I did what I wanted to do. It cost me though. LuAnn soon found out about Buddy and I, and she wanted to kill me. I didn't know it, but LuAnn and Buddy used to be together. I guess it bothered her to see me with him, or to see that he had moved on. Word got back to her and she let me have it. However, that wasn't the night which ended our long friendship.

"He could never love you the right way," LuAnn told me.

"Why, because I am Negro!" I shouted.

"Exactly," she said.

"I don't understand you LuAnn, why are you being so mean to me?" I asked.

"I'm just telling you the truth. It doesn't look right for you to be with someone else's man, especially a white man," LuAnn cried.

"Are you saying Buddy can't move on?" I asked.

"I need you to stop seeing him, Mattie," she requested. "I've never asked you for a lot, can't you do this one thing for me?"

"What about *my* happiness, LuAnn?" I cried.

"Please leave Buddy alone," she begged.

"I don't think I can do that," I said. "I won't do that!"

"I understand," LuAnn uttered.

She walked out of my face, and I never saw her again. She left upset because I wouldn't stop seeing a man who I was in love with. I didn't have anything to do with her and Buddy's relationship, and it bothered me that she was willing to throw a six-year friendship away over a guy whom she had been broken up with for a while. It didn't make a bit of sense to me.

The years passed one by one, and I didn't see, or hear from, LuAnn. I later found out that her dad was in fact the man who raped a twenty-five year old woman back when LuAnn and I were in high school. He got something like twenty years, to life. LuAnn's mother moved out of Louisiana, and didn't even say anything to LuAnn. LuAnn's aunt told me all this when I went to her house to try to talk to LuAnn, and see how she was doing. LuAnn's aunt told me that LuAnn had been gone for some time. She left one morning and told her she needed to get away. She didn't question her, being that LuAnn was a grown woman.

Buddy and I married, and had a son. My parent's grew to love Buddy. At first, they weren't accepting of the marriage, or my son. However, I told them that they were no better than any racist, because of how they were acting. How could they speak about injustice and inequality when they were carrying the same closed-minded, ignorant mentality as a bigot?

No matter how hard I tried, year after year, I just couldn't find my friend LuAnn. I even traveled back to Texas with Buddy, thinking she maybe went back to college, but she hadn't. It was like she had disappeared off the face of the earth. I was standing face to face with her, and then all of a sudden, she was gone. No one knew what happened to LuAnn Billings.

I played over and over in my head what I could've done differently. Except, I wasn't willing to give up Buddy. I understood that LuAnn was my best friend, and I knew her before I knew Buddy, but I didn't feel it was right for me to miss out on happiness because LuAnn said so. I needed to know what it was, that made LuAnn act territorial over Buddy. He told me the root of her anger.

It was when we were still in high school and LuAnn was seventeen years old. The guys had known her as the easiest girl. They knew it, and she knew it. It was when she met Buddy that changed her life dramatically. He accidentally got her pregnant according to LuAnn, and she actually wanted to have the baby. I never knew she was pregnant because she never told me. Buddy was willing to help her once he finished school. He was only a year older than both of us, and he wasn't going to college. He had plans to stay right in Louisiana.

Unfortunately, things didn't work out for LuAnn and Buddy. She ended up losing the baby two months into the pregnancy. She was devastated according to Buddy. I didn't seem to notice a difference, LuAnn was always sad. I thought she was just going through regular family problems. I tried to comfort her the best way I knew how. She was there for me, and I was there for her.

The miscarriage really affected LuAnn, and she had a connection to Buddy that I never really knew about. Buddy told me that she was the one who broke things off. He wanted to be with her, but LuAnn was the one who didn't want to be with Buddy anymore. I couldn't understand why she didn't want to be with him anymore if she had felt such a strong connection to him. It didn't make sense to me. Buddy says he didn't understand either. He just moved on.

From LuAnn's point of view, I could whole-heartedly imagine why she was so upset with me. It seemed like I took Buddy right from under her nose, but that's not how it happened. In her mind all she could see was betrayal from me. It hurt me that she walked out of my life, but I refused to give-up potential happiness. Maybe that proves what kind of friend I really was to LuAnn.

I wasn't measuring how much she did for me, and how much I did for her, we were friends. I loved her because of who she was, and I thought she loved me for who I was. I wonder how she could just throw away a friendship because of a guy. I needed to know more, but there was no way to find her. At first it didn't bother me, but now that almost fifteen years had gone by, and I hadn't heard from LuAnn, it bothered me.

After Buddy and I moved a couple of miles west from my hometown, I tried to look for LuAnn's mother. I knew some of her family lived in this part of Louisiana and I needed to make another attempt to try to get in contact with her. I was successful in locating LuAnn's uncle who she used to talk about. He told me the last thing he heard was that LuAnn was married with two kids, somewhere here in Louisiana.

I followed her uncle's lead but it didn't prove to be true. I remember sitting in my house one day getting a call from LuAnn's aunt. She told me she needed me to come by her house, because she had something she needed to give to me. I told Buddy I wanted to go by myself, he agreed, and I left the next day to go back into town.

I arrived at her aunt's house and she let me in. Before she explained to me why she brought me over, she went into this big to do about friendship and loyalty, and how no one is loyal these days. I didn't know what she was taking about, but I smiled and nodded and acted like I agreed with what she was saying to me. She eventually leaned over her chair to grab a stack of letters off of her desk.

The letters were stacked nice and neat and held by a rubber band. She handed me one letter, then surfs through a few more, and hands me another letter. Finally, she rummages to the very bottom of the stack, and pulls out a blue letter-sized envelope. As she hands me these letters, I find that all of the letters are addressed to me. I was in a state of confusion, why would anyone send me letters to LuAnn's aunt?

"You need to read these letters, they were mailed from this address, and have come back. I guess LuAnn had the wrong address," she said.

"You know where LuAnn is?" I said blissfully.

"Yeah! Well, I knew where she was, didn't you know?" she asked.

"No, I don't know where she is," I cried.

"Oh, baby, LuAnn died over ten years ago. I just found that out a few months ago," her aunt stated.

"Died," I stuttered.

I couldn't believe what her aunt had just told me. I needed a minute to think about what she had just said to me.

"How did she die?" I asked.

"LuAnn died of pancreatic cancer," her aunt informed me.

The tears rolled heavily down my face. I couldn't believe that my best friend had died, and I didn't know about it.

"Was she here in Louisiana?" I questioned.

"She was living in Texas at the time. Poor girl went back to school, got her education, and then two years later she died of cancer," her aunt said.

"Someone told me she was married, and had two children. Is that true?" I asked.

"Well, yes, she *was* married, but she only had one child, a little boy," she said.

Her aunt tried her best to console me, but I didn't want to be consoled, I had spent over ten years looking for my best friend, and I didn't even know she had died. I hated myself in that moment. I was the one who caused her to leave Louisiana. If I just would've broken up with Buddy, and found someone else, she would still be alive today.

I excused myself from the house, thanked LuAnn's aunt for the letters, and walked out of her house. Before I could make it to the car, I stopped on the bottom step of the house, sat down, and I cried and cried for my friend. In the midst of the tears, I pulled out all of the letters LuAnn's aunt had given me. LuAnn had addressed the letters to the wrong house; she had written the wrong address. I guess her aunt held on to the letters thinking LuAnn was going to come back for them eventually.

I opened the first letter, which she entitled, dear friend. As I began to read the letter, LuAnn explained to me how she was sorry for the things she had said to me in the heat of our argument. I didn't need the explanation from Buddy, she had given it to me in her letter. She said the reason she had to break it off with Buddy, was because she was leaving for college in Texas, and she didn't want to be in a long distance relationship. However, she explained to me that she still cared for Buddy. I read on, and she explained to me that she was going back to college, and that she didn't want to be a journalist anymore, she wanted to be a psychologist. LuAnn said she wanted to counsel people, because she had been through so much in her life. She ended the letter and told me to write her back.

When LuAnn didn't hear from me, she wrote me another letter. She begged for my forgiveness, and didn't want us to lose the friendship we had. She told me I wasn't just her best friend, she said I was her sister. It's funny, because that's the same way I thought of her. As I continued to read her letter, I grew more distraught, because LuAnn thought I hadn't forgiven her. It hurt that she had died thinking I hated her. I didn't know how I was going to go on living with myself.

I read page after page, thinking about what she must have felt during this time. I couldn't go to her and tell her that I was sorry for what I had done. There was another letter she wrote entitled, dear friend, which was the last letter she wrote me. She said she didn't want to bother me anymore, and that if she didn't hear from me, she would stop writing. She never heard from me, and so she cut all ties with me.

Why would fate let that happen to me? Why did my best friend have to die thinking I hated her? I gathered all the letters and headed to my car. I remember my mama's old saying about the clouds in the sky, the darkness over the land, and the swarm of birds means someone is in distress. The distressed person was *me*. I had to tell Buddy. He had to know!

As I was driving home, I had to compose myself. My face was covered in warm tears. I regretted so many things I did in my life when it came to LuAnn. I let her down. The one person who had stuck her neck out for me all those years ago was dead because of me. I rushed into the house with the letters in my hand. I found Buddy sitting in the kitchen reading.

"Buddy, it was me!" I shouted. He looked dazed and didn't know what I was talking about. I stood in the kitchen with my hands covering my face, as the tears continued to roll faster and faster down my face. Buddy got up and grabbed me.

"What are you talking about?" he said.

"I killed LuAnn," I said.

"What!" he shouted. "What are you talking about?"

I displayed the letters in my hand, and signaled for Buddy to take them.

"Read these," I cried.

Buddy took the letters, and threw them down. He was more concerned about me. He tried to pull me together. He dragged me to the table to have a seat. I was too upset to move on my own. He pushed back one of the chairs at the table, and put me in it.

"I need you to calm down, Mattie," Buddy stated. "I need you to tell me what in the world you're talking about."

After a while, I finally calmed down, and I began to tell Buddy what had happened. I told him all about the letters, and how LuAnn died. I explained to him that we should've never been together, and never should've gotten married. He looked at me in amazement, as if he couldn't believe what I was saying to him.

"Why, Mattie, are you saying you don't love me?" Buddy cried.

"I do," I muttered.

"Then why would you say something as mean as that?" he asked.

"She died because you and I broke her heart! She didn't want me to be with you, and she told me to stay away from you, but I didn't listen," I explained.

"Listen to me, Mattie. I truly understand your love for LuAnn, but you and me are not responsible for LuAnn's death. You also forget that I tried to stay with LuAnn, she left *me*. She told me she was leaving town," Buddy stated.

What he was saying was making sense to me, but I still wasn't at ease. My conscious will always be affected by the fact that, LuAnn died thinking I didn't love her anymore. How was I supposed to go through the rest of my life with that kind of guilt and hurt in me? Buddy said as long as I knew in my heart I didn't hate LuAnn, that's all that mattered. Now, Buddy was upset with *me*.

"I'm surprised at you, Mattie, how you could just dismiss our love like it's nothing. I can't believe you regret marrying me," he said.

"I didn't say that," I replied.

"But that's exactly what you mean. It wasn't easy for me to just casually start dating a black girl. I received hate from all sides, the whites, and the blacks of this town," said Buddy.

"What are you saying?" I asked.

"I don't regret one minute I've spent with you, but I resent you coming in here telling me that you and I are the cause of LuAnn's death. Heck, I miss LuAnn, but I wasn't going to wait around for her. And she wasn't a good friend if she expected you to deny yourself happiness, just because *she* couldn't find it," Buddy explained.

I knew I hurt Buddy that night, but honestly, I was still thinking about LuAnn, and how she felt betrayed. It bothered me for weeks and weeks. There was no one I could talk to about it. Buddy certainly didn't want to hear anymore about the issues in my friendship with LuAnn. I had taken her letters and stored them in a box at the top of my closet. I wasn't going to dare throw those letters away.

After a few weeks had passed, I went back to LuAnn's aunt's house, and talked to her briefly. I had to know where LuAnn was buried. With one swift phone call made by her aunt, I knew where to find her grave. Before she died, her aunt told me she wanted to be brought back to Louisiana. I got the address, and headed to the cemetery.

When I got out, I couldn't believe beautiful LuAnn was here. I was still stunned beyond belief. I circled up and down, trying to find the letter of the plot, where LuAnn was. After about ten minutes, I found where she was. The only thing left to do was find which grave was hers.

I walked humbly through the grass, trying to find the name, LuAnn Billings. I searched long and hard, until I finally discovered where she was. I made my way over to the pretty yellow and blue flowers that filled her grave. It was hard, at first, to look down and imagine anything but an elegant light surrounding LuAnn. She was my one and only true friend. I thought I had it rough, but her life was one I didn't envy as I got older. I at least had both of my parents, and they loved me. LuAnn couldn't say the same.

I brushed the dirt away from her name, and just stared at her name over and over. I couldn't believe it. When no one would accept me, or make me welcome, LuAnn did. I loved how she was so courageous. It didn't bother her that people would call her, "a nigger lover." She seemed unmoved. She still told me I was her best friend.

Whenever I endured problems from others, she was right there for me, helping me. When she needed a place to stay, food, and somewhere to escape to, I was there for her. In a way I was kind of mad at LuAnn also. She was the one who walked out on me, and took out her anger on me as well. If it truly bothered her to the core like she said, I would've given up Buddy. I was willing to, but she disappeared before I could make peace with her.

I had made a little wooden message for her that I was going to put on her headstone. I had Buddy inscribe it, 'dear friend.' LuAnn *was* my dear friend. I knew I would never find another friend like her. LuAnn allowed me to see beyond the, "racial lines" in Louisiana. When mama and daddy first told me about racism, and bigotry, I needed to see it for myself. I needed to see just exactly what it was they were talking about.

Spending my entire youth in Louisiana in the 1960's, I saw what mama and daddy were talking about. However, it was LuAnn who proved me wrong. I thought all of those white people were racist. LuAnn showed me not everyone thinks and acts the same. One conversation I can remember having with LuAnn will always stick out in my mind.

"I want you to get out of this town and move far away from here," LuAnn said.

"I'm working on it," I replied.

"There's nothing worse than being stuck in this racist town, with no way out, and no education," LuAnn told me.

"I'm not smart enough to go to college, or something like that," I said.

"You're going to have to try somehow to get out of here," LuAnn replied.

"I don't know if I'm ready to leave," I cried.

"No matter where I go, or you go, we'll always be best friends. There's no one that could ever take your place, Mattie," LuAnn told me.

"There's no one that could ever take your place either, LuAnn," I stated.

LuAnn wanted the best for me. That's how I know she was my true friend. I kissed her grave, left the flowers, and went back home. That would be the last time I would visit the cemetery. That's not how I wanted to remember LuAnn. I didn't go back!

A couple of years passed by, and I was able to do what LuAnn had wanted for me. Buddy, my son, and I, moved out of Louisiana, and moved up north. I left that racist town I was in, and started afresh. My sister and mother would later come join us, and daddy had already passed on by this time. He was buried in Louisiana.

I ended up finding LuAnn's son. He still lived in Texas with his father, and I didn't want to bother him, to tell him I once knew his mother. I just let things be. Everyone was well situated in their lives, and I didn't want to go stirring up old emotions.

I will forever be grateful to LuAnn's aunt. If she hadn't contacted me, I still, to this day, would have never known what happened to LuAnn. Irrespective of whether or not, I found out if she was dead or alive, I always carried her in my heart, and there is nothing in this world that could have prevented her from being my dear friend . . . I love you, LuAnn.

CHAPTER NINE
It happened at three

It's been tough on Brian ever since the accident. For months no one could get through to him. Nothing anyone said, or did, could make him just snap out of the terrible state of mind he was in. I tried everything I could think of to grab a hold of him, and tell him its okay, be strong, and live your life. It didn't work! The connection that someone has with another can never really be broken with the snap of a finger. I wish I would've known that. It wasn't so much that I was trying to push Brian into recovery mode, or that I was heartless to the fact that he, like the rest of us, had lost someone we truly cared about; it was the way in which Brian was dealing with his emotions.

People say it's not good to keep things bottled up inside, and everyone needs to release the emotions they feel. Not Brian! Brian was the opposite. He held everything inside until he just couldn't take it anymore. I know the exact day, time, and place I was, when I got the call about Brian. I'll never forget that day. I thought my mind was playing tricks on me. I was just in the emergency room six months ago receiving the worst news of my life, and now, I was back there again with the call that my brother had just been admitted.

If I wasn't the oldest, and the strongest in the family, I would've had a breakdown. I couldn't take the pressure to keep everyone together and to try to patch people's lives together. What about me, what about what I was feeling? Everyone was so concerned about Brian, and how he was taking things, no one even bothered to ask how I was dealing with the accident. The family automatically assumed that everything would be taken care of because I was the oldest, and I was seemingly the strong one. There were times when I wanted to cry alone, and not be bothered.

I didn't even get to grieve properly, because I was too busy taking care of a brother who thought shoving alcohol down his throat was the answer. I was always there for Brian, but when has he ever been there for me? When did he ever take the time to come and see about me? He's too wrapped up in his own miserable destructive life to care about anyone else. I wanted so badly to tell him to man up, and stop depending on everyone, but I couldn't. I watched him that night in the hospital. My little brother was in bad shape, and it was up to me to help him.

Brian's problems basically started when he picked-up a disgusting drinking habit. It was habitual for him to drink all morning, and all night, and waste his life away. When he had graduated from college and moved back home, my mom told him to pack up and go, because she couldn't take his dinking. Brian was a nasty drunk, and my mom wasn't going to put up with it.

My dad called me one day and asked if I would let Brian come and stay with me, just until he figured out what it was he wanted to do with his life. I didn't want him staying with me because I knew the type of person Brain was. He was a lazy drunk, and not consistent in anything he did. I told dad, "Six years in college wasn't enough time for him to figure out what he wanted to do?" My dad laughed, and told me I needed to learn what it meant to be a big brother. Maybe he was right? Maybe I should've been more sympathetic towards Brian. Maybe our relationship would have been better as brothers.

Brian was closer to our other brother Stewart anyway. Everyone loved Stewart. Even I, wanted to be like Stewart, and I was the oldest! Stewart was mom and dad's dream child. He was humble and quiet, and mainly they praised him because he was some big-time criminal defense lawyer in Washington.

I had plans to become an attorney, but things just didn't turn out right for me like they did with Stewart. My mom says if I had been more of a warm-hearted person, I would've got more blessings in life. I didn't necessarily agree. I was just too stupid to do well on that dumb law school admissions test. I ended up becoming a high school history teacher.

Eventually, against all my reservations, I let Brian come and stay with me. My dad thanked me and told me I was a better man than I gave myself credit for. I didn't feel that way. I was only doing a favor for my father, so mom could keep her sanity. The relationship between my mother and Brian was strained at times. I couldn't understand why. I didn't know if he wasn't living up to her expectations, but her patience ran thin with Brian. He was a screw-up in my eyes, but with a little guidance he could get back on track.

He received that guidance from my father. For some reason, dad had all the patience in the world with Brian, and I think Brian knew that. Whether Brian was changing academic majors, quitting a job, or falling into debt, dad was always there supporting him, and getting him out of a bind. Now, I'm not saying my mother didn't love him, but Brian knew whom he could go to if he had a problem. That's the way dad was. I think all three of us knew that to some degree.

It had been over five months, and Brian was still living with me, and things between us weren't good, but they weren't too bad either. I remember getting a call from mom one day telling me that dad was leaving town on business, and that he wanted Brian and I to come to the house. I asked when he was leaving, and she told me that weekend. We had made plans to get together the day before to come over.

Brian and I showed up and spent the majority of the evening with our parents, talking about different things. Dad talked about the company he was working for, and how they were finally paying for him to travel on business. It had been ten long years for him, and now he was finally getting the chance to feel a part of the team. I was excited for him. There was nothing unusual about that night, and nothing could have prepared any of us for the pain that would soon come our way.

It had been a week since dad left, and he was due to return today. I can recall one morning sitting at my desk, when I got a call from mom telling me she needed me to drive her to the airport to pick up dad. She didn't want to be bothered with the downtown traffic. I agreed, and completed the rest of my day. As soon as school was out I drove to my parent's house, picked up my mom, and we drove to the airport together.

When we arrived at the airport, we noticed two ambulances parked right in front of the airport. There were multiple police cars as well. We didn't know what was going on. I dropped my mom off at one of the other entrances and went to park the car. When I approached my mother we cautiously headed inside trying to avoid the chaos.

"Holden, wait here," my mom said.

I stood at the entrance and watched my mom make her way into one of the lines. It looked like she was going to ask for some information. I turned to one of the big screens to try to find exactly when dad's flight would be in. I became annoyed instantly. There was too much commotion going on in the airport. I saw all these ambulances parked outside, but the EMT's I spotted, were just standing as if they were waiting for someone to get off the plane.

My mom made her way back to me, and told me dad's flight was already here. We moved closer to the crowd hoping to see dad, but we didn't spot him. I continued to look at each person I passed. I was looking for an average height, thin, bearded, gray-haired man. I didn't see my dad. I continued to look, but I just didn't see him anywhere.

When I turned to look to see if dad was getting off the plane, I didn't see anyone, not even the EMT's that was standing there. I looked over my shoulder to see if they had left, but the two ambulances were still parked there.

Then, out of nowhere, I saw the guys carrying out a stretcher. They required everyone to move back and give them room to get through. They moved fast, and as they rushed past me, I saw who was on the stretcher. It was my dad!

I forgot about my mom still standing in the midst of the crowd. I ran to follow the EMT's, and once I got outside, I began to question them.

"Excuse me, what happened to him!" I said frantically.

"Will you please move, sir," one of the guys asked.

"This is my father, what happened?" I demanded.

"We can't release any information to you at this time. If he's your father, you need to go to St.Vincent's on Second Street, that's where we're taking him," the man replied.

Tears forming in my eyes, I ran back into the airport to find my mom. She was standing by the entrance with a worried look on her face.

"What's wrong?" she asked.

"It's dad," I said.

"What!" Mom cried.

"We need to get to the hospital right now, right now! We need to go!" I stated.

My mom didn't ask any more questions. She followed me, and she kept wiping her face, trying to fight back tears. There was silence in the car on the way to St. Vincent's. In my mind I'm thinking that dad had a black out, or that he felt weak from no food or something. I tried not to think of too many scenarios of what could be wrong, because I didn't want to stumble upon the worst. I kept glancing over at my mom. She didn't know what to do with herself. I could see she wanted to cry all over the place, but she kept holding herself together for some reason. I certainly wasn't going to stop her if she wanted to cry.

When we reached the hospital we both flew out of the car, and hurried to the first nurse who could help us. She said we needed to go down to the emergency room, because that's where my dad was brought in. We asked for directions, but the nurse was kind enough to take us down there herself. She checked some information, and pointed to a spot where we could wait. My mom took a seat, but I couldn't sit down, I was nervous. I didn't know what was going on.

Before I called Brian, or anyone else, I wanted to make sure I knew what was going on. I didn't want to scare anyone if there was no real bad news to give. We waited for close to an hour, before anyone came to give us any information. I kept repeatedly going up to the nurses and asking them if they had any information. They kept telling me to wait for the doctor. I was, but no one was giving us any information. I just wanted dad to be okay, I needed him to be okay.

A short, middle-aged man came through the double doors with his hands on his hips, and asked for the family of, Omar Rutledge. My mom jumped up and ran to where the door was. I followed right behind her. The doctor stuck out his hand and introduced himself. I didn't care about being formal, I wanted an update on my dad.

The doctor walked us behind the double doors into the emergency room, and took us over to a corner wall.

"Mr. Rutledge had a heart-attack," the doctor stated.

"Oh, my God," my mother blurted.

"How is he?" I asked.

"Right now, it's touch and go. He's holding on," the doctor said.

My mother propped herself up against the wall, and began to cry. I put my hand on her back trying to comfort her while listening to the doctor.

"Omar's heart is very weak, but we have some amazing cardiac physicians here, and we're doing everything we can to get him better," he said.

"When can we see him?" I questioned.

"We're going to try to get him into his own room once we get his test results back, but not before then. We'll let you know Mrs. Rutledge."

I thanked him, and he escorted my mother and I back into the waiting room. I sat her down, and she continued to sob. I left her momentarily to step outside and call Brian and Stewart. Brian didn't answer his phone, so I left him a message. When I got a hold of Stewart, he immediately informed me that he would be out on the next flight. I called all of the family, wanting them to send their thoughts and prayers to dad. I personally didn't feel dad was in any real danger. I was used to dad having health problems when I was growing-up. If it wasn't his kidneys, then it was heart problems, but he always seemed to pull through every time.

It had been hours, and there was still no word on dad's condition. By this time, Brian had showed up, and he was beside himself. He was a mess, just like mom was. If I didn't know how much they loved each other before, I knew it right then and there. It was hard for me to understand why things had taken such a turn for the worse in dad's life. One minute he's out of his mind happy, and the next he's in some operation room. I guess the hard part for me was not knowing where, or how, to put things into perspective, because it had all happened so fast.

What would've happened if my mom and I hadn't turned up at the airport when we did? We probably would've gotten a call from the hospital telling us about dad. Who knows what would've happened between their call, and our arrival. I was emotionally and physically drained, just sitting around while not knowing the condition of my father. It produced a large amount of anxiety.

One of the nurses finally came out, and told us that it wasn't going to be possible for dad to be moved and go to his own room. They were taking him to intensive care. He wasn't getting better. Our hearts sank. I was thinking to myself, come on dad, you've pulled through stuff like this before, come on! I had to watch myself, because I was beginning to grow angry with my father for having had a heart attack. As if he had a choice in the matter. I became blinded with panic, and my head was spinning out of control. The worse part of this ordeal, was knowing that there wasn't anything I could do to help him.

After the night had passed, we all awoke, having spent the night down in the waiting room. I got up early and sent Brian to go and pick up Stewart from the airport in the afternoon. When he arrived with Brian, I could see he was scared as well. He hugged all of us and wanted to know if he could see dad. We told him we still hadn't even seen dad yet.

A little after noon the doctor came and got us, and told us that dad still remained in the intensive care unit, but it was okay if we went in to see him. We each took turns going in to see dad. Mom went first, and then Stewart, Brian, and then me. I walked in and took a seat in the chair next to dad's bed. I looked him over and noticed he didn't look like himself. He was pale, he looked frail, and he had tubes all over his body. The tears just fell from my eyes. I couldn't believe dad looked like this. This wasn't supposed to be happening to him.

I gently placed my hand over his chest, and then I began to rub his head. I wondered if he was going to ever wake up. It was hard for me to imagine life without dad. I loved my father more than he could ever know. I didn't always show it, or say it, but I loved him. I needed him to know that. I promised myself the moment he woke up, I was going to tell him how much I loved him. I wasn't going to let another day pass by without telling him that.

The rest of the day passed by, and dad's condition didn't get any better. We spent the day in the hospital waiting, and hoping for good news. My mom was quiet, and didn't want to be bothered. I knew she was taking it hard. In the back of her mind I knew she was thinking the worst. I think we were *all* thinking the worst.

When night came, I went back into the intensive care unit. I sat down by dad, and just watched him sleep. After about an hour he woke up. I couldn't believe it. I was going to get the nurse when he silently told me to sit. The nurse walked over with the doctor and started doing something with the machines.

"I love you, Holden," dad said softly.

"I love you too, dad," I cried.

"I love you all," he said.

Without any notice, one of dad's machines went off. I heard a long alarm sound remain constant, and the doctor told me I needed to leave at once.

"Dad," I shouted. I stood up and felt a hand on my arm, trying to pull me out of the room. I kept trying to force my way back to dad's bed.

"Dad!" I shouted.

"Sir, you can't be yelling in here, this is an intensive care unit," one of the nurses said.

"Oh, God, oh, God, no!" I cried.

I couldn't feel my legs, and I was standing in the room looking at the doctors trying to bring my dad back. I realized dad had just died. I was escorted out into the hall and placed on a chair. My mom walked up to me. She saw me and didn't say anything to me. She kneeled down, and put her arms around me and rested her cheek on the top of my head. I felt her warm tears fall on my face. She knew dad was dead.

"It's okay," she said calmly.

I heard Brian crying, and then I saw him collapse to the floor. Stewart tried his best to comfort him.

"Oh, God, why dad!" I stated. I was crying so uncontrollably, I couldn't see anything.

"Just cry, its okay," mom said to me.

I put my arms around her and tried to soothe her, but she was more concerned about us. I heard Brian's voice, and how distressed he was. I had never seen him like that before. I dried my eyes, and then I saw him in a fetal position next to Stewart. Mom and I walked over to Stewart and Brian. I got down on the floor, and gently rested on Brian.

The doctor came out and confirmed to Stewart that dad had died. He had a severe heart attack and he wasn't able to recover. Stewart was trying to explain to the rest of us what the doctor had told him, but no one was listening to him at that moment. All we knew, was that dad was gone. I had never watched someone die right before me. It was the most disheartening thing I had ever witnessed in my entire life.

We all struggled to get Brian up, and out, of the hospital that night. He didn't want to leave. I didn't know if he thought he was going to lose some sort of connection with dad or not. I didn't understand why he wanted to stay in the hospital.

While Stewart and I struggled with Brian, mom went to make some calls. Everything happened so fast. I couldn't believe my father, who I loved so much, was taken away within a day and a half. Things weren't making sense to me. It took some time for me to play over in my head what had taken place tonight. I didn't know how to move forward, or what to do next. What was I supposed to do now?

We all went back to mom and dad's house that night. Brian and mom fell fast asleep that night, but Stewart and I stayed up and talked for a while. I explained to him the last words dad had spoken to me.

"He said he loved me, and that he loved all of us," I said.

"At least he got to see one of us before he passed," said Stewart.

"I can't believe dad's gone," I cried.

"Me neither. It all happened so fast," Stewart stated.

"I hate those doctors," I told Stewart.

"Why?" he asked.

"They lollygagged around pretending they knew what was wrong with him, they didn't know! They said they had the best cardiac physicians. If they're the best, then why is dad dead?" I shouted.

"Come on, Holden, they did everything they could do," Stewart replied.

"I don't think it was enough."

"Dad had a bad heart. You know all those problems he used to have when we were younger. This was bound to happen," Stewart told me.

I didn't agree with Stewart. The doctors said they could save him, and they didn't. I was mad as hell, and I wanted answers. I wanted to punch something. If I were a drinker I would have found comfort in the bottle, like Brian did. I was sitting right by dad's side when he woke-up, it wasn't until that nurse came over and started messing with stuff, that dad's machine went off.

The next night I stayed outside by myself, going over in my head all the times I had spent with dad. I was reaching all the way down from my childhood. I was trying to remember every birthday, Christmas, and all the time I had spent with him. I wasn't sure if it was enough. I pondered in my head what I could've done differently. It wasn't supposed to end this way. Dad didn't even get to see me live out my life. He'll never see me marry, nor have children. It was all over. He was gone!

A few days later I found out that my dad had wanted to be cremated. This upset me even more. I questioned my mother, because I didn't want my father to be remembered as nothing but a bunch of ashes. My mother wouldn't listen to anything I had to say. She was insistent dad be cremated. It was what he wanted. I begged Brian and Stewart to convince mom to not cremate him, but no one could get through to her. She was going to honor dad's wishes. In a way I had to respect the fact that she was sticking to what he wanted, no matter how much it upset me. Keeping dad concealed in some jar was not my idea of honoring him, but it's what dad wanted.

The fact that we had a memorial service for him bothered me for months. The whole process of burning dad up didn't sit right with me. I just couldn't convince my mother otherwise. I wondered if it had to do with cost, because I'll never be able to comprehend why in the world dad wanted to be cremated.

The problems in the family didn't really begin to unfold until Brian started drinking again. He was already unstable, and dad's death pushed him right over the edge. It was inevitable. I knew Brian was going to have to hit rock bottom before he could get better. It plagued me how the family was tripping over themselves with concern for Brian. Everyone wanted to know how he was taking it, and they wanted him to know they were praying for him. What about the rest of us? I thought. We all lost someone just like Brian did.

Maybe I was a bit more stable than Brian was. I fully understood he had issues he needed to work through. It was selfish of me to not recognize that he was in a suffering state, and he needed more consolation than the rest of us. All I could see was my own pain, and I think that's where my relationship with Brian was crippled. I didn't give him the space and time he needed.

I couldn't understand why he was crying throughout the night, and why he was so withdrawn all the time. Just because I was beginning to accept dad was gone, and he wasn't coming back, it didn't mean that Brian had. It took my mother to tell me this.

"You have to realize everyone goes through grief differently," she told me.

"I know that," I answered.

"No, you don't Holden," she said.

"What?" I said baffled.

"It might take years before Brian finally accepts that Omar is gone. It might be longer before he's ready to talk about it. I don't always show my emotions, but I suffer every night I get in the bed, and look over and don't see your father sleeping next to me," mom explained.

"I guess I didn't understand," I said.

"Lighten up on Brian. Do it for your father," she asked.

I should have taken my mother's advice, but I didn't. I thought I had really taken in what she had told me, but when I was put to the test, I completely ignored everything she had said.

About six months had passed by since dad's death, and things weren't getting any better for Brian. I thought he was purposefully acting up all the time. He would come home drunk, break things, and loud talk me. He didn't want to work, and he expected me to keep taking care of him. The fall-out would not only be dangerous, but eye opening for me.

One night, I decided I finally had enough of having to deal with Brian and the way he was acting. To me, there was a difference between needing time to grieve, and accepting the death of a loved one. By this time, Stewart and I had already overcome our acceptance period. It was time for Brian to do so as well. However, that night in particular, I should have kept my big fat mouth shut. It was just something inside me that boiled over when Brian began to disrespect me. Additionally, I already had built up anger from all this underserved attention Brian was receiving from others, who didn't see the real Brian Rutledge behind closed doors.

I knew he was a drunk and self-destructive. I was the one who put up with his ways, I knew who he was. Everyone else saw the outward appearance, which is why they didn't understand that some of Brian's actions had nothing to do with the death of our father. I'll admit that death strikes people in many different ways, and I'll buy what my mother says about grieving differently. But, no one can convince me it's necessary to take your frustrations out on your family. We were all in this together; we all lost someone, not just Brian.

The promise I made to my mother a while back was, that I would get off of Brian's case, and give him some room to breathe. She wanted me to avoid any unnecessary confrontations. It was kind of hard to do that since he lived with me, but looking back, I could have tried harder.

It was late one night when Brian came home and I had been waiting up for him. I wanted him to explain to me why he was being so destructive with his life. Maybe the middle of the night wasn't the best time, but I figured I would talk to him before I went to work and didn't see him for the whole day. He told me to leave him alone and to get out of his face.

"Listen, Brian, I've been giving you space because mom says you need it, but I think it's time for you to move forward," I stated.

"What do you mean move forward?" Brian questioned.

"Don't pretend like you don't know what I'm talking about," I uttered.

"What, Holden, dad's freaking death! Is that what you want me to move forward from? Huh," Brian asked.

"It wouldn't be such a bad idea if you started seeing some sort of counselor or something. You need help . . . serious help," I told him.

"Who are you to tell me I need help? You don't know what I need," Brain replied.

Brian started to become hostile with me, and that's when I should've ended the conversation. I just couldn't though, because I needed him to know all the pain he was causing the family. I love Brian, and I was tired of seeing him self-destruct.

"It's not right, nor is it healthy for a twenty-five year old male to be drinking every night, and having to be brought home by strangers," I said.

"Excuse me for wanting to numb the pain of not having my father around," Brian stated.

"You can use dad's death all you want as the reason for you to get drunk every night, but you and I both know you were a sloppy drunk way *before* dad died."

"Why are you acting like this, why are you jumping on me?" Brain asked.

"I'm tired of this."

"Tired of what?" Brian said.

"The late night drinking, the laziness, the excuses for not finding a job, and your reckless behavior. It's enough. I need you to get some help," I said.

"Or what?" Brian inquired.

"Dad's not here anymore! I don't have to accommodate your lazy butt anymore. I'll put you out," I stated.

"The truth comes out doesn't it, now that dad's gone? The *real* Holden comes out. I always knew you were a little pansy. You always wanted to be like Stewart!" Brian shouted.

"What?" I said in disbelief.

"You heard me! You're jealous of everything Stewart and I have," Brain said.

"Are you serious Brian? You think I'm jealous of *you*?"

"You're thirty years old, you have no wife and kids, and you're a history teacher. The only thing you have going on in your life is trying to make me feel bad. It gives you pleasure or something," Brian exclaimed.

"Get out!" I yelled.

Brian stood there looking at me, not knowing if I was serious. I looked directly in his eyes, and he knew then, I was serious. He walked towards me, and brushed up against me as he walked to his room. I didn't have to repeat myself, because he knew I was serious. Here I was taking care of him for months, and then he goes and disrespects me to my face. I didn't care where he went, I just wanted him out of my sight.

Brian packed a few things and got out as quick as possible. He was probably going to mom's house. After I went to bed that night I couldn't sleep. I didn't feel good about what happened between Brian and I. My mind started thinking about dad, and how many times he told me to love Brian in spite of his faults. I'd made a mess of things and I didn't even know where to begin to fix it.

It was around four o'clock the next day when I received a call from mom, telling me I needed to get to the emergency room over on Second Street. I didn't know what was going on. After I got off the phone with her, I paused for a second, and thought about the last time I was at St. Vincent's in the emergency room. I was there six months ago waiting to see if dad was going to recovery from his heart attack. I knew this call wasn't anything good, so I tried to prepare myself mentally.

When I arrived at the hospital, I found my mom sitting by herself with her head down.

"Mom," I said.

She looked up, and waved me over to sit with her. I gave her a hug.

"What's wrong?" I asked.

"It's Brian," she said.

In the back of my mind I knew it was Brian, and all the guilt started to pour over me. If Brian was in trouble, it was my fault. I was the one who kicked him out last night. It was me who started up with him for no reason.

"What happened?" I said fearfully.

"He's been in an accident. His car was hit by an eighteen-wheeler truck last night," she stated.

I couldn't believe what I had just heard. My heart was beating so fast I thought I was going to go into cardiac arrest. I was even more fearful than I had been with the news about dad.

"Oh, God, how is he?" I asked.

"I don't know, he's been in surgery forever," Mom replied.

"You've just been waiting?" I asked.

"All day!" She began to cry. "I don't think he's alive," Mom confessed.

"What? Don't say that!" I shouted. "Please don't say that."

Mom began to weep some more. She had scared me to death. I began to think maybe Brian *was* dead. I couldn't take this. I couldn't take someone else I loved, dying on me. I sat with mom, and we waited together to hear something from the doctor. When the nurse finally did approach us, she told us Brian was finally out of surgery and the doctor would be with us shortly.

The day my father had died, the doctor told us that had my dad received medical attention in a timely manner, he probably would've survived. Except, it happened at three o'clock. He had a heart attack at three in the afternoon, on the airplane, and didn't even get sufficient medical treatment until almost an hour later. I just hope Brian's accident wasn't as severe as mom was assuming. The way things sounded it didn't seem like things were going that well.

Night came upon us, and we were finally allowed to see Brian. I walked in right behind mom, and we saw immediately just how badly injured Brian was. I instantly started crying. His entire head was covered in a thick white bandage with visible blood spots seeping out. He had tubes in his mouth and his face was swollen and bruised, almost to where we couldn't recognize him. It didn't look like Brian. Mom left the room because she couldn't take looking at him. It hurt her to see her son looking that way.

I walked all the way to his bed, and stared directly at him.

"You better not die on us," I said angrily.

With tears in my eyes, I realized just how much I loved Brian. However, I wasn't just looking at him as a brother. I started to see him the way dad saw him. I loved my brother, and all the stupid, childish things I thought about him didn't matter. As he was lying there helpless and obviously in pain, I thought about all the hurtful things I had said to him, and realized I had disappointed my father. He told me to watch over my brothers, and love them unconditionally. I hadn't done that for Brian.

I took his hand and kissed it. He was my little brother, and I had spent years resenting him because he wasn't who I thought he should be. The reason he was so close to our father, and the reason it was so hard for him to accept dad's death; was because dad loved Brian through the good and bad in his life. Dad was the one who had the patience to deal with Brian. All these revelations were coming to me as I stood next to my brother's bed.

"I love you, Brian," I said.

It was a shame that it took tragedies for me to realize that my only job was to love Brian as a brother. I had spent so much time worrying about his life, I forget to love him just as he was. From that day on I promised myself that I was going to love Brian the way my father would have wanted me too. I couldn't fix the past mistakes I had made, but now it was up to me to start afresh with Brian.

It took a little over a year and a half for Brian to complete his physical therapy, and for him to get back to the way he once was. Although he walks with a limp, he expressed to me he was just glad to be alive. When he was released from the hospital I took him back home to live with me. Mom would stay with him and care for him until I was able to.

Eventually Stewart left Washington, and came back home. It was nice to have all of us living in the same area again. It's sad though, because there will always be one person missing. Dad was the person who held us together. Besides my mother, I've never known a greater love that someone could have for another human being. If I've learned nothing else from my father, I've learned to not judge others, and to accept people as they are.

The grieving period for one person, may not take as long for someone else. No one can tell someone how long to grieve. Through the death of my father I've learned that there is no time limit on the grieving or healing process. I work on my relationship with Brian every day, and I am able to love him as a brother. I can never replace my father, but there's nothing wrong with trying to be the kind of person he was, for the sake of my family.

I love my father, and I've never known a greater man than, Omar Rutledge!

CHAPTER TEN
Cynthia and Grayson

F inding true happiness in one's life can be a complex task at times, and trying to find a solid, genuine love, can almost be next to impossible. There are many different reasons why people in the world get married, and it's not always for love. It would be a challenging mission if someone were to actually sift through all the people they know who are married, and find out if they truly have love for one another. The kind of love that is unconditional. The kind of love that would make someone want to give up their life for their spouse, if they were put in a life or death situation. It's rare to find a love like that.

However, Brad Branson knew a love like that. He had found a love in Cynthia that would ultimately be put to the test. The kind of love they shared was unlike any other they both had ever known. Could it even be remotely possible to believe what the fairy tales say about happily ever after? Could it be possible to have a love so strong and deep, that nothing, or no one, could come between two people? With all the complexities of the world, it is possible to find an everlasting love.

It had been well over two years since Brad had experienced a loss that would affect him forever. He never believed love came with a price. Even though he knew nothing would ever come between him and Cynthia, there was always a tiny seed of doubt planted in the back of his mind, which didn't allow him to become fully content in life. Brad sometimes let the problems in his own life spill over into his relationship with Cynthia. At times it showed.

When Cynthia left for college, she claimed she didn't know who she was, and that she was trying to work on herself. She didn't have that many friends, and looking for a boyfriend wasn't something she was even interested in. She had heard stories of how people meet their future husbands and wives in college. Cynthia really didn't believe it was possible to find someone of quality in this lustful, sin pool, called college. She had already programmed her mind to hold up a cross against any guy who dared to come her way.

It wasn't until the last semester of her first year in college, that she decided to relinquish her thoughts about being with someone. Besides, she really didn't have a choice in the matter.

One warm spring night, as Cynthia was sitting outside her dorm on the curb crying, she couldn't help but look up when someone softly asked if she was okay. When she removed the tears from her eyes, she gazed up and saw a thin, six-foot tall, brown haired, green-eyed, young man, looking down at her.

"Are you okay tonight," he asked.

Cynthia didn't respond to the young man's question. She looked at him puzzled beyond comprehension. The young man looked down at himself thinking there was something wrong with him. He didn't understand why Cynthia was looking at him so comically. Cynthia wiped the tears from her eyes once more, and got the courage to speak.

"Um, I'm fine," Cynthia replied.

The young man didn't believe her. He kept looking at Cynthia, wanting her to tell him the truth.

"Well, let me not lie. I'm not really fine," Cynthia muttered.

"Yeah, I could tell," the young man said.

"I'm going to be fine. Thanks for asking," Cynthia said.

"Are you sure?" he asked.

Cynthia knew she was lying, and she also knew that he could see she wasn't going to be okay.

"I'm not going to bother you anymore; I just thought I would see if you were okay. I saw you crying," he said.

"I appreciate that," Cynthia said.

"What's your name?" he asked.

"I'm Cynthia, what's your name?" she asked.

"I'm Brad," he answered.

"Thank you, Brad," Cynthia replied.

Brad dropped his backpack, and took a seat next to Cynthia. She became uneasy at that moment. She didn't know what his intentions were. Cynthia dried her face with her hands, and scooted over away from Brad. He noticed her actions, but didn't pay attention to it. There was silence between the two of them for a brief period. Neither of them knew the next thing to say. In Brad's mind he thought things were going to go a little better now that they had introduced themselves.

"I was upset because I just found out my dad lost his job. I might not get to come back to college in the fall," Cynthia explained.

"Oh, I'm sorry to hear that, Cynthia."

"Plus, college hasn't been what I thought it was going to be," she exclaimed.

"What's wrong?" Brad asked.

"I don't know, maybe it's just me. Maybe I'm the reason why college isn't what I thought it was going to be. I have like one friend, and the classes are really extra hard. And now that my dad has no job, I may have to go to a community college next year instead. Things just haven't been working out for me," Cynthia said.

"I know how you feel, things were tough for me my first year as well," Brad said.

"Oh, you're not a freshman?" Cynthia sounded surprised.

"Sophomore," Brad answered. "Things will get better, you just need time to adjust. I would rather be suffering through hard classes, than go back home and get a job, and live with my parents," Brad stated.

"Yeah, I guess you're right," Cynthia answered.

"Listen, I'm going to a little get-together with a friend of mine tomorrow night, you want to come with me?" Brad asked.

Again, Cynthia was overcome with silence, and a host of awkward looks displayed on her face. By the time this night was over she just knew Brad was going to think there was something mentally wrong with her.

"Get together?" Cynthia said.

"Yeah, nothing big, just like music, food, and a couple of us just hanging out. There will be other people there . . . I promise," Brad said jokingly.

"Why not?" Cynthia said.

"Great!" Brad said excitedly.

From that moment on, Cynthia and Brad were inseparable. There was nothing that could keep them apart. When Cynthia learned that she would be able to return to school, she took an immediate liking to Brad. They spent holidays, summers and vacations together. Brad knew how to make Cynthia happy, and there was nothing he could do wrong in her eyes. It was as if they were soul mates. When Brad finished college a year before Cynthia, he had already declared his love for her. Cynthia loved Brad, but wasn't sure if their relationship was going to last.

Upon graduation, Brad had been offered a job outside of the State, and he was going to get the opportunity to work for a well-known advertising company. The plan Brad had came up with was, to wait until Cynthia was done with school, marry her, and both of them would move to where Brad's new job would be. Conversely, things weren't going to work out as he hoped for.

Another year passed, and Brad automatically assumed Cynthia was going to pick-up and follow him. He didn't count on the fact that Cynthia had made her own plans. It was in August when Brad had prepared a romantic evening for Cynthia out at their favorite park, that he finally learned the truth. Evening struck, and there was a glow which filled the sky with the gradual fading of the intense beaming yellow sun. The trees were gently swaying from side to side, and Brad had laid a thin, blue blanket over the bright green grass. He was more in love with Cynthia that night than ever before.

Cynthia met Brad that night, and they talked for hours. During their conversation, Brad interrupted Cynthia.

"Cynthia, I love you, and we've been together for almost four and a half years," Brad said.

Brad removed a tiny red velvet box, got down on one knee, and opened the box.

"Will you make me the happiest man on earth, and be my wife?" Brad said lovingly.

Cynthia seemed happy at first glance, but her expression soon faded to bewilderment. The smile had been removed from her face. Brad saw the sudden transformation of Cynthia's actions, and became embarrassed. Cynthia stood there in amazement looking at Brad, not knowing what to say.

"Cynthia," Brad called.

"I'm sorry, I was just shocked," Cynthia said.

"You love me, right?" Brad asked.

"Yes," Cynthia answered.

"Okay, then what's the problem?" Brad questioned.

"Come here, and close the box," Cynthia requested.

Cynthia took Brad's hand, and they sat back down on the blue blanket. Brad didn't know what to expect. He was unsure if Cynthia was getting ready to break-up with him.

"I truly do love you, Brad, and you are my best friend," Cynthia explained.

"But," Brad interrupted.

"But, I'm not ready to get married. I mean I want to go to graduate school. I'm not done with my education," Cynthia said.

"Graduate school? Why didn't you tell me this a long time ago?" Brad asked.

"I thought you knew what my plans were!" Cynthia said.

"No, I didn't," Brad replied.

Brad got up, and began to clear away the items he had brought for their picnic. In his anger, he threw the red box into his pocket, and tried to pull the blanket from under Cynthia. Cynthia got up and fell into Brad's arms. She embraces him tighter than she ever had before.

Brad released a few tears as he rested his head on her shoulders. Cynthia continues to hold on to Brad, and doesn't let him go.

"I love you Brad, and I will marry you. If our love is as strong in two years time as it is now, we'll still be together," Cynthia proclaimed.

"And if not?" Brad uttered.

"Then we'll know to go our separate ways," said Cynthia.

The wonderful evening Brad had planned for months didn't go the way he thought it would, and it did put a strain on their relationship for months. Nonetheless, Brad wasn't going to give up on Cynthia. He believed Cynthia was the one, and because of this, he waited for her.

Brad didn't take the job he was offered, instead, he stayed home, and Cynthia went on to graduate school. Brad took a local newspaper job in the advertising department and let go of the dream job he had been offered. He didn't resent Cynthia for her decision not to marry him until after graduation, or the fact that he had given up on his life-changing opportunities.

It was hard to tell if two people who had been together for so long could continue in the type of relationship Brad and Cynthia shared. Brad and Cynthia were able to see the worst and best in each other. They knew each other inside out. The fact that Brad was willing to wait for Cynthia proved how much he loved her. The fact that he gave up the opportunity of a lifetime to be with her, showed Cynthia that Brad was the one she was supposed to marry.

Two years had come and gone and the relationship between Brad and Cynthia had been put to the test multiple times. Brad endured the death of his mother, and Cynthia dealt with the pressures of going back home and taking care of her ailing stepmother. During Cynthia's time in school, she promised Brad upon graduation that she would marry him right away. However, there would be yet another obstacle they would have to endure.

Cynthia had every intention of marrying Brad, but it would be *another* two years before she would marry Brad.

"I have to take care of my mother," Cynthia stated.

"Stepmother," Brad corrected.

"Even so, my dad needs help," said Cynthia.

"I waited all this time, and now you don't want to marry me?" Brad asked furiously.

"I do, but just not at this time," Cynthia replied.

"I don't think you love me," said Brad.

"That's not true Brad!" Cynthia answered.

"You let me know when you can make me a priority," Brad said angrily.

There was something in Cynthia that made her not want to get married right away. The promise she made to Brad had already been broken, and in her mind she knew what she was doing to Brad wasn't fair. He spent four years waiting for her to make *her* dreams come true, and he had set *his* dreams aside. Their relationship seemed rocky, and it would take months for them to get back on the right track.

After nine years of knowing each other, and all the obstacles they both endured, Brad and Cynthia finally got married at a small, outside wedding. The day was perfect. The weather was calm and warm, and everything fell right into place. The love between two people had been tested, and both Brad and Cynthia knew that if they could withstand the pressures they had gone through already, they could endure anything.

Life for Brad and Cynthia seemed rather plain and simple for the first few years of their marriage. They were both hardworking people who loved each other unconditionally.

After three years of marriage, and a constant battle to conceive a baby, Brad and Cynthia would be expecting their first child. The news that Cynthia was pregnant made Brad happier than ever. He was sharing his life with his best friend, and now their love had grown, which allowed them to bring another life into the world.

However, Cynthia's pregnancy came at a price. The doctor had informed Cynthia that her pregnancy would bring her some complications, and that she probably wouldn't be able to carry her baby to term. No matter how much they kept receiving bad news, Cynthia and Brad didn't give up hope. They believed everything was going to work out for the best. They had to have faith, because no one else was going to have it for them. It was up to them to believe in the miracle they needed for their baby not only to survive, but to be healthy as well.

"Have you both considered your adoption options?" said the doctor.

"Why would we need to do that?" asked Cynthia.

"I'm not trying to go against you and your husband's hope, but things don't look good, Mrs. Branson," the doctor proclaimed.

"What is it that you're trying to tell us doctor?" Brad demanded.

"Your baby might not make it to term, and it's still not too late to consider all your options."

"You mean like an abortion?" Cynthia asked.

"Yes. Despite some people's moral code, abortion is still legal in this country. I don't want you two to have to go through the pain and devastation of losing a baby you've grown to love," the doctor stated.

"Thank you, doctor, and thank you for your suggestions, but Cynthia isn't going to be getting an abortion," Brad stated.

The news that their baby might not make it full term bothered Cynthia and Brad. Cynthia blamed herself, because she felt if she hadn't have waited so long to get married and have a baby, they wouldn't have been in this situation. Cynthia carried around this guilt for months. Brad couldn't convince her it wasn't her fault. Cynthia believed it *was* her fault.

As the months progressed, Brad and Cynthia began to make all the necessary preparations for the arrival of their baby. Cynthia found herself decorating the nursery every chance she got, and Brad was fixing and painting everything he could think of. It was no surprise to them when they would go to the doctor, and receive a negative report about the baby's growth. In spite of the doctor's report, they were just excited that the baby was still alive, and that the baby had a heartbeat.

It had been almost seven months into Cynthia's pregnancy when her worst fears would be confirmed. Cynthia was home alone one cold December evening, when she went into labor. Brad had been at work and was on his way home. Cynthia was able to contact Brad on his cell phone. Frantically, Brad's mind was working overtime. The only thing on his mind was getting home to Cynthia. He drove home fast, just fast enough to make sure he was still compliant with the speed limit though.

When Brad arrived at home, Cynthia was waiting outside by the door sitting on a rusty chair. Brad could see the distress on her face. He raced out of the car and went directly to Cynthia. Cynthia was holding the bottom of her stomach with one hand and signaling with the other hand for Brad to grab a hold to her, and help her to the car. Brad was scared because of the anguish displayed on Cynthia's face. He saw how much pain she was in. Cynthia could barely make it to the car. Brad walked her slowly, and tried to caress her head as they made their way to the car.

Cynthia tried to remain calm, but she was sweating, and she seemed as if she was going to pass out. Brad continued to talk to her and did everything he could to keep her awake. By this time, Cynthia and Brad were both frightened that the doctor was right. Once Brad pulled up to the emergency room entrance, he quickly opened the door, ran in, and requested help.

When Cynthia was finally in the hospital and examined by the doctor, it was confirmed that she was in labor. Brad was asked to step outside for a moment while they prepared for the delivery of the baby. Cynthia began crying.

"It wasn't supposed to be *now*. It's too early!" Cynthia cried.

Brad stepped outside and called his father, also Cynthia's parents, and asked them to meet him at the hospital.

Brad was haunted by what the doctor had said seven months ago, about the baby not making it to the full term. However, he wouldn't let his mind go to that dark place. He requested numerous times to be allowed to go into the delivery room with Cynthia. The doctor had denied his request until she was able to stop the bleeding. She didn't want any extra people in the room until the actual delivery was to take place.

It had been one of the longest nights in Brad's life, just standing around waiting. As the night progressed, all of Brad and Cynthia's family had come to be with them during this time. It had been over an hour before Brad was allowed to be in the room with Cynthia. When he walked in, he saw Cynthia crying her heart out. It didn't look like happy tears. He kissed her forehead and looked around the room at all the machines, and all the doctors in the room. This isn't how he imagined Cynthia's delivery would be. The calm and pleasant atmosphere with his camcorder he had envisioned was tainted by Cynthia's screaming, an operating table covered in blood, and doctors moving all around the room.

One of the doctors approached Brad, and told him it wasn't going to be possible for Cynthia to deliver the baby vaginally. She was going to have to deliver by c-section. Brad grabbed Cynthia's hand, and told her he loved her. Cynthia was given some medication which relaxed her before the anesthetic was given, and enabled the doctors to perform the necessary surgery to remove the baby. The baby wasn't fully developed, and the doctor explained this to Brad as he was standing by Cynthia's side.

Once again, Brad was asked to leave the operating room while the delivery took place. He begged and pleaded to be able to stay in the room, but they wouldn't let him.

"Sir, we're going to do everything we're medically trained to do to deliver you a healthy baby. Your wife is going to be just fine. Trust us," said the doctor.

"I can't lose them," Brad cried.

"Do you know what you're having?" asked the doctor.

Brad paused for a moment, and looked over at Cynthia lying on the table.

"A baby boy. We picked the name Grayson," Brad answered.

"Okay, your wife and baby Grayson will be fine," the doctor stated.

Brad left the room and joined his family in the waiting room.

"Everything is going to be just fine," said Brad's father.

"But you don't know that dad," said Brad.

"I believe it will, you have to have faith," he stated.

"I'm tired of hoping for the best. Why can't things ever work out the way they're supposed to? Why did this have to happen to Cynthia and I?" Brad questioned.

"Sometimes good people are given obstacles in life, if you go through them, it only makes you that much stronger," Brad's father explained.

"I don't want to lose my family," Brad cried.

Brad waited patiently hoping to hear the crying of his baby, but he didn't. He stood outside of the door to the operating room, thinking one of the nurses or doctors were on their way to get him.

"I love you, Brad," said Cynthia's father.

"I love you, too," Brad replied.

Cynthia's father reached out and hugged Brad. Brad needed that comfort, because he had become weak and was losing his confidence in the belief that Cynthia and Grayson were okay. All he had was his love for his family. He hoped that was enough to get him through.

A lady dressed in green scrubs, wearing a yellow medical gown covered in blood, a green plastic cap, and bloody latex gloves, walked out to the waiting room. She pulled down a white mask that covered her mouth and nose. Brad stood up in haste to meet her half way. She wasn't wearing a smile.

"Mr. Brad Branson?" She called.

"Yes," Brad answered.

Brad stood face to face with the doctor, and looked directly in her eyes without blinking.

"Please, no! Oh, God, what happened?" Brad yelled.

"I'm sorry, we did everything we could," the doctor began.

"Dad!" Brad interrupted.

Brad's father saw Brad was about to fall, and caught him before him hit the floor. Brad was flooded with emotion. Brad began to moan. Soon, the tears rolled down his face. The nurse kneeled down to finish what she was telling Brad.

"Sir, your baby's heart stopped," said the doctor sympathetically. "We did everything we could to revive him."

Brad was in a state of hysteria, but he was able to process what the doctor had just told him.

"Your wife is still holding on. Were monitoring her. She's lost a lot of blood," The doctor explained.

"No, no, no!" Brad yelled.

"Brad, its okay, son," said Brad's father.

The whole family gathered around Brad and his father, crying, and trying to comfort Brad.

"How's my daughter?" Cynthia's father asked.

"We're doing everything we can to save her," The doctor exclaimed.

"Can I see her?" Brad asked.

"Yes. Come with me," the doctor replied.

When Brad entered the room, he saw Cynthia hooked up to a number of machines with an oxygen mask on her face. Brad leaned on Cynthia, weeping for her to wake up. No matter what Brad said or did, Cynthia wouldn't wake-up. As the night ran on, Brad stayed with Cynthia. He tried not to dwell on the fact he and Cynthia had lost Grayson. In a way he felt guilty. He pondered if Cynthia should've had an abortion when they found out all of the complications Cynthia would endure.

Having to go through the death now, was more painful than if they would've ended things earlier. How were they supposed to recover from this heartbreak? The nursery was already painted blue and yellow. All of the little baby clothes they had received, were hanging in the closet. It didn't matter anymore. Grayson had died, and Brad wondered if Cynthia even knew.

Everything they had planned for fell to pieces in one day. One day was all it took for Brad to lose the son he never even got to know. It was good for Brad to be focusing on Cynthia, because it relived his mind from having to think about Grayson. Brad had spent the night beside Cynthia's bed, and waited for hours for her to open her eyes the next day. As Brad sat next to her, he didn't know how he was going to tell Cynthia that Grayson had died. How could he possibly give her the worst news of her life? Brad waited and waited for Cynthia to wake-up, but she kept resting serenely like an angel.

By the second day, the doctor declared Cynthia had slipped into a coma. Both Brad and Cynthia's families had been back and forth throughout this time, trying to be a rock for Brad. Cynthia's father fell into a state of shock when he learned the diagnosis of his daughter. No one knew what to expect, or how things were going to turn out.

While Cynthia was comatose, Brad secretly asked his father and father-in-law to handle anything necessary for the burying of Grayson. Brad couldn't effectively take care of anything. His focus was on Cynthia. Yet, he remembered all too well, the very night when he said good-bye to Grayson.

After the doctor took Brad to see Cynthia, he went to go see his baby boy. He was allowed to hold Grayson. He held the small, lifeless body he had grown to love. Grayson had only weighted two pounds. He cried while he held Grayson. He hated the day he and Cynthia decided to pick a name. Everything the doctor said had come true. Brad was living the nightmare he and Cynthia had hoped would never happen.

It was now three days, and there was no response from Cynthia. Brad never left her side, and believed in his heart she was going to wake-up. The doctor didn't make any promises, but she had indicated that it was a good sign that Cynthia was still holding on. The doctor had restored some of the hope Brad had lost. Cynthia had lost so much blood she needed a blood transfusion. Brad realized just how serious her condition was.

There was no time to grieve for Grayson; Brad was scared that he might also lose his wife. In order to help him stay focused on Cynthia, he tried to block out of his mind the fact he had just lost his son. However, when he thought about being able to take Cynthia home he was reminded of the life he and Cynthia had built for themselves. It would be hard for them to go back home knowing there wasn't a baby. A baby they had been preparing for.

It had almost been a week, and one night while Brad was sleeping next to Cynthia, she peacefully slipped away. Brad didn't know at first. He awoke to a nurse and a doctor opening the door and quickly rushing over to Cynthia. The doctor had asked Brad to please wait outside. Brad was petrified and overtaken in anxiousness. He calmly did as the doctor had asked, and waited by the door. After ten minutes, the doctor came out.

"Mr. Branson, I'm sorry, but Cynthia just passed away," said the doctor.

Brad stood there face to face with the doctor, as if the doctor was lying to him or something.

"She's dead?" Brad asked.

"She's passed, yes sir," the doctor replied.

Overtaken in rage, Brad lashed out at the doctor.

"I thought you said everything looked good? I don't understand!" Brad cried.

"She held on as long as she could, but her body gave out," said the doctor.

"I don't think I can take this," Brad revealed.

"I'm sorry sir," said the doctor.

"I'm lost. I don't know what to do. I don't have any more tears to cry," said Brad.

That night Brad called his family and told them that after five days in the hospital, Cynthia was gone. Everyone tried to console Brad. No one could believe that in the span of a few days he had lost his son and his wife. It didn't make sense to anyone. Why would God let this happen to him? Brad didn't deserve this. He was a humble, caring, loving man, and an even better husband.

Brad spent two weeks living with his father, and his father took care of him. Having to bury two loved ones, was more than Brad was able to handle. It was his father who got him through this difficult time. The connection between Brad and Cynthia's father and stepmother didn't change one bit. He loved them, and they loved Brad just the same. They all mourned together.

Brad's father opened up about the deaths, and how he knew what it was like to lose a spouse.

"It's indescribable what you're going through, son, and I know what it's like to lose a wife. I know the pain and the hurt I still feel, even though your mother is gone," said Brad's father.

"I'll never be able to understand why this happened to me . . . never," Brad replied.

"I can tell you that the people we love are just loaned to us for a short while. Everyone belongs to God," he explained.

"Dad, that doesn't make me feel any better. I'm mad at God anyhow. How could He take them away from me," Brad questioned.

"Because he has the power to do that," said Brad's father.

When Brad returned home, he walked around his empty house crying, and not knowing where to go. He visited the nursery first, and then quickly tore down the nursery, and threw every last item in that room in the trash. He shoved clothes, books, bedding, and stuffed animals, into a long black trash bag. He didn't want to give anything away, because it was all Grayson's. He felt that if Grayson wasn't here to have it, no one else deserved it. He threw everything out of the nursery that day.

Next, he went into his bedroom, sat on the floor, and flipped through his wedding album, and old pictures of him and Cynthia. Brad reminisced about the happy times he spent with Cynthia. He tried to ease his hurt by starting to reflect on the negative in Cynthia. He knew Cynthia was nothing less than perfect in his eyes, but he needed to be angry with her, to help him cope with her death.

He blamed her for not being able to pursue his career. He blamed her for them marrying so late. He blamed Cynthia for the complications with Grayson. He tried his best to be mad at her, but it didn't work. He loved Cynthia from the bottom of his heart, and wanted her back more than anything in the world.

Brad didn't know how to adjust to life without Cynthia. His best friend was gone, and he couldn't bring her back. Brad didn't know where he could direct his anger. He didn't know where to release the hurt and pain Grayson and Cynthia had left him with. Brad believed it was unfair for him to have to go through this life without having the one person who he shared his dreams with. The one person who he believed understood him the most. The person he knew who would love him regardless of his faults. There was no one else like Cynthia.

Even though they had only been married for three years, it was as if they had spent a lifetime together. The connection they had from the time they met, never faded, and only grew stronger. There wasn't anyone else out there for Brad. No one could love him the way Cynthia did. Furthermore, he didn't want anyone else to love him the way Cynthia did. It wasn't anyone's place to try to love Brad, how Cynthia had loved him. It wasn't going to work.

Now that Brad was alone, he used the time to reflect on what he could've done differently. He beat himself up, coming up with ways he could've avoided the loss of his wife and son. What he didn't realize was that there wasn't anything anyone could have done to save Cynthia and Grayson. It was their time to go. It was their time to go back to Heaven.

It's been a constant struggle for Brad to move on. Time is what he needed to accept, and move past the death of Grayson, but the love he shared with Cynthia was still right in the middle of his heart. Is it possible to find another great love in one's life? The death of Cynthia was for a reason, and it took years before Brad was able to accept the fact that Cynthia could still remain a part of him, even though she wasn't here physically.

Brad didn't believe that it was okay for him to move on and be with someone else. His father wanted him to be happy, but Brad felt the opposite.

"Cynthia would want you to move on with your life," said Brad's father.

"I don't know that, Cynthia's not here. I don't know what she would've wanted," Brad stated.

"You're never going to be with anyone ever again then?" asked Brad's father.

"I spent most of my adult life with the person I loved, I can't just forget everything we had. My heart and mind won't let me," said Brad.

"The love you have for Cynthia will never go away as long as you carry her in your heart, but you are allowed to move on son, and be happy," said Brad's father.

"I know I can. I don't think I want to," Brad replied.

Brad spent years alone, wanting to go back to the way things used to be in his life. He had a hard time letting go of Cynthia. It wasn't that he felt he would be dishonoring her, or that he would be disrespectful to the memory of Cynthia. He knew he was entitled to move on, but there were two things that prevented him from doing that.

Brad didn't want to share who he was with anyone else the way he had with Cynthia. He truly opened his heart and let Cynthia in. He didn't want to do that again. Secondly, he didn't want to risk making a connection with someone, just to have them taken away from him again. Fear played a vital role in Brad's life after the death of his wife and son.

There's no magic timeline on when someone is supposed to move on from the death of a spouse, or a child. In Brad's case, he has spent years being content by himself. Maybe in order to safeguard his heart from disappointment, he leads a lonely life, but as a man who had everything taken away from him unexpectedly, he felt it was his own decision.

Brad, still to this day, holds a special place in his heart for Cynthia and Grayson. The love he has for both of them will never die. Unlike the things in this world which are replaceable, removable, and erasable, Brad's love for Cynthia and Grayson will always be everlasting.

CHAPTER ELEVEN
On The Battlefield

The life I had envisioned for myself always included a husband and kids. I had a hard time coming to terms with my childhood, and overcoming the devastation my mom, my brother and I, had been put through. I watched my mother raise my brother and I alone, with no help when my father left. Actually, he didn't leave of his own volition. My mother kicked him out when she found out he was messing around behind her back. I always wondered what she expected, considering she and my father weren't even married.

Living in sin might have worked for her, but dad probably wouldn't have cheated if he knew he was tied down. Some men need that reminder. That vow of fidelity helps some men remember they have a wife at home. She basically gave him free reign to wander around town and impregnate all the women he could get his hands on. He did just that. I really actually don't know how many half-brothers and sisters I have.

I didn't want the kind of life my mother had made for herself. I witnessed her depression, and her lonely nights longing for a man to love her and hold her. She was the type of woman who needed the touch and affection of a man to be whole. I didn't so much need the reassurance, or the confidence boost, I wanted a different life than what my mother had. My mother needed a man to validate her, and that's why she went from relationship to relationship never being truly happy.

Watching *her* life made me realize I needed to set higher standards for myself. I wanted a man I could truly be happy with. My insurance to keep him was to marry him and have a baby. I wasn't trying to trap him, but I knew that if I wanted to hold on to him I needed him to know that his family was the most important thing in his life. My father didn't get that concept. He didn't believe that my mom, and my brother and I, were that important.

When I first met Matthew I knew he was the one I wanted to marry. At first he didn't feel the same way. Once we started dating for a while he used to complain that I would hover too much over him. He used to whine about his personal space. I didn't agree with his assertions about my actions. I felt he should've just been happy that I was willing to spend so much time with him. We had known each other since high school, and after graduation we went our separate ways, but then reconnected. That's how I knew he was the one for me. We spent a good four or five years apart, but we ended up back together.

The first time I confessed to Matthew that I loved him he didn't say it back to me. He outright told me that he didn't feel that way about me just yet. It tore me to pieces that he didn't love me.

"I love you with all my heart, Matthew, and I hope you feel the same way," I revealed.

He looked at me like I was naked in the midst of a winter snowstorm. I called out to him several times. He was acting like a mute, and I didn't appreciate the way he was disregarding my love declaration.

"I don't think I love you," Matthew replied.

I was hurt, and distanced myself from him for a while. By this time we had been together a year. His response let me know he was probably holding out for someone else, or he was secretly with someone else. It upset me, and I spent weeks playing over in my head what I could've possibly done for Matthew not to love me the way I loved him.

It wasn't an overnight revelation, but I began to come to the conclusion I wasn't the dream girlfriend I thought I was. I was Matthew's smothering worst nightmare. It took his rejection of my love, for me to see I wasn't the best thing that had ever walked into his life. The reason I knew Matthew was the one for me, was, because he wasn't like any other guy I had ever known. He was different.

Matthew was going places, and he wasn't like the rest of the boys I knew who weren't trying to make anything of themselves. My ambitions lead me right to an office job as a secretary after high school. I wasn't going to work any harder than I had to. Life was hard enough, and I knew trying to get a college degree was going to be a task I wasn't ready or willing to undertake.

Three years into our relationship Matthew revealed to me he was going into the Army. I guess the classes at the local community college wasn't stimulating and challenging enough for him. I didn't understand why he needed to go get shot in order to feel successful in life. I will admit that I gave Matthew a hard time about going into the Army. I didn't understand how a life filled with violence was going to be gratifying for him.

"So, you're telling me that you are being shipped off to god knows where, and fighting in a senseless war is going to make you feel accomplished?" I asked him.

"Why do you have to be so negative? I'm going to go fight for my country," Matthew replied.

"You can fight for your country here. There are other things you can do for your country besides going to war," I said.

"This is what I want to do! I've made up my mind that this is what I want to do. No one is going to persuade me to back out," Matthew said.

"What about our plans for a future?" I asked.

"I want to be with you, Leslie. I'll marry you after my tour in Afghanistan," he explained.

"Why not now?" I groaned.

"I have my reasons. If you love me like you say you do, you'll wait for me," Matthew insisted.

That night I spent hours trying to convince Matthew to stay with me. He wouldn't relent. We had been together three and a half years and spent almost every day together, and now he was leaving me. My love for Matthew was stronger than it had ever been before. I knew it, and so did he. It was easy to love Matthew. He was generous, one of the most handsome men I had ever known, and intelligent. Perhaps, I loved him because he took an interest in me. He had shown me the kind of affection I had never known from a man.

I wasn't going to lose him, and I did everything in my power to hold on to him. I didn't completely change who I was, but I gradually removed myself from being omnipresent in Matthew's life. I'm not sure if my absence made his heart grow fonder, but I needed to be constant, but not always present. Eventually, I would hear the most beautiful words I had ever heard from a man. The night before Matthew was set to deploy to Afghanistan, he confessed his love to me. It took four years, but he told me I was the one who he wanted to spend the rest of his life with.

I knew he truly meant it, not only because it took him so long to say it, but also I could feel his love. It was some sort of connection we had that I couldn't explain. That connection we shared lasted from that night on. I never knew what true happiness was until I met Matthew. He was the one who completely changed my life.

I remember standing with Matthew, his parents, and his brother, as he was leaving to go to Afghanistan. It was one of the most heart-wrenching things I had ever been through. I didn't know what to expect. I was worried that Matthew might not come home to me. I didn't care about the rest of his family. I wanted Matthew to come back to me. I was the one who loved him with all my heart.

Fear and sadness took over my mind as I was standing there waiting for Matthew to finish saying goodbye to his family. I watched him tightly embrace his mother, with a kiss to the forehead. He hugged his father, and kissed his neck. I watched him say goodbye to his brother as if he was never going to see him again. Matthew's family was hurting inside, but it didn't matter to me. I stood off to the side, and pretended as if I was studying the map I held in my hand.

Once Matthew said goodbye to his family, he eased his way over to me. I acted as if I didn't see him creeping up behind me. Then he pulled me towards him, and began to confess his love for me, and all I could do was gaze into his light brown eyes. I purposefully looked Matthew up and down, thinking that I would forget what he looked liked physically. I held him as close as I possibly could. I didn't want to forget the way he felt upon me. We both cried and wanted nothing more than to be with each other.

It felt like everything I tried to do, to keep Matthew from enlisting, didn't pay off. Those first few months passed by so fast, that I can remember the conversation Matthew and I had about him leaving. What I didn't know, was that he was already in basic training. The day had finally come when I had to say good-bye to the love of my life. However, I did so with grace, and a meek heart. I never once gave Matthew an ultimatum.

Of course I was upset and wanted him to stay, but I eventually realized my efforts would be a waste. That was actually one of the things I loved about Matthew. His ability to not take down from what he believed in, or to not give in. He was one of those bull-headed, stubborn, individuals, but he also knew when to be loving, caring, and compassionate.

I remember standing and waving to Matthew as he departed, along with what seemed like a bus load of people all dressed in their Army uniforms. It was hard to watch him looking back at me. In a way I was letting go, but at the same time our relationship was going to be tested. Matthew promised to marry me when he came back, which was going to be at least seven or eight months, or even a year from now. I didn't know if he felt as if he might die, and he was trying to spare me the hurt of being a widow, or if he was putting me through some sort of test. I wasn't sure if his reasons for waiting until he came back were truly genuine. All I could do was wait.

During the time Matthew was gone, I wrote him almost every day, and tried to remember what he felt like. It turned out to be a rough seven months. No matter how hard I tried, I couldn't seem to make myself happy. All I wanted was for him to return to me and marry me, so we could start our lives together. Upon his return, I expected everything to be the same. In my mind we would pick up right where we left off.

As the seasons changed from month to month, I eagerly anticipated Matthew's return. It was challenging trying to seemingly move on with my life, without the one person who I loved the most. I centered myself around my family, but my mother and brother could only provide a portion of comfort to me. I wasn't going to be the same until Matthew returned.

After nine long months I would finally get my wish. After tons of letters, sleepless nights, and a mind in a state of worry, I saw Matthew. I finally got to hold him, and see the man whom I longed for day after day. The love between us was still there. I felt it, and I could see it in Matthew's eyes. He still loved me. I wasn't worried that he would go off and lose interest in me, I was more afraid that he might not want to get married.

My worries were put to rest five months later when Matthew and I got married. It was the happiest day of my life. Matthew and I were now one, and there was nothing that could tear us apart. Our relationship had endured one of the biggest hurdles any couple could endure. Our time apart actually made us closer. I know for me, having to spend every day without him, hurt me emotionally, mentally and physically. It was a pain I didn't want to have to re-live. I made Matthew promise that he would not go back. He did his best to try to give me peace of mind, but I knew deep down he was making a promise he couldn't keep. Even I knew the rules of being in the military. You go when you're told. I tried my hardest to plan a normal life for Matthew and I.

Six months into our marriage, I found out I was going to have a baby. Matthew was beyond the moon with excitement when I told him the news. It was hard for me to be completely happy under the circumstances. In my heart I knew that Matthew would be leaving again. I didn't know when, but I knew he would be gone. I didn't want to have this wonderful life, and no husband to share it with.

With all the blessings I had been receiving in my life, things were going the way I wanted them to. It was important to me not to be stuck in the same position my mother was. I didn't want to raise a child all on my own. More than that, I wanted to be with the love of my life. During my pregnancy, I was truly never content or happy for a while. My life had been overtaken by apprehension. My biggest fear was having Matthew called off, and not returning to me.

It was a hot summer day, when I made the brave move to go and see my mother, and talk to her about all my fears and what was stressing me the most. I confided in her, something I didn't ordinarily do.

"I know he's going to leave me," I cried.

"But you know he'll come back to you," my mother replied.

"I don't know that for sure. I spent months just waiting for the news that Matthew had been killed on the battlefield," I answered.

"I've never known you to be so fearful. I actually admire your courage. I wish I would've had some of your courage," my mother said.

"Well, things change. It's no longer just about Matthew and I. We're going to have a baby pretty soon. I don't want my child to have to grow up without her father. I know what that's like," I said.

"I know you blame me for your father leaving," she stated.

"I blame dad for him and I not having a relationship. It was up to him to see about us. He didn't care," I proclaimed

"All I can tell you is to be optimistic. I've never seen a love between two people as strong. I do know that he loves you. You're just required to love him, your baby, and be happy. You're not supposed to live your life in fear," my mom exclaimed.

Her words of encouragement gave me a little hope, that maybe I could begin to be happy again. After the birth of our daughter, Lily, things remained calm. I had moved past the fear which plagued me, and took on the role of mother and wife more seriously than I had before. Life couldn't have been much better. I had everything I wanted out of life. Matthew was constantly around the house, and we spent those months after Lily's birth, developing our marriage, and learning how to be parents. I couldn't have prayed for such a perfect life. However, wherever there's good . . . destruction must come.

After two years of having Matthew home, my worst fear played out right in front of me. Matthew had sat me down, and causally tried to bring up the fact that he was being deployed again. It was foolish of me to believe that something good could last. Matthew didn't even need to tell me, I had already played the words over and over in my head. As he was explaining to me what was to come in the next month, I sat emotionless, and unmoved, about what he was telling me.

"I leave in a month," Matthew revealed.

I couldn't even face him. I focused my attention on the beautiful beaming sun that was shining right through the small square window.

"I'm not going to Afghanistan this time, I'll be going to Iraq," said Matthew.

In that moment I turned to him, face-to-face and eye-to-eye. All I could do was look at him. I couldn't muster up anything to say to him.

"Did you hear me, Leslie," Matthew cried.

"I heard you," I replied.

"Well, then you know how hard this is for me then," Matthew confessed.

"No, Matthew, I don't know how hard this is on you. I know how hard it is on me and your daughter," I cried.

"I don't want to leave, but I have to. It's what I signed up for," he said.

"I haven't forgotten. I was the one who tried everything in my power to stop you from joining," I exclaimed!

"This is not my decision. It's what I have to do. I have to do this. Surely you understand that," Matthew explained.

"What I don't understand is why you couldn't just pick something else to do with your life. You came home to me last time, what if you don't this time? Then what Matthew?" I proclaimed.

"I will come home. God wouldn't take me away from you and Lily. He just wouldn't do that," Matthew stated.

"Do you believe that Matthew? Because God wasn't the one who told you to go and join the military, did He?" I said abrasively.

"I have an obligation to my country," he cried.

"I can't be happy about this Matthew, and the more we talk about it, the more I get angry about it," I exclaimed.

"You're upset with me?" Matthew asked.

"Yes, I am! Don't think I will ever get used to the fact that you're putting your life on the line, because I won't!" I shouted.

I suddenly released all the anger and frustration I had been battling with all at once. I couldn't pretend to be happy in the acceptance of the kind of life Matthew chose. I was tired of playing the good wife, the sympathetic wife, and the understanding wife. When it was just Matthew and I, I could minimally accept he was fighting for his country, and I needed to accept it and suck it up. Now, things were completely different. We had a daughter, and within the blink of an eye, Lily's father could be dead.

Before Matthew could continue to try to make me feel better about his leaving, I got up and walked out. I didn't want to hear anymore anyway. It's sad to say, but I didn't care about some other country and their problems. I didn't care about those families over there. I only cared about *my* family and what we were getting ready to go through. I wasn't in the slightest moved by all of the praise and honor these men and women in the military were getting. So what! I thought. It didn't make a bit of difference to me who was courageous and willing to put their life on the line. I remember seeing all of the posters around town telling us to support our troops. I didn't care about the troops. I just wanted my family to stay together.

Throughout the next couple of weeks, I kept wishing something would happen to Matthew physically, so that he wouldn't have to leave. It was wrong of me to hope for bad things to happen to my husband, but I did. I didn't want anything drastic to happen, but I wanted it to be enough so that he couldn't be deployed. I wished he would've endured a twisted ankle, a broken leg, a sprained arm, or a concussion for a couple of days. These were the terrible things I wished on my husband. I justified my impure thoughts by convincing myself it was all for Lily. I wanted Lily to be close with her father. Who knows when Matthew was going to come home.

Day after day I wouldn't speak to Matthew. I shunned him, and acted as if he didn't exist. He couldn't understand why I was upset with him. In all honesty, I wasn't upset with him, I was upset with the military. However, Matthew held some of the blame in my eyes as well, because I told him before he enlisted to take another route. He was too smart to waste his talents by signing on to spend his life in combat. I begged him with everything that was in me. He ignored me. So I guess if I was upset with him that was the reason.

Matthew was putting me in a position like the other wives who have husbands in the military. I didn't want to be an Army Wife. No way was I going to live my life in constant fear day in and day out, wondering if my husband laid dead somewhere on the battlefield. I didn't want to have to raise a child by myself, or have to move around all over the country. All this was going through my head the last couple of weeks I was supposed to be spending with Matthew. I knew in my heart I would regret not spending this time with him, but I was trying to make a statement to him without communication. I wanted him to leave the military, and I figured if I were nasty enough to him, he would remember my actions and want to please me.

Matthew didn't seem bothered by the fact that I was ignoring him, and not spending the last couple of weeks with him. If he was hurting inside he didn't dare show it. He wasn't suffering like I thought he was. I was confused, but I remained stony-faced and unloving, until the time he was ready to leave.

I didn't want to be like Greta Barnes down the street. She didn't see her husband for months, and when she finally got word that the troops were on their way back, she learned her husband had died. I went to the funeral, and it was one of the most depressing experiences I had ever witnessed. I can still hear those loud shots being fired, and the ringing sensation which covered the air. I watched Greta sit on the front row at the cemetery, holding a United States flag, and crying silently as she rocked back and forth. Her two little children cried until I saw their faces turn a light blue. I remembered that, and I didn't want to have to go through the same pain.

I also blamed myself as I was carrying on this act of malice and frustration. I was mad at myself, because I chose to marry Matthew. I knew when he came back the first time I couldn't handle him being away from me, and the pure stress of having to worry about if he was going to be okay; or if I was going to receive the news that he was dead. I can recall almost every night I cried for him. Yet, I still chose to make a life with him. I was in love though. I wasn't willing to let Matthew go because of some fears I had. I wasn't going to lose the love of my life, because I was afraid of whether or not he would return to me. In the back of my mind, I guess I thought he would never be deployed again.

Now, I was hoping something would happen to him so he could never go back. My thinking was skewed. I was thinking irrationally, and I allowed my emotions to take over my sound judgment. I didn't want anything to happen to Matthew. I just wanted a good life with no problems. I wanted to be happy. At that present time, I wasn't happy. I had worked so hard to create the kind of life I wanted for myself, and it was being threatened. I could lose everything!

Two days before Matthew left to go to Iraq, I made it a point to go to a meeting at one of the counseling centers in the neighborhood for women who have either lost a husband in war, or women who have husbands in the war. I received an invitation from Greta Barnes a long time ago, but I never went because Matthew was home with me. I didn't see the need. However, I needed some support and guidance this time around.

When I was in the elevator by myself, I kept thinking about all the time I had wasted being angry with Matthew, for something I know he had no control over. I knew it was wrong at the time, but I was too mulish to give in and be the kind of wife I needed to be. I'll never get those weeks back ever again, and I only had myself to blame.

I got off the elevator and walked through the long hallway, trying to find the room number. When I approached the right door, I stood there for a few seconds trying to gather my thoughts, and trying to fix my face. I didn't want these women to see I had been crying. I didn't know what to expect as I was walking in. I wondered if I was going to have to speak first since I was new. I didn't know if there was going to be a speaker. I thought about Matthew leaving in two days, and got the strength to go in.

When I walked in, the first person I saw was Greta. She got up and walked over to hug me. She kissed me on my cheek, and told me to take a seat next to her. I laid my things down, and immediately felt everyone's eyes on me. The atmosphere was inviting, but sad at the same time. I heard one woman crying behind me. There was a lady speaking at the podium, and the room had an unusual calmness about it. As the woman neared the end of what she was saying, Greta was holding my hand, and I saw tears drop from her eyes. I caught the tail end of what the woman was saying, but it sounded as if she had a husband serving right now. I instantly identified with her.

Greta released my hand and walked up to the podium. Before she began speaking she started crying. She held her head down and just began to cry. I didn't know if I should go up and comfort her, or just let her be. Eventually, she ceased crying and immediately began talking.

"I lost Eric a year and a half ago," Greta stated. "It has been hard to move on without him. I try so hard every day to push forward and be content with the fact that he's gone, but nothing I do helps me accept his death. Everything reminds me of him. I don't know *how* to move on," Greta confessed.

As I was listening to Greta, I didn't want to have to go through what she was going through. I wanted to have Matthew with me for the rest of my life.

"This group has been a lifeline for me. I have been able to find comfort in each and everyone's story. We have all struggled in some way, and we all know what it's like to have to say good-bye, whether they have been deployed or have died," Greta said.

Greta mentioned how she wondered how she was going to be able to be truly contented in this life. I connected with her when she stated how she felt emptiness within her heart. Even though Matthew was still here, I felt the emptiness already. I knew it was coming, and I was trying to prepare myself. I was trying to put on a brave face and be mentally ready for what this long journey of separation may mean.

After Greta finished, one woman told us how she resented her husband in death, because he left her behind. She blamed him for getting killed, and mocked the memory of her husband. It wasn't until she came to the realization that he did his job, and was protecting us, that she let go of her hatred. He didn't ask to die, but through his fighting and death, he made our country that much safer. I didn't believe the love ever left. I put together that she was having the same reaction I was for the past couple of weeks. I was bitter and blamed Matthew for something that was out of his control. It wasn't as if he asked to be deployed, he was being obedient to his responsibilities.

After the support group wrapped up, I went home with a different outlook. When I got home, I rushed to find Matthew, and embraced him with loving arms. I couldn't let go of him . . . I wasn't going to let go of him. He began to shed a tear. I guess my actions surprised him.

"I love you, Matthew, and I need you to forgive me."

"I love you too. I don't need to forgive you, you're entitled to be upset," Matthew replied.

"I shouldn't have treated you like that, I let my emotions take over," I explained.

"I get it, Leslie, I really do get it," he said.

The remaining time I had left with Matthew we spent as a family. There was no greater joy in my life at that time then when I was with Matthew. I didn't even want to think about him leaving tomorrow. I tried to make the best out of the situation the best way I knew how. Matthew and I confessed our love for one another time and time again. I made him promise he would come back to me. I did everything I could to try to hold him to a promise. All he told me, was that he was going to do his best and that his intentions were to come back. I accepted that.

I rose early the next morning and sat out on the porch holding one of Matthew's shirts that had his scent on it. I held it close to my heart and closed my eyes. I reflected on the first time we ever met, and how nervous he was to talk to me. I thought about our first date and how we kissed for the first time. I was trying to remember all of the blissful moments we shared while he was still alive. It was what I needed to do at the present time. I needed to think about all the good times we had together, in case I wouldn't see him ever again.

Matthew finally broke down and told me, this time he was going to be gone a year or two. I could hardly catch my breath when he told me that. A year or two was too long for us to be apart, but there was nothing I could do to stop him from going. He was leaving in a few short hours and there was no telling when he was going to come back home. After I went inside, I lounged around the house with Lily. I was trying my best to be brave and accept that Matthew was leaving. I went back into our bedroom, got into bed and held Matthew's hand as he lay resting on the bed next to me. I couldn't fight back the tears any longer. I cried right before him. He tried to comfort me, but there was no way I was going to be comforted.

When the time came for Matthew to say good-bye, I met his parents there with Lily, and we all said a prayer for Matthew's safe return home, and Matthew hugged all of us. Matthew's mom put her arm around me and saw that I was visibly upset, and couldn't contain myself. My emotions were all over the place. I didn't know whether to keep crying, laugh, or stop and put on a courageous face for Matthew, and show him that I was strong. Matthew knew I wasn't strong enough to watch him go without crying, and I didn't worry about being strong in front of him.

I waved, and watched Matthew leave for a second time. The tears just kept rolling down my face. My heart grew heavy, and my thoughts were mixed up beyond my control. I couldn't understand how this could be happening all over again. I wanted this nightmare to end, and I didn't want to live in a house without my husband. We were a family now, and life wasn't going to be the same without him. I was always relying on a miracle to bring Matthew home, and if he did come home this time, things were going to be different. I wasn't going to let him go back. There was no way I was letting Matthew go back into war. I didn't know exactly how to accomplish this, but something was going to have to be done.

The first few months were the hardest to get used to without Matthew. I had to adjust to life with just a toddler and myself. It was hard at first. I missed Matthew too much to be an effective mother. I just went through the motions, and I didn't give Lily the kind of attention she needed. I felt guilty. I felt I wasn't being the kind of mother she deserved. I didn't know how to fix it. Life was just complicated those first few months.

Matthews's letters went from almost every day, to every two or three weeks. I was disappointed, but I figured he was in the heat of the battle. I didn't want to be a hindrance, so I followed Matthew's lead and only wrote him every two weeks. My mom and Matthew's mother would often come over and help me with Lily, and sometimes allow me to have a break away. I needed their help, and relied on them more than I should have, but in those distressing times their help was needed.

After five months had passed by fast, the rest of the months just sort of flew by. Before I knew it we were already in another year. It still would be some time before Matthew was due home, so I continued to go through my daily routine with the motivation of Matthew's arrival. I spent the remainder of my days waiting for him. All I did for the next couple of months was wait. I lived my life in waiting. The fear of Matthew dying wasn't even a factor in my mind anymore. I just wanted him home.

After thirteen and a half long months had come and gone, Matthew was on his way back home to Lily and I. He was finally returning to me. I had held out on nothing but hope and faith. Those two things allowed me to get through the agony of having to live without my husband, and the separation between my daughter and her father. Things were going to be normal now, and I felt as if I had deserved it for all of the hard times I had put up with.

On the morning that Matthew was to come home, I received a call from the Veteran's Hospital, and a lady asked me to make my way down there as soon as I was available. I automatically knew it was something about Matthew. The lady confirmed it was about Matthew, and told me I needed to come quickly. I called my mom to come over to the house as soon as possible to watch Lily. As soon as my mother stepped inside the house, I dashed out and drove in a rage. What could have possibly happened to Matthew? I didn't know, and I tried to think of the most minor thing I could think of to give myself hope that everything was okay. Maybe he was treated for some kind of sickness and he needed a ride home, or maybe he needed to heal after an accident or something.

When I got into the hospital, I checked-in, and was escorted by one of the nurses to a big room filled with hospital beds, and white long curtains separating each individual bed. It looked like every person had his, or her, own cubicle. I saw all of these people lying in those beds looking as if they were in pain. I glanced from bed to bed trying to find Matthew, but I couldn't find him. The nurse stood at the entrance into the room and told me to wait right by the entrance. She walked inside with a clipboard and talked to one of the doctors. I stood at the entrance carefully looking at all the patients in their beds trying to find Matthew, but I couldn't find him. Where was he I thought? Maybe she brought me to the wrong place, maybe he was somewhere else, I thought. I looked at each patient and still didn't see Matthew.

Finally, the nurse waved me over and told me I needed to sign some forms. She told me Matthew had been here since yesterday. I was nervous. I didn't know what was going on. Why wasn't I meeting Matthew where I normally do, and why wasn't he waving to me dressed in his uniform? I didn't understand. The doctor explained Matthew was badly injured over in Iraq. I wanted to see just how bad.

"Madam, your husband Matthew is the third bed from the right," the nurse stated.

"Are you sure, because I didn't see him," I replied.

The nurse looked down at her clipboard and checked something, and looked back up at me. She shook her head, yes.

"Matthew Prescott, right?" the nurse asked.

"Yes," I answered.

"Yes, that's his bed, I'll take you over there," the nurse directed.

We walked only a short distance, she stopped and pulled the curtain back even further, signaling that it was okay for me to see him. I was confused because I had glanced over and didn't see Matthew in this bed.

"Now the doctor thinks with some reconstructive surgery, he may be able to restore the entire left portion of his face fully," the nurse said.

As I turned myself to see Matthew, I saw an ugly man with half of the left side of his face missing, lying there in the bed. He was missing his left arm, and he had bruises on his right arm. I instantly threw-up on the right side of the bed. The nurse grabbed something to clean it up with, and another nurse took a hold of me and removed me from the bed. I began to cry.

"That's not my husband!" I shouted.

The nurse didn't answer me. She got something to wipe my mouth, then got a cool cloth and rested it on my head.

"That is Matthew Prescott," the nurse said.

After thirty minutes had passed, I went back into the room and stared at Matthew. I looked at the right side of his face first. Yes, indeed it *was* Matthew. I looked long and hard, trying to remove any doubt that this wasn't Matthew. But it was. I then moved over to his left side, and saw that his ear was hanging lower, and his jaw and cheek were almost gone. I could see directly into the side of his mouth. I looked at his arm which was gone. My gorgeous husband was gone. The handsome man with the light brown eyes and tanned skin was lying in this bed looking like a monster.

How was I supposed to love someone who looked like this? I watched Matthew sleep for hours, waiting for him to wake-up so I could ask him what happened. All I could do was cry. I brought this on Matthew. I wanted something bad to happen to him, and it did. I sat by his side holding his right hand. He finally came to.

"Hi," he said.

I smiled at him.

"Hi, Matthew," I replied.

"How long have you been here?" he asked.

"A while," I stated. I couldn't hold back any longer, I had to know what happened.

"Matthew how did this happen to you," I questioned.

"Well, my arm had to be amputated after I got it stuck. Then, I got shot in the face. I survived almost an entire year, and all of a sudden my luck ran out," he cried.

"I'm sorry this happened to you," I said.

"I came back to you tough. May not have been the way you wanted, but I'm here," Matthew told me.

All I could do was sit and look at him. I felt an immeasurable amount of guilt overtake me.

"I caused this Matthew to happen to you," I revealed.

"What? Don't be inane, Leslie," he replied.

"No, you don't understand. I wanted something bad to happen to you so you couldn't go back to war. I never meant for this . . ."

Matthew interrupted, "Don't talk like that, and you didn't do this to me. You just wanted me at home. Don't you dare blame yourself," Matthew proclaimed.

I rested my head on Matthew's left shoulder, and cried the whole night. I didn't know how I was going to love him. It was like he was literally a different person. Plus, he had been away for so long, but even before I saw how he looked, I still was in love with him. I couldn't stop being in love with him just because he didn't look the same. In an ironic way I got my wish. Now Matthew can't go back to war! I guess I should've been happy, but I wasn't.

I spent months grieving for the man I once knew, to come back. He wasn't the same. Our life wasn't the same either. Matthew's love didn't change, mine did. When I saw Matthew in that hospital my love became conditional and vain, and that's not what we had built our love on all those years ago.

I eventually found my way to loving Matthew again the way I was supposed to. It took a year just to get Matthew's face to even look remotely like a human's face, but I labored with him. His face might have been different, and he may have lost a limb, but he was the same Matthew I had grown to love back when I was a teenager. Our love didn't die, and the most precious gift I received was getting my husband back. I was blessed. At least he was still alive and able to share in the beautiful moments in this life. Not many wives have been blessed like I was to have my husband return to me.

Although Matthew was honorably discharged, he will always have an eternal reminder of his time on the battlefield.

CHAPTER TWELVE
He Was Alone

With so much hurt in the world, and with all of the suffering people go through, I wondered why God even bothered to give us life in the first place. Why were we put here to suffer and endure so much pain? I didn't have the answer to this question, and I doubted anyone did. I believed in an array of things throughout my life, but believing that pain was a part of life, was something I couldn't accept. Not everyone had to go through pain and suffering. I chose to believe that. There was someone out there who didn't know what it was like to lose a loved one, a friend, or someone important in his, or her, life. There just had to be someone out there.

I witnessed my mother stay by my grandmother's side when she was in her final stages of cancer. The indescribable pain my mother went through couldn't be understood by anyone. No one knew what she was going through, nor did we try to pretend we understood. I hadn't really been close to my grandmother, and I didn't know how I was supposed to feel about the fact she was dying. My way of showing that I cared, was to help my mom with anything she needed at the time. I played the role of a good daughter for weeks, hoping my mom would see my efforts and appreciate me just a little more.

I couldn't muster up any tears, or act like I had some emotion when I really didn't. It wasn't that I didn't care; I just didn't have an emotional connection with my grandmother like the rest of my family did. After my grandmother's death, my mom sent my younger brother and I to stay with my dad for a couple of weeks while she got herself together. I couldn't understand why she couldn't be with us just because grandmother died. I was like eleven or twelve at the time, but I remember thinking to myself that I didn't want to have to go through what my mother had gone through. It literally broke her. I didn't understand at the time just how powerful death was.

When my mother sent for my brother and I, I chose to stay behind with my father. I didn't go back to live with my mom. It wasn't that I didn't love her, I just wanted to be with my father. Living with him allowed me to explore who I was without restrictions. My mother held the reins on me and didn't allow me to experience the fullness of becoming a teenager. I loved her, but needed to be away from her. Of course she thought I was an outright heathen for leaving her, and she did everything she could to get me to come back to live with her. I didn't want to go back though, and I was happy being with my father. Besides, being with my father allowed me to meet Jonah.

Jonah was my cousin from my father's side, who I met one summer when he came to live with my father and I. Undoubtedly, we formed one of the closest relationships I had ever formed in my life. After having spent so much time with him, I actually considered him to be a brother. I was seventeen, and he was about twenty-two years old. However, he looked like he was in his mid-thirties. Jonah was the talk of the family for years ever since I could remember. Everything about him was kept secret, and I wondered why he was living with us when he had parents who lived in the next town. Whenever I would question my dad about Jonah living with us, he wouldn't give me an answer. He would just tell me to mind my own business. Something was wrong in the family, and no one wanted to talk about it.

For years I lived in the dark about the big secret no one wanted to talk about. Everyone in the family wanted to talk behind Jonah's back, but no one wanted to talk openly about what was going on with him. He ended up living with us for close to a year, and then he suddenly left. Again, my dad wouldn't tell me where he went. I didn't know what was so secretive about Jonah.

I finally got my answer unexpectedly one afternoon when I was home from school. The way I found out was completely by accident. Some lady had called dad's house asking to speak to him concerning, Jonah Maurer. I picked up the phone and talked to the lady.

"Hello," I said.

"Yes, can I speak with Carson Maurer?" the lady asked.

"He isn't here right now, can I take a message?" I stated.

There was a long pause on the phone between the lady and I. It felt as if she didn't want to give me any more information. I pondered what could she possibly want to talk to my father about.

"This is a matter regarding Jonah Maurer," she stated.

Why was Jonah a concern to my father? Jonah had been gone for some time.

"Who am I speaking with?" the lady inquired.

"This is Carson's daughter, Emily," I replied.

"When your dad gets in sweetie, it's very important you tell him to call Ms. Kale back. He knows the number," she said.

I replied with a firm yes, and let her know that I understood. Yet, before I could get off of the phone, I had to ask her a question.

"Excuse me, ma'am," I stuttered.

"Yes," she said.

"Where are you calling from?" I questioned.

"This is Ms. Kale, I'm calling from the Langston Hospice," she exclaimed.

"Thank you," I said.

I hung up the phone and took a moment to replay what Ms. Kale had just told me. I didn't understand why dad had any dealings with a hospice. He wasn't dying. Nothing made sense to me. I wrote the message for my dad, got in my car, and headed for the Langston Hospice. I had a bit of a drive ahead of me, and I used the time to try to piece together what could possibly be going on?

I sat in the parking lot scared to go in the hospice. The very last thing I remember about this hospice was coming to see my grandmother right before she passed away. I hadn't been here in years. I was nervous to go in. So I sat outside for close to an hour, contemplating whether or not to go in. I wasn't going to get any answers by sitting in the car I thought to myself. I unlocked the door, got out, and headed for the entrance.

Upon entering, I could smell the unpleasant odor named sickness. I could hardly stand to be in there, but I needed to know what was going on with Jonah and my father. I found someone who looked like they were on the staff, and asked them where I might be able to find Jonah or Carson Maurer. The man directed me to a room in the last hall, at the very end. I walked as fast as I could to get to whoever was in that room. I didn't realize just how daunting it was for me to witness first hand someone I actually had a connection with, lying in his sick bed. I knew it was Jonah. I knew it had to be him.

I had to be strong in that moment, because I didn't know what was awaiting me. However, I just couldn't get the courage to go in. I started thinking of all the worst possible things that could be wrong. Why wouldn't Jonah tell us he was sick? Why was my dad involved with a hospice? The only way I was going to get any answers was to walk through the door. I gently turned the cold, brown knob on the door, and walked in.

When I first stepped inside I didn't see anyone in the room. I walked in a little further and looked behind the door, and realized the bed was situated in a corner off to the side. There he was looking feverishly tired, weak, pale, and sweating immensely. I was right; it was Jonah lying in the bed looking very ill. I walked closer to him, and dropped my purse on the floor right next to me. I couldn't even say anything to him. All I could do was stare at Jonah right in his face.

Jonah was resting, and hadn't opened his eyes yet. I took a seat at the end of the bed near his feet, and touched him on the soles of his feet hoping he would wake up. His feet felt cold and his legs were bunched up underneath a thick blue blanket which had Jonah's name sown into the fabric. I began to cry. I didn't understand what was going on, and I needed Jonah to wake-up so that I could ask him questions. He lay there close to two hours, just sleeping. I watched his chest softly go up and down. I watched him sleep until he finally awoke.

Jonah didn't say anything to me when he first opened his eyes. I felt uncomfortable and distressed that all Jonah did was look at me, as if he didn't know who I was. I waited for him to speak to me and acknowledge the fact that I had waited all this time for him to wake-up. He looked at me quizzically, and I responded with my actions in the same manner.

"What's wrong, Jonah?" I asked hesitantly.

Jonah didn't answer me right away.

"Jonah," I proclaimed!

Jonah turned over in his bed and faced the wall directly in front of him. He was really starting to hurt my feelings, but there was no way I was about to leave. I got up and walked over to the other side of the bed, and looked Jonah squarely in the eyes.

"What's your problem," I cried angrily.

Jonah began to shed some tears.

"What is it? Are you about to die?" I inquired.

Suddenly, after receiving the silent treatment, Jonah spoke in a moderate tone of voice.

"Yes," he replied.

"You're going to die?" I asked.

"Yes," he said again.

I immediately threw myself across his chest, and could feel the warm tears streaming down my face. Jonah tried to put his arms around me, but he was too weak.

"What happened?" I asked.

"I only have forty-eight hours to live," Jonah informed me.

"Forty-eight hours! Does the family know?" I said.

"Yes, everyone knows," Jonah answered.

"Where are your parents?" I questioned.

"They've already been here, plus I don't think they want anything to do with me," Jonah cried.

"What! Why not?" I asked.

"It's a complicated and depressing story you don't need to know about," Jonah stated.

"I have time," I insisted.

"All that matters is that you and your father are the only family I have left," Jonah said.

"That's not true, everyone in the family loves you. Why wouldn't they?" I asked.

"You don't know the true me," Jonah exclaimed.

"Yes I do," I stated.

"No, you don't!" Jonah replied.

The back and forth conversation of trying to convince Jonah that I knew who he was, became tiresome. I didn't know what he was talking about. I knew exactly who he was, he lived with my father and I for a year. I became close with Jonah, and we formed a bond. For him to say I didn't know the 'true him,' upset me greatly. Conversely, he kept holding on to the fact that I didn't know who *he* was.

"Tell me who you are?" I said.

"If I told you, you would think the same way the rest of the family does. I don't want you to think badly of me," he said.

"You were just going to die in two days and not tell anyone?" I cried. "How dare you Jonah!" I shouted.

"Your dad was going to tell you," he said.

"So my dad was keeping this a secret as well?" I asked.

"Yes," Jonah replied.

What Jonah was talking about was something I could never grasp happening within a family. He tried his hardest to keep from telling me what happened to him, and why he was about to lose his life. He wasn't banking on the fact that I would find out while he was still alive. He wanted me to find out everything *after* he died. He wanted my father to explain everything. However, things didn't work out the way Jonah planned.

"I'm a homosexual," Jonah revealed.

"What," I said stunned.

"I'm gay, Emily, and I'm dying because I have AIDS," Jonah declared.

"You have AIDS?" I asked.

"Yes," he said.

When Jonah was a teenager he admitted to his parents that he was gay. His mom and dad didn't accept him for who he was, but they tolerated his lifestyle. It wasn't until he contracted HIV/AIDS that his parents kicked him out, and basically disowned him. No one in the family wanted anything to do with Jonah, but my father was the one who stepped in, and took Jonah in when he had no place to go. I finally learned the secret everyone wanted to keep hidden. I also learned why Jonah came to live with us.

I didn't know how to react to Jonah's revelation that he was going to die in a matter of days because of this virus. More than that, I was brutally devastated by the actions of my family. There was no way I was going to understand how family could turn their back on someone in need, much less his own parents. They literally kicked him out and wanted nothing more to do with him. For years this is what Jonah had to endure. Not only was he fighting to stay alive, he was dealing with the hurt and pain of having no family.

There was only two days left for Jonah to enjoy the world before he would be gone forever. He was confined to a bed weak and sick, and didn't look like he was getting any better. His last days on earth were going to be spent lying in bed. I don't think my aunt and uncle understood the seriousness of death, and that they were never going to see their son again. In my eyes they were stupid. They were willing to give up the little time they had left with Jonah all because they were upset their son was diagnosed with an incurable disease. It didn't make sense to me.

I left Jonah that night and returned home, heated and ready to confront my father about holding this information from me. I knew there wasn't a reasonable explanation. I wasn't willing to accept and understand any excuse as to why he didn't want me to know the truth. I arrived home to find my father sitting in his bedroom in a relaxing position.

"Why didn't you tell me Jonah had AIDS, and he's going to die?" I demanded.

My father was stunned beyond belief that I knew the secret.

"Who told you that?" Dad asked.

"I found out. Why, dad? Why weren't you going to tell me?" I asked in distress.

"I didn't want to lie to you, and Jonah didn't want you to know. He's embarrassed," Dad explained.

"Why should he be embarrassed?" I asked.

"Because, he's dying. He blames himself, and he just wanted to go peacefully," Dad stated.

"How did you find out?" he inquired.

"A lady called," I answered.

"You weren't supposed to find out this way," Dad explained.

"That's heartless, dad. I can't believe you were going to let my cousin die and wait to tell me," I said.

"I was respecting what Jonah wanted," he answered.

"He was one of the few people I actually felt close to. I feel betrayed by both you, and Jonah," I told him.

"It's what he wanted. I *had* to respect his wishes. Don't spend the last days of his life being upset with him," dad begged.

"You don't have to worry about that. I'm not like his scumbag parents who turned their backs on their son!" I shouted.

"Don't you talk about your aunt and uncle like that," said dad.

"The truth is the truth," I replied.

We ended our conversation that night both of us angry at one another. I was mad at the fact dad had kept this to himself all these years, and that he was willing to let Jonah die and not tell me. He was going to make me find out when everyone else did, and try to smooth the truth over with a pack of lies.

Dad was upset with me, because he felt I butted in on his business, and that I went to go and see Jonah. I guess it made him feel as if he was a liar, since he had told Jonah no one would know. The family already knew. Everyone practically forgot about Jonah when he was deemed the worst human being to walk the face of the earth, because of the lifestyle he chose to live. It didn't matter who Jonah was in his personal life, he was still the cousin I thought of as a brother.

My only hope was for his parents to realize they rejected Jonah at one of the most critical times in his life. There had to be something that could be done to bring Jonah and his parents back together. He only had less than two days to live. It disgusted me how no one wanted to be around Jonah because they thought they were going to catch AIDS. That didn't matter to me. I was going to go see Jonah tomorrow, and I didn't have any fear which kept me from spending the last few days with him.

The next morning I got to the hospice early, and watched Jonah sleep peacefully like I had done yesterday. By looking at his face, I knew he wasn't going to hold on much longer. He was too young to die. He was too young to be treated like this. I became outraged with the world. I hated everyone and everything. I didn't know why, but I did. That day I spent in the hospice with Jonah, was the day I began to question God, and all that He stood for. Why would he give Jonah life just to take it away? My grandfather on my dad's side always talked about God to me and my brother, and we learned from an early age who was in control of the world.

This was someone who I looked up to, and who I thought was going to be around forever. It was hard for me to accept Jonah was dying tomorrow. I had a misconception about death before I understood what dying meant. I thought it was only supposed to happen to elderly people. I never would have thought it would've happened to a young man like Jonah. Jonah didn't want to talk that much while I was there. I understood he was weak, but I needed to spend all the time I could with him.

I needed Jonah to talk to me about what he was feeling. I wanted him to open up to me and tell me about what he was going through. I wanted to know everything. How he got AIDS, when he got kicked out, where he went before he came to live with us, and where he went after he left. Jonah had to tell me, he needed to tell me, because I wasn't going to be able to have rest in my mind until I knew everything, and his emotions. He wasn't being treated fairly, and he needed to know I was here for him. He was alone.

As the afternoon approached, Jonah became more talkative and was able to answer some of the questions I had for him. He was careful not to let me in on all of his personal business, so his answers contained multiple pauses, and starting and stopping his sentences. I knew what he was trying to do, but I was grateful that he was even opening up to me. I started by asking him did he regret being a homosexual.

"No," he replied.

"But don't you feel things would have worked out differently for you if you would've not liked men?" I asked.

He paused for a second.

"I could've gotten AIDS even if I was a straight male," he answered.

"You think this is your punishment?" I questioned.

"Having AIDS?" he replied.

I shook my head, yes.

"My punishment was being born into this world to the kind of parents I have," Jonah answered.

"What do you mean?" I asked.

"My parents wanted nothing to do with me when they found out I had HIV. They treated me like I was the plague. They kicked me out, and rarely ever kept in contact with me. My mom tried to be a constant in my life, but I know my dad made her distance herself from me," Jonah explained.

"And that's when my dad took you in?" I asked.

"Yes. Uncle Carson literally saved my life. I had nowhere to go," Jonah told me.

"Why did you leave us?" I inquired.

"I was getting worse. They didn't catch the virus in time, and it had already taken over my immune system. I had to leave, and I've been here ever since," Jonah cried.

"Why didn't you want me to know? Why did you tell my dad not to tell me?" I asked.

Jonah took one of those long pauses, and I guess he didn't know how to answer me. I thought he was battling whether or not to tell the truth or make up some lie.

"I didn't want you to think different about me," Jonah confessed.

I nodded my head as if I understood his reasoning for not telling me. Honestly, I didn't understand, and I wanted to express that to him, but there was no need. He was going to die any day now. I felt a heaviness glide over my heart as I kept thinking how this might be the last day I ever see Jonah alive. One of the most caring, loving, friendly, and forgiving people I knew, was going to die.

I had only dealt with death once before, whenever my grandmother had died. I had to face it all over again. However, this time was different. I wasn't too young to remember Jonah. I loved him, and had a relationship with him that was special. This wasn't like grandma's sickness, where I could be the strong one, and help my mom any way I could. I was the mess this time, only there was no one there to comfort me.

Before I left that night, and making sure that I had my curiosity satisfied, I had to ask one of the most gut wrenching questions I knew Jonah wasn't going to want to answer. Yet, I needed to ask for me. I wanted to know what it was that caused my cousin to end up in this position. With all the courage within me, I asked him.

"I have to know something, Jonah," I muttered.

"What's that," he replied.

"How did you get AIDS?" I exclaimed.

I felt the uneasiness by looking at Jonah's body language. I could tell he didn't want to answer. I got up and headed for the door.

"I'm sorry, don't answer that. I don't have a right to know that," I said.

"Come here, please," Jonah stated.

He motioned for me to come back to his bed. I went back and took a seat.

"Maybe if I tell you this you may be able to help someone else, or even yourself from the unintelligent mistake I made," Jonah explained.

"I mean, I'm not stupid Jonah. I know how it's spread. I just . . ."

He interrupted me.

"You just wanted to know how I got it," he said.

"Yes," I replied.

"I was in a relationship with someone who had the disease. I was an idiot to believe he was clean," Jonah said.

"Was he committed to you?" I asked.

"Yes, he was committed to me. He just didn't protect me," Jonah answered.

"Did he die?" I questioned.

"Yes, he died," Jonah replied.

"It's not fair. I can't believe there's a disease that kills lovers. It's just not right!" I proclaimed.

"The sad thing is, once I moved away from him, he died shortly thereafter. I never got the chance to say good-bye," Jonah revealed.

"My mom told me I needed to pray to God and ask him to forgive me for my lifestyle, and ask him for mercy." Jonah cried.

"She thinks you're going to hell?" I asked.

"Yes," he said.

"Do you think you're going to hell because you're gay," I questioned.

"I know right from wrong, and I knew deep inside my lifestyle was displeasing to God, but I kept living this way anyway." Jonah exclaimed.

"Have you asked for forgiveness?" I stated.

"I already prayed and asked God to forgive me for being a homosexual, and also asked him to forgive me for going against the Holy Bible. I knew being gay was wrong." Jonah confessed.

As I went home that night, I couldn't stop thinking about all the problems Jonah had faced since his diagnosis. I believed that Jonah suffered silently. He put on a brave face, but I know he was hurting from the way the family kind of just let him go into the wilderness. It bothered me that they were willing to let him go over something he couldn't control. It hurt me to my heart that Jonah was going to die alone. In a way he still had my father and I, but he was without his own family, the family that abandoned him. He needed them more than he knew.

I stayed up all night thinking about Jonah, and how he could slip away at any time without anyone being there for him, but the caregivers at the hospice said stages of life are sometimes unpredictable. She gave me hope that maybe, just maybe, Jonah might live long enough to be reconciled with his family. Even though he did nothing wrong against his family, he still needed to mend fences with his family, and I was determined to make that happen.

The next morning my father and I drove to the hospice before I went to school. When we arrived, my dad took care of some paperwork, and I went to Jonah's room. I anxiously went to him and rested my head once more on his chest. I could feel his heart beating, it was faint, but I could feel each beat. I watched him sleep like I had done many times before. I made it a point to call my aunt and uncle, and get them here as fast as they could. Jonah was going to slip away at any moment. His mom said she would be right there.

By the afternoon of that same day, Jonah was still holding on. His mom had spent the latter half of the morning talking and sharing photos with him. I could see the bright smile on Jonah's face which had been lost for some time. Once Jonah fell asleep for the night, his mother stayed with him and didn't leave his side. I went home feeling good that Jonah had finally got the chance to reunite with at least his mother. Also, by her being right by his side, if he did slip away, she would be there.

I rose the next morning a little later than usual because it was the weekend, and found my father about to run errands. I decided to get in my car and go see Jonah. We hadn't gotten a call from anyone, or Jonah's mother, so I assumed everything was alright. When I arrived at the hospice with my pictures for Jonah, I was redirected to go back up to the front and wait for one of the caregivers to come and talk to me. I suspected the worst. All of the other days I had come in without any problems, and now I was being told to go wait in a room. I knew it wasn't good.

The tears just came to my eyes. I tried to fight the tears back, telling myself Jonah was going to live one more day. I knew he had one more day in him. I knew it. I just knew he did. The caregiver walked up front with a nurse, and they informed me that they had just called my father. They wanted him to get here as fast as he could. Jonah only had about an hour to live. My dad was the one who oversaw Jonah's care, insurance, and all that stuff. If I didn't know how much of a good man my father was, I would, after this whole experience.

Even though Jonah was family, my father still allowed him to come into our home and live with us, knowing he had HIV. Then, he assumed all of Jonah's personal and medical bills. Not many people in this world would do that. My father now had a special place in my heart that wasn't there before. His sacrifices, humility, and caring heart, lead me to see him in a different light.

The caregiver and the nurse went over just some routine things to expect, once Jonah passed away. They didn't go into grave detail, but they informed me about why certain parts of the body were going to shut down, and how that was going to cause Jonah to slip away. They were saving the bulk of information for my father. I just sat with them, hoping they would let me see Jonah before he died. However, for some reason they wouldn't let me go until my father came. When he finally did arrive, I sprinted to Jonah's room and made haste to see what kind of state he was in.

He didn't look like himself. He was tiny, pale, shivering, and I could see the veins in his head protruding out. He was no longer the Jonah I once knew.

"If nobody else tells you Jonah, I want you to know I love you," I cried.

I was trying to be strong in front of Jonah, but the tears just kept coming. I could barely get my words out.

"I love you, too," Jonah said gently.

Jonah took a hold of my hand and kissed it. I could tell he was in an enormous amount of pain. In a way, I wanted Jonah to be released from all this pain and suffering, but the only way that would be possible was for him to die. It was inevitable. He was going to die. Time stood still as I was in his room. I was trying to absorb all the last minute precious moments with Jonah I could. He was barely hanging on.

"This isn't fair," I told Jonah.

He shook his head in agreement with my statement.

"I want you to fight to stay alive, Jonah. The doctors were wrong before. You weren't supposed to be here today," I said.

"My time is up, I'm not going to be here much longer," he replied.

"Can't you fight?" I begged.

"There's nothing to fight for. Besides, the doctors did everything they could to help me," Jonah explained.

"What about me," I asked.

Jonah began to cry. It was the first time I saw him break down emotionally. He was finally releasing everything he kept inside.

"I can't, Emily. There's nothing I can do," he proclaimed.

"Our bond isn't worth fighting for?" I questioned.

"I've already seen the death angel appear before me. I know it's my time," Jonah stated.

I picked up his right hand, and held it to my heart. I knew there was nothing I could do to help him.

"Promise me you won't let the lies that are going to be told about me after I'm gone make you think different about me?" Jonah requested.

"That could never happen," I said.

Another hour had passed, and Jonah had gone to sleep. My dad joined me in Jonah's room, and we talked silently about the family and how Jonah's mother was on her way back up to the hospice. Jonah's father said all he could do for Jonah was pray for him. However, I doubted God would answer the prayers of a man who cut off contact with his son just because he was a homosexual. Jonah's father reached out to him once before my dad told me, but his attempt didn't lead to a father-son reconciliation. Jonah needed all the family he could get, and my father and I were going to be the support he needed. I accepted Jonah for who he was, and it didn't make a bit of difference he was infected with an incurable disease.

When I got up to use the restroom, I walked away from Jonah's bed, but as I opened the door, I heard a startling gulp. I quickly turned back around, and looked at my father.

"That was Jonah?" I asked.

"Yes," my father said.

"He died," I asked.

"He's gone," Dad replied.

I rushed to his bedside, and studied his face. I didn't see his chest go up and down as I had seen so many times before. Jonah passed away at six o'clock that evening. My dad went to get the nurses.

While he was gone, I used that time to look and remember Jonah's face in the natural. I was never going to see his fleshly body again. I immediately felt sad, angry, hurt, disgusted, and vengeful all at once. I wanted to kick and scream and throw something, or hit someone. I felt the same way my mother did when she lost grandma. I didn't feel a strong connection to grandma, but I knew what it was like to lose someone you love.

I wasn't stunned in any way, because I had three days to prepare myself for Jonah's death. The only thing that bothered me was the fact that Jonah was willing to die without saying goodbye to me. I'm not a believer in trying to ease the pain on others by holding back the truth. That notion doesn't work for me.

Everything after Jonah's death seemed to move pretty quickly. He was taken out of his room, and picked up. My dad and Jonah's mother were responsible for all the funeral arrangements. I felt bad for her. I saw her crying her eyes out when she pulled up to the hospice. She couldn't control herself. I saw the purest form of emotion I had ever seen. I saw her head turn bright red, her eyes flowing like a river, and her holding her chest. I could tell she was deeply grieved by the death of her son.

Poor Jonah lived the last few months of his life in distress. He couldn't have focused on getting better, even if he wanted to. He was struggling with so much. I could see why his health got progressively worse. I admire Jonah for being who he was, and not letting others determine who he should've been. I know it took guts for him to go against his parents, and have to bear the burden of being the joke of the family. I'm glad I got to see my family for the kind of people they really were.

Jonah's funeral was nothing how I imagined it. I thought a ton of his friends were going to show up and say something positive about him. I thought the atmosphere in general was going to be more about celebrating his life, and remembering the kind of person he was. Instead, it was more of a sorry your gone, we expected it. I was disappointed in my father, because I thought he could've done more in preparation for the funeral.

I sat there dressed in my black clothes, listening to a few different people tell about their close relationships with Jonah, and how he was their best friend. I thought to myself, what a crock. These people were standing up there in a church, lying about how seemingly close they were to Jonah. I thought to myself, was that before or after they found out he had AIDS. I didn't see any of those people who got up to talk, at Jonah's bedside once this past week. None of them were there. Even though my father and I were there by his side, he was alone.

People's true colors come through when faced with life altering information. I bet none of those people wanted to be around Jonah anymore, because they were afraid they might get AIDS. I hate stupid, fictitious people. I looked ahead a couple of rows, and saw Jonah's mean-spirited father sitting there with Jonah's mom. I was surprised to see him there. It was so typical of my uncle to want sympathy from others when he really didn't even care about his own son. I just wanted to get out of my seat, walk to that podium, and tell everyone in this church to leave.

You don't show someone you care for them or love them when their dead. People are supposed to give others their flowers while they're alive, and can smell them. All of these nice loving words didn't mean a thing now that Jonah was gone. I can almost guarantee he would've loved to have seen all of these people come see him while he was alive. I know he would have.

After the funeral and burial, I took up a project on HIV/AIDDS, and educating myself about this deadly disease. Also, I volunteered a couple times a week at the hospice where Jonah spent his final days. I can never forget the images I have planted in my mind about him. I'm happy with myself, that I was able to be there with Jonah in his last days. I think having been there with him for those couple of days helped me to prepare for his death.

I don't go to the cemetery to visit him. I don't like death, and I know Jonah's body isn't in that grave anyway. He's in a place where AIDS can't hurt him anymore. There's no way in this world I could ever forget Jonah. I still have those questions for God that I would like answered, but now I have a different outlook on life. I truly hope God answered Jonah's prayer and forgave him for his lifestyle.

I spend my days not questioning things as much, and being thankful for the time I have with my family. It's never promised that I will get the chance to have a long good-bye like the one I had with Jonah. I could lose them in an instant. I make it a point to cherish them and make sure they're not alone.

CHAPTER THIRTEEN
I Thank A Teacher

Ever since I could remember, my heart's desire was to become a teacher. It wasn't that I had such a special love for children down in my heart, or that I thought children were easier to work with, I loved the school system. I grew fond of the notion of getting to have my own classroom, and being able to be any kind of teacher I wanted to be. I had outlined what I wanted for my life, and I knew all the plans I had set for myself.

I spent four years of my life after high school working on getting my degree in education. I labored night and day to obtain all the knowledge I would need, in order to become a successful teacher. I was entering a profession that didn't pay well, had long hours, and very little recognition for the difference I would be making in a child's life. It never quite made any sense to me why society pays an athlete millions of dollars, to either dribble a ball up and down a basketball court, or a football player to simply run with a football, but a teacher's pay is at the bottom of the barrel.

I was so dedicated to becoming a teacher that I rarely had any time for a social life. I tried the boyfriend thing, but I wasn't into giving up my free time for some man, when I could've been studying or researching. I remained alone for a while. It didn't really bother me until I found myself all alone in my apartment on the weekends, with no one to do anything with. I started to feel bad about myself, and I questioned everything I did, making sure it was what I *really* wanted to do.

Becoming a teacher means having at least a like for children. I can remember one of my college professors telling me that loving children that are not your own doesn't come instantly. In fact, he said there would be some children we hated. I didn't know if he was completely being honest, because I couldn't see myself hating a child. Undeniably, there would be some challenges, but I wasn't going to let some kid ruin my dream of becoming a teacher. I worked hard to obtain all the credentials I needed, so that I could get the best teaching job I possibly could.

My desire was to always work with small children, but when I graduated, and couldn't find a job, I decided to look for employment at the high school level. I had to work hard just to get my foot in the door. There were so many people who wanted to be teachers I thought it was going to be impossible for me to ever find a job. I was disappointed in myself, because six months after graduation I still hadn't found a job. None of the old teachers were retiring yet, and every school I applied to in my community, was fully staffed.

I knew my problem wasn't because I was going to be a first year teacher, because the good thing about the teaching profession is; everyone has to be a first year teacher in order to get the experience they need. After having talked to career services at my university, he recommended that I stop looking for work locally. He suggested that I look for a teaching job outside of my community, but within reason. He even gave me a list of potential schools. I didn't want to venture out elsewhere. I wanted to teach in a community I knew—a community I was familiar with.

I remember calling my parents and complaining about not being able to find a job. My mom was the one who gave me the push I needed. She told me to stop being lazy and if I really wanted to be a teacher, I would stop wasting time and find a job wherever I could. I was upset that she didn't try to comfort me, or that she didn't tell me everything was going to be alright. What I really wanted was for someone to try to convince me not to seek employment elsewhere. However, even my dad wasn't on my side. I knew what I had to do.

Here I was, twenty-four years old, and I was simply a substitute teacher. I wanted my own class, and I wanted to be a teacher more than anything. I applied at every school I could possible think of, and I also utilized the list 'career services' had given me. I told myself the first school to call me for an interview, was the school I was going to work at. I no longer cared about where I would be teaching. I just wanted to teach.

Three weeks had passed before I received a call from a school district, it was about forty-five minutes away from where I lived. It was a high school over on a rough side of town. I listened to the principal's message over and over again, excited that someone had called, and wanted to schedule an interview with me. I spent all weekend preparing for my interview and what I was going to say. I was going to get this job, and I knew I had to bring my best.

The morning of the interview I left early, and decided to drive around town to get a feel for the neighborhood. I passed by several run-down homes, and the streets had multiple holes in them, while the buildings were filled with graffiti. I drove a little further, thinking the school was going to be in a better section of the neighborhood. I was wrong. I pulled into the parking lot and stopped my car, before I could even find a spot to park.

The school was two levels, and the outside of the building looked like someone had purposely scraped the paint off the building. I drove a little closer to the school to check the address, to make sure I was at the right place. Everything was correct. I pulled into a parking spot, got out, and headed towards the door. The building was a disgusting brown color, and the windows were rusty, and looked liked they hadn't been opened in years. I approached the front double-doors, and saw that the doors looked liked they hadn't ever been cleaned. I was instantly turned off by the condition of the school. I thought the inside would be better.

I walked in, and saw that at least the tile was shiny and white, but the walls were covered in dirt. It looked like they were supposed to be white, but almost looked gray from all the dirt. The smell was like an old 1960's boy's restroom. I could hardly hold myself from vomiting on the floor. This school was not what I expected. I was highly upset, and knew that if I were offered the job, I wouldn't take it.

Once I found the office, the secretary escorted me to wait outside principal Deed's office. He kept me waiting for close to an hour. I was uneasy, irritated, and wanted to go. I wanted to get my stuff and walk right out the door, and tell Mr. Deed to shove his job, but I didn't. I stayed, and waited for him to shake my hand and invite me into his office.

"I want to welcome you to, East Brook High School," Mr. Deed said.

He was a short, Caucasian male, with a receding hairline, and a small thin build, and looked like he was under an immeasurable amount of stress, and not to mention pain.

"Thank you," I replied.

"I was quite impressed with your resume. You got your bachelor's degree and master's, and you're only twenty-four. Pretty impressive," Mr. Deed stated.

He went on to ask me about why I wanted to be a teacher, and all kinds of questions about discipline, and my philosophy on education. He told me I would be teaching sophomore English. During the interview, I started to change my negative attitude and realized that I was being offered the job I had dreamed about so many years before. Then, as I was smiling within, Mr. Deed changed the tone of the conversation.

"I don't want to lie to you about our school," he started out.

"Lie," I said, stunned.

"Well, you'll be working with minority students, and some of my white teachers have a problem with that. Is that going to be a problem for you?" he asked.

I took a moment to think, but I didn't take too long, because I didn't want him to think I was scared, and consider giving my job to someone else.

"Um, no sir, that shouldn't be a problem," I replied.

"I also want you to know a lot of our teachers quit, right in the middle of a semester. Some don't even stay for a full two months," Mr. Deed said.

"What?" I stammered.

"Yes, I have six more interviews today. I need all the teachers I can possibly get," he revealed.

My excitement faded as fast as it came.

"I tell all my teachers its okay to be tough as nails. At this school, you have to be," he explained.

"I'm sure I'll be fine. I just want to teach," I said.

"Well, there's no need to beat around the bush, I need you, and I would like for you to be a teacher here. The job is yours if you want it," Mr. Deed exclaimed.

"Yes, thank you, sir," I answered.

I left that afternoon not knowing what I had gotten myself into. A school where teachers were quitting in the middle of a semester didn't sound to inspiring. Working with minority kids, working in a rundown school, this was not the ideal teaching job I had planned for. However, I was ready to take on the challenge, and begin my first year as a teacher.

On my first day of school, I stood with my door open and I was leaning up against the chalkboard with a smile on my face, ready to greet the students as they walked in. When the first bell rang, I felt the nerves overtake me, and I became a little scared. I didn't know what to expect. Before I had the chance to calm myself down students just started flooding in one by one. Some looked at me and smiled, some just looked, others acted like they didn't see me. I thought to myself, here come the hormones!

"Good morning class, I'm Ms. Blake," I introduced myself.

No one said anything, the entire class was silent.

"English 1302," I said.

"No one's gonna say anything to you," a voice in the back said.

"Who said that?" I asked.

No one responded to my question.

"Don't be acting like you gonna be here teaching us, when you prolly jus' gonna leave," a male voice said.

I finally was able to spot the direction of the voice, and saw a young male Latino student slouched in his chair.

"Why would I leave?" I inquired.

"Cause, all our teachers leave. Then they just keep sending new people like you all the time," he said.

Suddenly, the whole class agreed with him in unison. The students began talking, and the talking lead to shouting, and the shouting lead to them getting up and conversing with one another. Some were arguing, some were playing music, some were sitting, and the little snot nose ringleader of it all, just sat in the back like he had nothing to do with it. I had lost control of the class. The amount of foul language I heard that day was enough to make me want to prove the class right, and not show up tomorrow.

Aside from the catastrophe I had early that morning, the rest of my three classes weren't nearly as rebellious and rude as my first period students. By no means were they sweet angels, but I was at least able to get them to open a book.

The first few weeks had raced by, and I spent almost every day crying in my car during my lunch period. This school, and these students, wasn't what I had hoped for. This wasn't the dream I had wanted when I was little. I didn't want to teach a bunch of Mexican and Black students.

No matter what I did, I couldn't get my first period class under control. I brought educational videos, I played music, I created word games, and I even let them bring food. Nothing worked. I had to get to Elias Ochoa. Elias was seemingly the one individual who commanded the attention of the class, he was the leader, and they followed whatever he did. I couldn't stand him. I thought back to what my professor had said about having a student we might hate, I didn't think it was possible, but I was close to hating that little sixteen year-old deviant. He would always get the students pumped up to defy me, and once he got them distracted, he felt as if he had accomplished something.

One day after class, I told him I wanted to speak with him after school. I wasn't sure if he was going to show up, but come four o'clock, there he was standing in the doorway.

"Come in, and sit down please," I said firmly.

He walked slowly, as if he was trying to agitate me. He fiercely took a seat in a desk in the front row right across from my desk.

"What, man? I got to go home," Elias said.

"It will only take a minute," I stated.

"It better," he replied.

I didn't know how to approach him, or what to say. I didn't want him to get abusive with me, and I didn't know how he was going to act if I said something he didn't want to hear.

"Your behavior in my class is really unacceptable, and I'm asking you nicely if you could just come to class, and not say anything to the other students," I requested.

"You don't want me to talk to my friends, Ms. Blake?" Elias asked.

"You can talk to them, but can it be after class?" I questioned.

"I don't know Ms. I don't know if I can do that," he said in a laughing manner.

"Well, I'm telling you that your behavior needs to change, or else . . ."

"What, what you gonna do?" Elias interrupted.

He got up out of the desk, and violently pushed the desk towards my desk.

"What you gonna do, uh?" he said again.

I stopped speaking for a split second, to give him a chance to calm down. I didn't know what he was going to do next.

"I was just going to say, we might have to talk to your parents," I said quietly.

"My parents," he laughed. "I aint got no parents!" Elias shouted.

"What do you mean?" I asked.

"Can I go now?" Elias yelled.

"Yes," I said.

I watched Elias leave that day, not really believing what he had told me about not having any parents. I passed it off as him being a fresh mouthed little teenager.

The next day in class, Elias didn't listen to anything he and I had discussed yesterday. In fact, things got worse. He purposely would start physical altercations with the other male students, and then while I was teaching, he would throw wads of wet paper at the back of my head. I tried my best to get him removed from my class, but every other class was filled to capacity.

I was pushing the four-month mark, and things hadn't gotten any better. Elias took his disrespect to another level, and he would start cursing at me, and threatening me. Yet, I never sunk to his level.

I'll never forget the day that changed my life as a teacher. It was a rainy afternoon, and I was driving home, and as I was driving through the East Brook neighborhood, I saw a teenage boy getting beaten up badly. He was on the ground being kicked in the head, and stomped on. There was about fifteen to twenty boys all huddled around a fence watching as the two boys fought. I didn't know what to do. Should I get out and stop the fight, or just pass by and get help?

With the rain dropping intensely on the roof of my car, and with fear in my eyes, I started honking my horn at the boys, and flashing my lights. I saw the boys disperse and run, as if their life depended on it. I didn't stop honking until I saw the last boy turn the corner and run away. I stopped my car, got my umbrella, and got out the car. I could feel the cool drops of rain splashing my face until I was able to open my umbrella. I checked my surroundings, and quickly went over to the boy, who looked like he was in serious pain. He was lying on the ground with a bloody tee shirt and ripped pants, and I could see the top of his head was bloody as well.

I bent down to turn the boy over, and when I did, I discovered it was Elias. Elias had a swollen black eye, his lip was cut, and his left arm looked limp. He didn't notice it was me at first, because he barely opened his eyes.

"Elias! Elias!" I screamed.

He wouldn't respond to me. I tried to pick the top half of his body up and situate him, so that I could communicate with him. He wasn't responding to me. I left him on the ground and went to the nearest house I could find, and banged on the door. I asked a woman to call the police. She did, and in a matter of minutes, Elias was being taken away to the hospital. I followed EMS to the hospital, and told the hospital that I was Elias's teacher. I asked the nurse, had she gotten a hold of his parents to let them know what happened. There wasn't a way to reach his parents, so the hospital got in contact with the school, and principal Deed pulled Elias's file, and gave a contact number to the hospital. Elias had been telling the truth. He didn't have a mother or father, at least living with him. The hospital contacted Elias's grandmother, who came up to the hospital right away.

I spent time with Elias's grandmother, who told me Elias's father was in prison, and his mother was deceased. His grandmother revealed to me that Elias had recently joined a gang, and she had told him to get out, but he wouldn't listen. The hate I had been carrying in my heart for this sixteen year-old boy was shameful. This young teenage boy was going down a path which could only lead to destruction. I had spent so much time trying to correct his behavior, I had failed to get to the root of why he was behaving the way he was. After Elias was placed in a room, I asked his grandmother would it be okay if I saw him only for a second. She allowed me to see him.

When I went into Elias's room, I was instantly drawn to the heavy cuts and bruises which covered his face. The left side of his face looked like he had been hit multiple times with a baseball bat. His arm was in a cast, and his head was bandaged. I sat down in a chair in the corner of the room waiting for him to wake up and see me.

"Why are you here?" Elias said softly.

"I was the one who stopped the fight, and got you help," I answered.

"You did?" he said, stunned.

"Yes," I said.

"You don't care about me. Why would you help me?" Elias asked.

"I care about all my students," I stated.

"Not me! You tried to get me kicked out of your class, now you calling for me to get help and stuff," he said.

I felt ashamed, and couldn't look him in the eyes. He was right. I guess I didn't do such a good job of hiding my disdain for him as well as I thought I did.

"I was only trying to help," I said. I got my stuff and left the room. There was nothing else to say. The one student who gave me such a hard time was wondering why I was there to help him. I really didn't know the answer to that question myself. All I knew was that there was a young boy who was in trouble, and I helped him. I would've done it for anyone.

For the next few weeks Elias didn't come to class. I actually was worried about him, and decided to go to his house and check on him. I knew it would probably be the worst mistake of my life, but after hearing about his problems I needed to know he was okay. I pulled his file from the office, got his address, and went to his grandmother's house. Before I got to his house, I printed information about gangs and violence, hoping Elias would read it, and want to get out of the gang he was in.

When I got to his house, his grandmother invited me in. It was a two-bedroom home, which looked like it hadn't been cleaned in months. The carpet was filthy, and the walls looked like they were covered with mildew, and I saw two little boys running around. Elias came out.

"Why are you here, man?" he said.

"I just wanted to see if you were okay, the class missed you," I told him.

"I'm fine. I really don't like you being in my house. I don't want no teacher in my house!" he shouted.

"I'm not staying long. I only came to see you, and give you this," I explained. I extended my hand with the information about gangs. He looked at it, and grabbed it away from me.

"Can I talk to you outside, Elias?" I asked.

Elias looked at his grandmother, and was about to tell me no, but he glanced back at me, and nodded his head yes.

We went outside, sat on the front steps, and I did most of the talking.

"Listen, I know you're in a gang," I said.

"Who told you that?" Elias inquired.

"It doesn't matter. I know how dangerous they can be. I once knew someone who ended up dying in a gang. I don't want that to happen to you," I stated.

"I aint gonna die, cause I aint in no gang, Ms. Blake," Elias proclaimed.

"Will you just read this, please? Please, Elias, please," I begged.

He glanced at it, looked up at me, and then once more at the paper.

I turned to walk away, realizing he didn't want to be bothered with anything I had to say. Suddenly, as I was making my way down the stairs, he called to me.

"I thought you said this had to do with gang violence!" Elias shouted.

I stopped and turned around.

"It does, Elias," I replied.

"Naw, this says something about gone violent," Elias said.

I walked back up the stairs towards Elias, and glanced at the reading I had given him.

"Look, didn't you read the title?" I asked.

"Yes, gone violent," Elias stated.

"Elias, it says, gang violence," I said. "Why are you acting like you don't know what this says?" I questioned.

He put his head down, and threw the packet on the ground. I stared at him for a second, and suddenly realized that Elias couldn't read.

"What grade level do you read at, Elias?" I asked.

"Bye, Ms. Blake," he said abruptly.

"Look at me Elias! Look at me!" I demanded.

He looked up with humiliation written on his face.

"What does this word say?" I pointed.

He struggled trying to say the words in the first paragraph. He tried his hardest to say the words, but he couldn't make the connection. I told Elias when he returned to school I wanted him to stay after school so that I could help him with his reading. He agreed. The tough, macho, troublemaking exterior Elias had, was starting to fade fast. He didn't reject my help. Elias was silent and thankless, and had no gratitude to show, but I knew deep within I had made a connection with him that night. Things changed for me that night. I found myself breaking from my comfort zone, and the four walls of the classroom, and was reaching out to one of my students, especially a student who had caused me so much trouble.

When Elias came back to school, he tried to fall back into his old habits of being the tough rebel and class jokester again. However, I had seen him in a vulnerable state, and knew two very personal secrets about him. His antics eventually ceased, and my first period class actually became my best class. For months it would take an entire class period just to get through even part of a lesson. But now, I commanded the attention of every student, every day, and their respect for me had grown. In a way I was glad that Elias was absent from class those couple of weeks, because it gave me a chance to get to my class without distractions and constant interruptions.

I spent the remainder of my afternoons and part of my evenings helping Elias with his reading. He was a sophomore reading on a fifth or sixth grade reading level. I knew exactly what had happened to him during his time in school. He was simply passed along and made someone else's problem. I tried my best to help as often as I could. It wasn't easy, because Elias felt as if I was treating him like he was stupid. My ultimate goal was to make sure he was learning. I met resistance from him in the beginning, and some days he would keep me waiting for an hour, and some days he wouldn't show up at all. Nonetheless, I still wanted to help him the best way I could.

One night I recall having a conversation with my mother in which she told me that what I was doing was what was expected of me. I didn't really agree with her, because I felt like I was going over and beyond my teaching duties, by helping a sophomore student learn to read on his grade level. I complained to her to no end that night.

"I hate this school," I cried to my mother.

"You should be used to it by now," my mother replied.

"If I can get out of here next year, I'm gone the first opportunity I get," I said.

"Why, so you can go help the white kids? So you can have it easy and be around your own kind?" my mother exclaimed.

"You make it sound as if there's something wrong with me wanting to be around an environment in which I'm more comfortable," I claimed.

"You're a teacher, it shouldn't matter what race your students are. A teacher teaches whoever, wherever, and does it because they love it. You told me you loved teaching," Mom said.

"I do," I replied.

"Good, than it shouldn't matter what school you're at, or who your kids are. Help that boy. You might make a difference in his life. You could probably be the first person to make a positive difference in his life," My mom stated.

I thought about what she said, and it didn't really sink in until about three weeks before school was about to be out. I was helping Elias with his last reading lesson. We had finished up, and he was on his way out the door.

"You gonna be here next year, Ms. Blake," Elias asked.

"I don't know yet," I replied.

"Well, I jus want to say thanks and stuff, for helping me with reading," Elias said.

I was puzzled, and didn't really know how to respond to Elias.

"You're welcome," I replied.

I spent the next couple of days teaching my class like I had never done before. It had taken me months to get them where I wanted them, and now it was all about to be over in less than two weeks. In a way, my students grew a special place in my heart. It took me awhile to get to a point where I could go into work at least liking my job. There were so many days throughout the year when I literally wanted to walk out, and give up teaching all together, but I persevered. I pushed through my weakness, and actually ended up gaining the respect of my students . . . even Elias!

The very last week of school, it was on a Monday, one of the secretaries came to my classroom and told me she was going to stay in my room and watch my students because Principal Deed wanted to see me. I couldn't have possibly known what he wanted. I told her to give me one second, and let me finish teaching my lesson. She insisted that I drop what I was doing and head over to his office immediately. I told my class to listen to the secretary, and that I would be back momentarily.

All the bad things that could happen I began to play over in my head. Maybe he was going to fire me on the spot for something. Maybe someone accused me of something like being sexually inappropriate with a student. I didn't know what to think. When I arrived at Mr. Deed's office, I stood outside the door for a second, and gave myself a minute to mentally prepare myself for what was about to come. I knocked on the door.

"Come in," Mr. Deed shouted.

I opened the door.

"Thank you for coming so quickly," he said.

"What's wrong, sir," I said hastily.

"Well, I received some horrible news about nine o'clock this morning," he explained.

I focused all my attention on him, listening to each and every word he was saying to me.

"What?" I said anxiously.

"One of your students died this morning," Mr. Deed blurted out.

I sat in silence for a moment trying to replay the words he had just spoken. Died, I thought. I've never known anyone in my life to have died before.

"Oh, my God, who?" I asked.

"Elias Ochoa," Mr. Deed stated sympathetically.

I burst into tears. I couldn't believe what he was saying to me. I put my hand over my eyes because I didn't want the principal to see my crying, but I couldn't stop the tears from coming down my face. I felt a slight pain in my head, and I felt my heart begin to race. I just taught Elias yesterday morning, how could he be dead?

"He was stabbed seventeen times in the chest, and twice in the head," Mr. Deed told me.

I couldn't say anything else. All I could do at that present time was cry. I was in a state of confusion as he was delivering this news to me. Never in my life had I experienced losing someone to death that I actually knew. I was scared. I didn't know why, but I was too terrified in that moment to be sorrowful. I didn't understand death, and now I had just lost a student . . . a student I had actually grown to love.

"It appears Elias was involved in some gang activity, and he met an early death because of his involvement," Mr. Deed explained.

"So he *really* is dead?" I asked.

"Yes, Ms. Blake, he died late last night, and his body was discovered early this morning over by a creek in his neighborhood," he said.

"Why would they kill a sophomore high school student? How much of a threat could he be?" I yelled!

"Gang life is tough for any age," he said.

"Do they know who did it?" I cried.

"They haven't found anyone to charge," Mr. Deed replied.

"I can't believe this," I said.

"By the way, Elias's grandmother wants to speak with you tonight, if you can make your way over to her house," Mr. Deed told me.

I nodded my head that I understood, and made my way back to class. The students saw that I was visibly upset. My face was red, and I was too shaken up to go on teaching. I told the class what happened, and many students began weeping, and I felt the sadness all over the room. I guess I was partly mad at myself, because this was a student that I once hated. I felt bad because I should've cared for Elias more than I did.

At the end of the day I sat in my room until it was dark outside. I sat just staring at Elias's seat. I'll never see him again. He'll never sit in this classroom again. I wasn't going to be able to see him flourish with his reading and excel. A sixteen year-old boy lost his life, and this time, there was nothing I could do. I couldn't simply put together a reading lesson to help Elias, like I had done to help him with his reading. He was dead, and I would never get the chance to see him ever again.

I packed up myself that night, and headed over to Elias's grandmothers house. I sat in the living room talking with her for what seemed like hours. She was already grieving. She kept telling me how she told him to get out of the gang, and she expressed to me how angry she was because she knew no one was going to be charged for his murder.

"I want to thank you," his grandmother said.

"For what?" I asked.

"You helped him read, and you tried to save his life," she stated.

"How did I do that?" I inquired.

"I saw him reading what you gave him about gang violence. He was trying to make a change, but I guess he couldn't do it fast enough," she said.

"Elias was reading what I gave him?" I said in disbelief.

"He sure was. I know for sure he was trying to leave that gang he was in, but for some reason he couldn't escape," she explained.

"I'm sorry for your loss," I said.

Elias's grandmother cried until the time I left. She had taken care of him practically his whole life, and now he was permanently removed from her life in such a horrific way. I couldn't imagine the police weren't going to do their job in trying to catch the people who did this to Elias, but all hope seemed lost when another teenage boy died from gang violence a week later. It was beyond me how someone could be so cold and mean to kill someone as if it was a natural thing to take someone's life away.

Elias's death made me take a different approach to teaching. I had spent so much time during the year trying to outthink and plot ways to connect with the students, instead of just doing my job, which was to simply teach. However, I found that being a teacher required much more than just teaching a lesson. I was also taking on the task of being a mentor, friend, and confidant. Some of my students needed more than an English Literature teacher. Elias was a special student that I didn't realize needed help, until it was too late. My tutoring him in reading, and giving him literature on gang violence didn't even touch the surface of the kind of help he needed.

It was okay for me to form relationships with my students. It was okay to go above and beyond my teaching duties in order to help a child succeed. My relationships didn't form until it was almost time for school to be over. I missed out on the joy of teaching. Additionally, I had to learn to prepare for the unexpected. My first year of teaching was filled with experiences I could never, or will never, forget.

Death was something I never understood until I lost Elias as a student. I didn't think it would affect me as much as it did. I felt this way because I always thought there was a separation between teachers and students. I didn't think it was possible to become emotionally invested in the well-being of a child beyond the classroom, but that notion was dispelled once I met Elias. I didn't care about his unruly behavior anymore. I saw he needed help, and it was my duty to help him. There could only be a separation if I allowed it.

What I understood about death and grieving was that there were certain times to grieve, and then there was a healing process. I always knew death was real, but it wasn't until I actually felt the pain of having known someone, and then realizing that they weren't ever coming back again, that I understood death for the first time in my life. It's my responsibility to cherish my students, and see some of them as more than just challenges. If I learned nothing else in my first year, I learned to treat every child as a special individual.

I stayed at East Brook the next year, and gave myself a chance to redo what I had done the previous year. I didn't run away like I wanted to; I stayed and developed my teaching style, so that I could not only be a teacher, but an effective, caring, teacher. I keep Elias's memory alive in my classroom with a picture, and I tell all my students about Elias, and his struggle to escape gang life, and his determination to succeed.

I hope by telling Elias's story I help someone from making that one wrong decision which could impact them, or someone who loves them, forever. Teaching is not a thankless job even if I only help one student.

I will always remember Elias, and my comfort comes from the fact that he tried to make the right decision in his life. I now understand the goal of an educator is for a student to one day say, "I thank a teacher."

CHAPTER FOURTEEN
Out On the Steps

This life is filled with heartache and pain, and there are too many of us who spend countless nights crying and trying to understand death. The Angels in Heaven are busy day after day preparing for the arrival of another graceful, innocent, soul, to spend eternity in peace and love. I know all too well the emotional damage losing a loved-one can have on a family. Especially, a family who never believed death could be a part of their lives. The most shocking thing about having to go through losing a family member, was trying to wrap my mind around the belief that they actually made it to Heaven. It was a task I soon learned I was unprepared for.

Talking about God and Heaven was something that I was used to, but I never fully grasped the absolute significance of how someone truly leaves this earth. I didn't know if what I was being told was the truth. How does a person really know if someone they loved made it to Heaven or not? Where's the evidence? It sounds good at the time to hear those comforting words people usually whisper to you, telling you that they're in a better place now. Giving you the hope they're already an Angel in Heaven. Or, that they're just resting, away from the pain of the world. Who really believes this?

It took some time for me to identify with the fact that death was something scary I wasn't ready for. I was unsure of the afterlife. I couldn't believe theories about where I would end up. Was it possible for a good person on earth to end up in hell? Was it possible for a person who didn't live such a good life to end up in Heaven? Was our final resting place contingent upon how horrific our death was on earth? I wanted answers to these questions, and it seemed like every time I would come to terms with forming a final answer, I would find something else to question.

Being afraid of death was something I was terrified of. In my heart I wished that no one had to die. I wished there wasn't a cut-off time for us. All these thoughts and questions soared through my mind when I first received that life-altering piece of news.

It had been just over a year, when Shelby, my sister, had moved to Seattle to start her career in law. She had labored so many years to become a lawyer, and she was beside herself with joy when she was offered a job in Seattle. It was always her goal to make some sort of difference in the lives of others. Shelby's goal was to start off in law, and eventually move into politics. I admired her ambition and her determination to be successful. Lord knows, I didn't have the mind, or the strength to accomplish even a fraction of the things Shelby set out to do. I watched her beam with joy when she told our parents the good news that Thursday night. Her career was finally taking off.

Moving to a new state was something my mom and dad didn't want my sister to do. She was fresh out of law school and didn't know a single soul in Seattle. However, my sister didn't let our parent's fear and worry hold her back from taking the job. The conversation I had with her a week before she left, didn't matter to her either.

"Are you sure this is what you want to do?" I asked.

Shelby looked at me, and gave me a cold stare as if she was looking into my soul.

"I've never been so certain of anything in my life," she replied.

"It's just such a depressing State," I muttered. I thought if I were to give her some negative conversation she would want to rethink her decision. Conversely, Shelby wasn't buying into anything I had to say.

"I want to experience life. It's time I saw the world on my own. I love mom and dad, but I have to remove myself from being under them," Shelby stated.

"I guess you've already made up your mind?" I questioned.

"Ally, you understand," she said to me.

I really didn't understand why she needed to leave her hometown just to be out on her own. She could do that in another city. Experiencing life didn't mean she had to leave the State, but I guess I understood why she felt she needed to be free. There was nothing no one could do to stop her from leaving. Come Monday, she was heading out to go start her new life. I wasn't envious of my little sister, I was trying to protect our mom. Our mom cried night and day because she didn't want Shelby to go. I saw how upset she was and I didn't want to keep seeing my mother in that kind of distress.

Perhaps, I was jealous in a way. My life amounted to nothing more than being a manager at a local grocery store. If I had the drive to be like Shelby, maybe I could've been something great, but my time was over. I was too settled in my own personal comfort to become something else. I lived a contented life, and my main goal was just to see my family happy. I truly meant that in my heart. All I wanted was, for my family to be happy. It gave me joy to see that others were enjoying life. I spent so many years resenting my life, and I hated who I was.

Before I became an adult, I wanted to die so many times when I was a teenager. I was depressed growing up, and my way for me to accept certain things was for me to cut myself. I don't think my intention was to kill myself, but I wanted to hurt physically rather them mentally and emotionally. My mom called me her basket-case, but I knew she meant it in a loving way.

I was unhappy with myself, and couldn't understand why I felt inadequate . . . as if I didn't belong. I watched my sister grow into a beautiful young woman. She was the kind of person I wanted to be. She was funny, intelligent, and loving. We were the best of friends and loved each other unconditionally as sisters. There wasn't anything we wouldn't do for one another. Shelby's leaving wasn't going to only affect our parents, but it was going to affect me greatly as well. I was going to miss having my sister around.

The day Shelby left, I met our mother and father at the airport, wishing Shelby a safe trip to Seattle as we said our good-byes and kissed each other. I saw the look of terror in my parent's eyes, as Shelby was getting ready to leave. We had all planned to come visit her the following week once she was settled in. I watched my sister take off, and I was thinking to myself what a wonderful life she was about to embark upon. A door full of opportunities awaited her, and she had the power to be whoever she wanted to be.

That night I went over to my parent's house to check on them, and make sure they were holding up okay. I found my dad watching television, and asked him where mom was.

"Do you have to ask," he said silently.

Once he said that, I knew exactly where to find my mom. I casually walked to the back of the house, out of the screen door, and found my mother sitting on the steps. Anytime my mother is dealing with anything stressful in her life, she makes her way to the back steps to 'clear her head' she tells us. I thought her serene territory was a bit odd, but everyone is different and needs to find comfort any way they can. Besides, my comfort used to be hurting myself, who was I to judge?

I slowly crept up behind my mother and found her resting comfortably on the middle step, with her back leaning up against the top step and her feet stretched out in front of her. At first I took a seat on this old rusty white rocking chair, but found it to be a bit uncomfortable. I took a seat on the top step behind my mother and put my hands across her shoulders. She reached for my arms, and tilted her head slightly on my bare arms.

"Are you going to be okay," I asked.

"Oh, I'm going to be fine," she replied. "It's just going to take some getting used to," she explained.

"We all know Shelby is an independent strong woman. You don't need to worry about her," I suggested.

"It's just hard having to let one of your children go," said Mom.

"But at least she's going away for something good. She's not trying to escape her life here, she's going away to make herself better and become successful," I stated.

"My heart is racing having to think about her being alone in a city she knows nothing about?" Mom cried.

"You and dad taught her well, Shelby is going to be fine. I promise you," I said.

"I just don't want my greatest fear to become a reality," Mom told me.

"Greatest fear?" I questioned.

"Yes, the fear of losing a child. I don't know what I would do if I ever lost you, or your sister," Mom explained.

"We're grown women now, mom, you don't have to worry about us as if we're little kids," I exclaimed.

"True, but just because you're both grown and moving on, doesn't mean you're not still my daughters. My love for you two is the same today as it was when you both were born. A parent's love and concern just doesn't stop when their child becomes an adult," Mom replied.

"I'm sorry," I said.

"Don't be sorry, you need to know there are many dangers that await a young twenty-six year old woman. If you never believed in prayer before, now's the time," Mom stated.

I sat on the steps with mom the rest of the night, listening to her talk about all of the memories she had of Shelby and I. I listened to her tell me how proud her and dad were of us, and how she just wanted us to be content. I returned home that same night thinking about what my mom had said about the dangers awaiting Shelby. I chose not to believe that Shelby was going to be living in danger. If I focused on all of the bad things that could happen, they would inevitably come to pass.

Time seemed to have flown by, and before we knew it, Shelby had been living in Seattle for well over a year. She became adjusted to life in Seattle, and she said she loved the city, but missed home even more. Mom's fears seem to have ceased after the one-year mark, and she was able to come to terms with the fact that Shelby was living her own life away from us. I finally was able to accept it. Nonetheless, I've always been one of those people that believe, for every good moment, there's a bad moment waiting to strike. No one in this world can deny the fact true happiness never lasts forever.

Aside from the fact that my family was a humble, caring, giving, and loving family, destruction still found its way into our lives. No one can be exempt from heartache and pain . . . no one. This was something I knew to be true. It doesn't matter how good any of us are, we will all have to encounter some type of suffering in this life. I just wasn't programmed for it yet.

It was a cold, clear, December night when my dad called me around two o'clock in the morning, telling me to get over to the house as soon as possible. He didn't go into details, but in order to give me peace of mind right then and there, he assured me that it had nothing to do with mom. Without thinking about changing, I rushed out of my home still wearing my nightclothes, and tried to get to my parent's house as fast as I could.

When I got to the house everything looked calm and peaceful, but something was terribly wrong. My father has never pulled me out of my bed in the middle of the night. I knocked and knocked on the door, and rang the doorbell until someone came to the door. Dad answered the door and told me to come in.

"What's wrong?" I blurted out.

"Come in here," my father pointed.

I cautiously followed my father into the living room, where I found my mother sitting on the couch with the phone clutched tightly in her hands, and she was weeping. Tears began to come to my own eyes.

"Dad, what's wrong?" I demanded.

"We just received a call from a police officer in Seattle," Dad began.

"Oh no, what is it, dad?" I said hysterically.

"Shelby was admitted to the hospital earlier tonight," Dad said.

He paused, and started to get choked up. I could see the pain in his eyes. He didn't want to say the words . . . he wanted to stop. I already put the pieces together in my mind from the actions of my parents. Shelby was hurt. He didn't have to tell me anything else. I already knew.

"She was raped and stabbed," dad cried.

"What?" I said. I was wiping my face, trying to hold back the tears, but the tears just came pouring down my face. I didn't need a second to process anything. I had already heard the devastating news.

"How is she?" I asked.

My mother looked up at me and began shaking her head. My father fell to the floor holding his heart. I was mystified right then and there. That very moment is something I'll never forget. I literally felt my heart stop for a second.

"Mom, no! No, no, no!" I said.

My father was resting on the floor, crying and trying to get himself together.

"She died an hour ago," Dad informed me.

I wiped the tears from my eyes, and used my hand to brush my hair out of my face. I felt like I wanted to throw-up, my knees grew weak, and I couldn't catch my breath. Mom got up from the couch and helped me to a chair. She cried with me and let me rest my head on her lap, just as if I were a baby. I didn't want any details. I was too emotionally drained to try to understand what had happened. All I knew that night was my lovely sister had been raped, and now she was dead. That was the part that astonished me beyond belief. Hearing my father say, "Shelby died an hour ago," gave me the shock of my life.

I spent the night at my parent's house, and awoke to an empty house the next day. I didn't rise until about almost eleven that morning. For a few hours in my sleep, I was able to forget about the news I had received. As soon as I woke, all the sadness and anger welled up again. I was experiencing the same kind of pain I had last night. I walked through the house looking for my parents, but I couldn't find them. I passed by Shelby's old room, hoping I was strong enough to go in there, but I bowed my head and went straight past her room. I made my way outside onto the porch.

An hour later my parents arrived back at home, and waved me to come to the car. My mom told me to get dressed and meet them outside in fifteen minutes. I rushed back into house, took a quick shower, and put on some clothes from my old room. I raced back outside, and got in the car.

"Your mother and I went to the police station this morning, to meet with an officer who gave us more information about Shelby," dad explained.

"Dad, I really can't handle the details right now," I replied.

"I understand, but we're going back to the police station right now," dad whispered.

"What, now?" I asked.

"Afterwards, your mother wanted you to be involved when we go to make the funeral arrangements," Dad said.

I could hear mom start to cry as soon as dad said, "funeral." I looked out the window, and started to become irate with Shelby. I was mad at her. How could she do this to us I thought. Why wasn't she more careful, and watchful? There I was blaming my sister for her own death, when all she did was try to live her life. I had to re-evaluate my thinking, and stop harboring on the idea of blaming my sister. Deep in my heart I knew she wasn't to blame for her death, but I was angry, and since I didn't know any of the details, I blamed Shelby. I needed to ease my mind, and going against my first instincts, I asked dad to tell me what happened.

Dad told me to wait until we arrived at the station and listen to what the officer had to say. Mom didn't come into the Police Department, she stayed in the car and insisted that dad and I get any information the officer wanted to share with us. As we walked in, I could feel a chill pass over me. Dad walked ahead of me and spoke with a bald headed man. Dad called me over, and the three of us entered a room. The officer instructed us to have a seat at the table.

"We were able to retrieve some more information about your daughter's attacker," the officer said.

"What else did you find out?" dad asked.

"Someone saw him leave your daughter's apartment that night. One of the tenants said they saw a man running from her apartment," he said.

"Have they made an arrest?" dad inquired.

"No, but the leads we have are guiding us in the right direction. I know that's not any comfort to you at this time, but it's all we have," the officer explained.

"What happened to my sister?" I asked.

"Are you sure you want to know?" Dad nudged me.

"I need to know," I said.

The officer began telling me how his Police Department received a call from a detective in Seattle, who found Shelby's cell phone with mom and dad's number in it. He told me how he needed to get in contact with them, because the hospital needed to inform someone about Shelby's death. The police in Seattle learned Shelby wasn't from that State. It was the police who made the phone call to mom and dad that night, not the hospital, to inform us about Shelby's accident.

It is unclear what Shelby was doing at the time of her attack, but the officer told us she was in her apartment, dressed in night pants and a tee shirt. Someone had broken into her apartment from one of the windows. There was shattered glass all over the living room floor. Shelby was raped and stabbed twice in the back, and her throat was slit. I couldn't take anymore, but I stayed because it was crucial for my sanity that I knew who did this to my sister.

The police believed it was a crime of passion, and that Shelby may have known the person, because of the meanness of the crime. Shelby didn't have any enemies, and she certainly never talked about a boyfriend. I believed whoever did this was a psychopath, who not only needed to be castrated first, but also deserved to be put to death. Hearing the police officer talk about this was a nightmare. I was living a nightmare. Someone out there just took a precious life away. Who could live with themselves knowing that they brutally killed someone? The officer paused for a second to take a call. He left the room, and I fell into my father's arms. I cried and cried. One minute I'm making Christmas plans with Shelby, and the next minute she's gone. I couldn't comprehend it at all.

The funeral arrangements were going to be made in Seattle, and that's where Shelby was going to be buried. There was no sense in having her body transported back here, my dad explained.

We were all scheduled to leave for Seattle the next morning, when the officer walked backed in the room; he was holding a letter size manila folder, with some white papers sticking out.

"I have some crime scene photos if you would like to take a look," the officer asked.

What an insensitive move on his part! Looking at pictures of my dead sister, and my dad glancing at photos of his dead daughter, was not something that was going to make us feel any better.

"Let me see one, please?" dad asked.

"Are you sure sir, these are pretty graphic?" the officer asked.

"I need to see for myself," dad answered.

The officer opened the folder and pulled out a handful of photos, and spread them across the table. I got up from the table and went to stand by the window. I turned my back and I could hear dad crying.

"My pretty daughter," dad cried helplessly.

All I could do was continue to look out of the window.

"These are the photos we just received from Seattle PD," the officer informed us.

I got the answers I needed that day. Some lowlife broke into my sister's apartment, raped her, and then slit her throat. This was the kind of stuff you watch in movies, and read in crime books. This wasn't real life. This wasn't something that could ever happen to my family. I tried to make myself feel better by telling myself maybe they have the wrong woman. Maybe it wasn't Shelby; besides, we hadn't actually seen the body yet. I tried to live in denial for about ten minutes, but when dad almost fell over in his chair from looking at those photos, I knew I had to face reality.

Shelby's murder was an ongoing investigation, but I didn't believe the police had any leads. All they had was someone from the apartment building saying they saw somebody running from Shelby's apartment. That wasn't enough for me. What we were going through as a family was the most painful ordeal we had ever suffered. Why us? Why did my family get picked to have an experience of having to live a life without someone we loved? It wasn't fair. We were good people, we lived good lives, and this sadness and pain shouldn't have been bestowed on us.

We arrived in Seattle late in the afternoon the next day, and headed straight to the Police Department. This time mom was right there with us. The detective assigned to the case told us we wouldn't be allowed to get any of Shelby's things until later that week, because the apartment was an official crime scene, and they were still combing the apartment for evidence. Shelby's body had been laying in a mortuary after the autopsy was performed.

"Was it really necessary to perform an autopsy?" Mom asked the detective.

"Your husband asked for one," he replied.

"She was already cut up, how much more cutting can the poor girl take?" Mom asked rhetorically.

Mom had grown bitter from the time we arrived, until the time we reached the funeral home. Dad said Shelby needed to be cremated, and mom said she needed a proper burial once her body was brought back to California. They argued back and forth, unable to come to common ground about something so serious.

"Mom, maybe it would be best if she were . . ."

Mom interrupted me, "Don't you dare even say those words! Don't you say it to my face," mom said devilishly.

Mom had completely lost it. She was lashing out at me, when all I was trying to do was make things easier for her.

"There is no way my beautiful daughter is going to be burned up. It will happen over my dead body! And anybody who thinks they're going to cremate her, better think again. I'll meet them in hell before it happens," mom boldly stated.

Dad and I ceased trying to convince mom what we felt would be best for Shelby. If Mom wanted Shelby to have a funeral, and be buried, who were we to stop her? Maybe mom needed that tangible comfort of having a grave to visit. It wasn't my place to persuade her otherwise. Besides, I had lost a sister, and she had lost a daughter. Our losses were totally different. I wasn't a mother, and I didn't know what it was like to lose a child. I didn't give birth to Shelby, I grew-up with Shelby. I was going through a different kind of pain than my mother and father. Undoubtedly, the death of a loved one affects all of us, but in different ways.

At the end of the week, once the police let us into Shelby's apartment, my mom, dad, and I worked tirelessly to clean out her stuff. Mom and I took the things we wanted, like jewelry, photos, keepsakes, and got rid of everything else. Dad spent his time loading up and throwing out things we didn't want. It was a sad time for us, but we came together as a family and just worked. It was silent the whole time as we were cleaning up. We had always been a close family, but we were together now under the most horrific of circumstances.

Shelby's body was brought back to California, and we had a memorial service for her once we returned home. She was laid to rest in a cemetery not too far from the church where we had her memorial. Family gathered at our house and brought all kinds of food, thinking it would make us feel better. We didn't want to eat; we wanted Shelby back. We all sat and talked for hours with family members we hadn't seen in years. It was shameful that the only time we were able to come together as a family was under distressing conditions. We were saying good-bye to a sweet, loving woman, who should've never been taken away. Her life was cut short for no reason other than some revolting human being thought it necessary to take her life.

I spent the next few weeks with my parents, and I didn't go home. I couldn't sleep, and every time I did fall asleep, I had haunting nightmares about death and I dreamed that my death was around the corner. I truly believed my time to die was next. I wasn't sure how it was going to happen, but I felt I was going to die. To keep my mind occupied, I lived at the police station, trying to find if they had any new leads on Shelby's attacker. The police here in California worked intensely with Seattle, but they could only move as fast as Seattle PD. I made it a point to go to them every day. Even if I was told they had nothing new, I wanted to find who did this to my sister.

Mom and dad didn't give-up on trying to find who murdered Shelby, but they were entrapped in a state of grief. I left them alone, and I took on the task of finding my sister's killer. Months went by, and there was still nothing new on Shelby's case. I tried not to give up, but when a solid year had gone by, and no one had been charged for her murder, I knew it was hopeless. It was impossible. Investigators really didn't know who they were looking for. How was justice supposed to be brought forth for my sister when authorities had nowhere to turn? I gave up, and so did my parents.

After the anniversary of my sister's death, I enrolled in some grief therapy classes to help me cope with her loss. I thought time was the answer, but every day got worse for me. I was going backwards! Instead of moving forward, and learning to accept the fact that my sister was gone, I longed for her day after day. I needed to center myself around people who could help me and share with me how they overcame the grief of losing a sister.

I listened to several people talk about the loss of parents, siblings, friends, and even pets. The one thing I found to be constant among each individual, was the fact that they didn't know how to move on. I was in the same predicament. We didn't know if we were supposed to smile day in and day out, were we supposed to move on in such a way that forced us to forget about them, or were we supposed to think about them every minute of every day? For me, I didn't have a problem thinking about Shelby every day, I wanted some advice on how to stop the pain of missing her, and I wanted to know how I was truly supposed to move on.

"I miss my sister every day, and one of the worst things about her death is not being able to punish the person who did it," I told the group. "She was a young vibrant woman who didn't deserve what happened to her. She didn't deserve it," I repeated.

After my first couple of meetings, people began coming up to me, and began to sympathize with me. Some of them gave me encouraging words, and told me Shelby's killer would be brought to justice. That part I didn't believe, because it had already been a year and there was nothing.

Time continued to fly by, and it would be another two years before we could finally rejoice as a family. It was during the middle of the day, when my dad received a call from one of the detectives who had been assigned to Shelby's case, telling him Shelby's case was going to trial because they had caught the man who killed her. When my dad told my mother and I the news, we cried tears of joy and relief.

Someone was finally going to be held responsible for what happened to my sister, more than three years ago.

The following week, my mom, dad, and I, gathered into a courtroom with about thirty other people seated. It was silent when we walked in. I felt people's eyes looking me up and down. Could it have been possible that they knew I was the victim's sister? I was questioning whether or not to sit in the front or in the back. I didn't want to be stared at during this trial. Once everyone was seated, and the trial was about to begin, I glanced over to my right and saw two muscle-armed policemen bring out a man in handcuffs. He was a repulsive looking man, with long brown hair pulled into a ponytail. He was pale skinned, average height, and had a strong build. Just because he was dressed in a buttoned down shirt with a tie, and slacks didn't mean he wasn't guilty as sin.

I didn't lose eye contact with him, I watched him until he sat down in his chair at the table. There he was, the twisted individual who took my sister's life for no reason. I was sitting in the room with a monster, and there was nothing I could do. All sorts of bad things raced through my mind as I sat there looking at this man. I wanted to bring my gun to court tomorrow and blow his brains out, or I wanted to stab him the same way he stabbed my sister. I was thinking purely evil thoughts. I quickly snapped back to reality, because spending my life in prison was not the way I wanted to spend my time on earth. I thought about Shelby, and how she wouldn't want me to use violence with the justification of an eye for an eye. It was up to the courts to punish him.

We learned his name was Alex Shogan. He was a thirty-five year old unemployed bum. He was thirty-two at the time he committed the murder. According to the prosecution, Alex had a previous charge of a sexual assault against a minor. The prosecution painted Alex as a sane individual, who knew exactly what he was doing. His defense team said he was disturbed, and oftentimes he would act randomly, not knowing what he was doing. I was getting sick to my stomach with the way these attorneys were trying to pass off Shelby's death as nothing more than one of Alex's random disturbances. Her injuries clearly indicated that someone knew what they were doing, and meant to kill her. He slit her throat knowing she was going to die. My only interest was finding out why he did what he did.

After three days in court, the prosecution presented documents which indicated that DNA evidence was able to link Alex to Shelby's apartment, and also his DNA was found on her body. When he broke the glass in order to enter into her apartment, he cut himself, and he dripped spots of blood in certain places. Alex was arrested because the cops received an anonymous call from someone stating they had the name of the man who was responsible for Shelby's murder, and the fingerprints taken of Alex, matched the prints at the crime scene. This anonymous tip lead police straight to Alex Shogan.

My family and I had to sit through gruesome details of how Alex raped Shelby, stabbed her, and slit her throat. According to the medical examiner, it wasn't even the stab wounds or the slit across the throat which killed Shelby. Shelby bled to death, and that's what killed her. We had to look at the crime scene photos displayed on a large screen for the jurors to see. I had to look at my precious sister lying in a pool of bright crimson blood. Looking at those photos and having to hear how vicious her attack was, opened up old wounds I thought I had suppressed.

Paying for therapy wasn't the answer to my problems. At the end of the day, grief counseling may be effective for some people, but it hadn't worked for me. I still felt the pain, rage, and a need for revenge. I thought I had moved on, but all I had done was push Shelby's death down deep, and blocked it out of my mind. That wasn't the right way to heal. Not only was I supposed to accept the fact that she was gone, I was supposed to be living with it. I was supposed to be able to talk about Shelby, and relive the happy times I spent with her, without becoming upset and wanting to be vengeful. I realized in that courtroom that I hadn't healed from her death like I thought I had.

After about three weeks of the trial, the case was over. The jury got the chance to deliberate. Even though I thought it was a pretty open and shut case, I had my doubts. Both sides did an outstanding job. I was terribly disgusted at how well Alex had been defended. My sister died, why were these men trying to set this monster free? I didn't understand it. All of the evidence pointed to Alex, a man with no life. So what, he didn't have much family, and people believed he was mentally delayed. I didn't care! He was sane enough to plot to break-in, rape an innocent woman, and kill her. I wanted him to burn in hell.

Alex never got a chance to speak during the trial. There was no emotional connection between him and Shelby, and they didn't know each other. This was just a random act of violence. He didn't deserve to live, I kept telling myself. I wanted him to be executed. I wanted his family to ache and suffer the way my family and I have to for the rest of our lives.

The very same day the case was turned over to the jury, a verdict was reached in a matter of an hour and thirty minutes. Dad, mom, and I, had barely finished our lunch, before we were racing down the street to get back to the courthouse. The courtroom was filled with people, like it had been throughout the case. I saw Alex being walked back in with shackles, with his head to the ground. There was nothing wrong with him that a couple of years on death row couldn't cure. I seriously wanted him to die. However, when I saw the jury file back in, and looked at Alex looking back at an older woman, I felt sadness. She had to be his mother; she was sobbing and whispering that she loved him. Did I really want him to die? If he were to die, his mother would be facing the same pain my mother was feeling.

The verdict was in, Alex was asked to stand, and the verdict was read. Alex Shogan was found guilty on the charge of first-degree murder. He had no emotion on his face. I saw him look straight ahead at the jurors with a look of, "I am guilty." My mom couldn't contain herself, and she yelled out in a loud voice, "Thank you, Jesus!" I couldn't hold back the smile on my face, and I hugged my dad. Justice had finally been achieved for my dear little sister. It took three long years, but the man who brutally raped and killed her was going away.

When we all filed back into the courthouse to hear the sentencing phase of Alex's punishment, I still wasn't persuaded that he shouldn't get the death penalty. Even though I saw his mother and the tears in her eyes, it didn't change the fact that he killed my sister. I chose to speak during the victim impact statement. I didn't need a piece of paper to write what I was going to say, because everything I needed to say was in my heart and mind.

"You'll never be able to understand the amount of pain you've caused my family and I, by what you did," I started off. "You took away one of the sweetest people I have ever known, and for what? So you could have a few moments of pleasure," I continued.

As I was standing at the podium, projecting everything that was bottled up inside of me, I could feel Shelby's presence around me.

"Life is not the same without sweet Shelby, but you don't care, because you're a spineless coward, who has the intelligence of an acorn, and the soul of Satan. You deserve to be punished, and only the good Lord is the one who can have mercy on your soul," I finished.

Alex was given life in prison, without the possibility of parole. As soon as the trial and the sentencing were done, we all headed back to California to quickly leave the horrible memories of Seattle. We returned home early the next day, and made a trip to the cemetery. I'm actually glad now that dad didn't have Shelby's body cremated. It's nice to talk to her in a place where I can still feel connected. I like knowing exactly where her body lays. It gives me the comfort I need. Mom and dad were able to sleep a little easier at night knowing justice for their daughter had been served.

Before I went back home to my own place, I had to try to make sense of the past month, and process everything that happened. In order for me to do that, there was one particular place I had become fond of which seemed to give my mom clarity. I needed some clarity and rest for my troubled mind. I was able to find that serenity, at my parent's house . . . out on the steps.

CHAPTER FIFTEEN
Will We Meet Again

Four years had passed since I had last seen my grandma. When we moved from Colorado to Virginia, it became almost impossible for me to visit Grandma Ruth. Having to adjust to a new life in Virginia was hard for me. I wanted to go back to my old home, my old school, be with my old friends, and most of all I wanted to be with my grandma. Our relationship was special, and she was one of the few people I could feel completely comfortable around to be myself.

Some of my first memories with my grandma took place in our old house on Silver Leaf Drive. Grandma used to live with us for a period of time after grandpa died. Mom didn't want her to be alone, and grandma wasn't herself for a long time. I didn't understand why grandma spent so many days and nights crying. It felt like every time I saw her, she was crying. Mom told me one of the greatest loves of her life was gone. Grandma and grandpa had been married for forty-five years. Grandma Ruth had to learn how to adjust to life without her husband. It was hard for her, after having spent almost her entire life with someone.

At the time I wasn't able to comprehend the fact, that grandpa wasn't coming back any more. I only knew that Grandma Ruth was sad, and I felt sad too, just because I knew she was hurting. Grandma's depressed state for several months was my first introduction to death. It was something I didn't want to ever happen in my family again, because of the way it affected people. If only someone would've told me that death is a part of life, then, I would've been prepared for the awful feeling I would later have to experience. My parent's tried their best to explain the concept of dying, and how people have to lose people they love. All I can remember asking over and over was 'why?' I wanted to understand, and I don't think even today, I will ever understand why people have to die.

Living miles away from my grandma, proved to not only be hard on us, but grandma as well. She had become increasingly sick in her old age, and needed constant care, and we weren't there to help her. Grandma refused to leave Colorado. She said that it was her home, and she wasn't going to dare leave grandpa. He was buried in Colorado, and she was going to stay there until she died also. We had no choice but to leave her alone.

The reason grandma and I became so close, was because I spent more time with her than my brother and sister did. Not to say that they didn't care about her, or that I loved her more, we just connected in a way that was special. Grandma would often tell me that I was the splitting image of mom. Grandma Ruth would tell me stories about my mom as a little girl, and how she and I were exactly alike. Of course mom would constantly deny grandma's claims every time I would ask her, but it was still nice to hear grandma tell stories about my mom, and about her own younger days.

I can recount almost every story that grandma ever told me. I would spend hours with her, listening to her talk, and I would ask her questions. It was interesting to hear her talk about her life, and how she spent so many years hating who she was. She resented her parent's for how she grew up, and the struggles she had to endure as a young woman, with barely any education and no skills to make it on her own.

"What was so hard about your life?" I asked grandma.

"The fact that I grew up in a one bedroom, run down little home. I don't think I can really even call it a home," she replied.

"Why?" I inquired.

"It didn't feel like a home. It was more of shack, or a hut. I hated it. I wasn't grateful for a roof over my head like my parent's said I should've been," grandma said.

"I can't imagine living in something that small," I stated.

I wasn't trying to appear rude, but I figured I had to say something to seem sympathetic.

"I vowed I would make something of myself no matter what it took, but I could only do so much, with an eighth grade education," grandma answered.

"You only have an eighth grade education?" I asked.

"I'm ashamed, but yes. Things were really tough for us back then. My dad made just enough money to keep us fed, and for a decent warm place to rest our heads," Grandma proclaimed.

As she was telling me about her life, and all the problems she experienced growing up, I could see the tragic look in her eyes. It was a mixture of embarrassment and deep-rooted pain. A pain no one would be able to understand but her. Through her stories I became upset with her parents, and I didn't even know them. Grandma was one of seven children, all living in a one bedroom, one bathroom little house. Why would her parents do that to her I thought? Having all of those kids, and not having enough room to let them grow up comfortably. It was selfish I thought. I could tell as grandma would tell me her stories, how hurt she was. I wasn't trying to bring up old wounds, but I was curious for her to tell me about her life as a young girl.

One Friday evening, I can remember when grandma told me one of the most horrific stories I had ever heard. It was hard for her to tell it to me, but getting a feel for how life was back then was fascinating to me. Grandma Ruth reflected on the time when she found out about her sister's secret.

"What secret, Grandma Ruth?" I inquired.

"Well, my youngest sister was the victim of molestation," grandma said.

"Molestation?" I said bewildered.

Grandma stopped, looked at me with tears in her eyes, and acted as if she didn't want to finish. She took a breath and started to stutter a little.

"My grandfather had sex with my eleven year old sister, and there was nothing I could do," Grandma stated.

My heart began to pump faster and faster, my body was overtaken by a swift cycle of heat all over. Tears came to my eyes.

"What! Why would he do that?" I asked.

"Because he was a pervert, that's why. No one did anything about it," she said.

"She didn't tell your mom or dad?" I questioned.

"We were sent to my grandparent's house every summer, my mom trusted her father, and there was no one she could tell. Plus, she was afraid of what my grandfather might do to her," grandma answered.

"She told you?" I asked.

"Yes, and I witnessed it," grandma answered.

Grandma told me her grandfather waited until it was night to come into their room and sexually molest her sister. My grandma said even though she was older, she was defenseless. He never touched grandma, but he would always touch her younger sister. Grandma also told me part of the real reason she didn't tell, was because her sister was embarrassed and felt dirty. All she could do was comfort her sister, and try to spend more summers at home. The very last summer they went back, my grandmother said she became wiser and outsmarted her grandfather. She instructed her sister to start sleeping in the same bed with her and to wear multiple clothes underneath her nightgown. However, there was no need to be on top of things that final summer, because their grandfather would die of a heart attack.

"His death was the best thing that ever happened to this family. I actually spat on his grave soon after he was buried," grandma revealed.

Grandma Ruth exposed her life with such intense emotion. Revealing her life was the only other time besides my grandfather's death that I saw my grandmother become emotional and unusually passionate. It hurt her to have to relive a host of traumatic events, but I believed it helped her in a way to be able to release all of these issues she had concealed for so many years. She admitted to me she had told me things she had never told anyone before. I guess that's one of the reasons why I felt so close to Grandma Ruth. She entrusted me with secrets no one else knew. Why me, I thought? Why did she trust me so much?

I kept what grandma said about her sister to myself. I have never told anyone, and will never tell anyone. Part of our bond was being able to trust each other, and to confide in each other. I was still her granddaughter, and she loved me the same, just like my brother and sister. I knew it, and they knew it as well. Yet, I still always felt like I had a special place in grandma's heart. I never told anyone I felt this way, but it was something I chose to believe. I wasn't as close to grandpa, partly because he died when I was so young. I really can't remember many conversations we had, like the way grandma Ruth and I talked. Although, I do have a few fond memories of sitting on grandpa's lap in church, and receiving birthday presents.

Grandma worked hard ever since she was eight years old. She didn't have a blessed and normal childhood she felt she was entitled to. Her education was cut short so she could perform laborious duties at home, and help raise her sisters and brothers. She knew what it was like to work hard from the age of ten. She didn't know what it was like to celebrate her birthday with nothing more than a small homemade two-layered cake. Grandma Ruth felt she missed out on a lot growing up. For years she carried around a disdain for her parent's. She confessed she loved her sisters and brothers, but it was her parent's who she had a problem with.

She explained to me that she never told them how she felt about her childhood. Her parents died not knowing how she felt about them, but she said it was probably for the best, because in her heart she knew her mom and dad couldn't do any better. They were both hard workers, but she felt like they produced a large amount of their own problems. Her dad was always starting a new job, and her mom was unable to work after she gave birth to her seventh child. Her mother was partially paralyzed in her legs and wasn't mobile enough to hold a job, which is why Grandma Ruth had to quit school and help raise her siblings, and then work out in the fields during the day, and help with the house chores in the evenings.

When Grandma Ruth turned nineteen, she met a man named, Garrison Salinas. Grandma called him a strapping man, with all the right qualities. He would liberate grandma from her life.

"When I met Garrison that rainy day walking home from the store, I knew it was love at first sight," grandma said.

"You believed in that grandma?" I asked.

"Yes, darling, it happened to me," she replied.

I didn't know how sure she was, but I took her word for it.

"Your grandfather saw me walking home in the rain, and offered me a ride. That was the one ride which changed my life forever," Grandma confessed.

Against her better judgment, grandma took a ride in grandpa's old blue Ford truck. She had never met him before, and didn't know why she got in his truck that day. Grandma's sense of humor shines through unknowingly sometimes, because she claims she took the ride because she was tired of being rained on. However, I knew it was more than that. I saw her face light up when she began to talk about grandpa, and the great love they shared.

After their first kiss, the first day they met, one rainy day, they were never apart until grandpa's death. Forty-five years they spent together. They loved each other no matter what kind of circumstances they faced, and their relationship was, of course, met with opposition from so many people. The fact that grandma was a white woman, who was dating a Mexican man, was not something people wanted to see. Grandma told me the whites believed the Mexican's were beneath them, and people in the town hated the fact grandma was dating a Mexican man.

"I hate racists," I told grandma.

"Don't say that, Julie," grandma replied.

"Why grandma? I hate 'em," I emphasized.

"You're not supposed to hate anybody. Don't let someone else's hatred become your problem, you'll spend your life hating people," grandma stated.

"What did Grandpa Garrison do? How did you both handle those people?" I asked.

"We didn't," Grandma answered.

"What do you mean?"

"The only thing we did was live our lives," grandma said.

Grandma's parents didn't care so much, but her relationship became a problem with them when she announced she was going to marry grandpa. They tried their best to keep her from marrying Grandpa Garrison. Their empty threats and futile talks about ruining her life went unheard. Grandma married Grandpa Garrison in May of 1952, when she was nineteen, and grandpa was twenty-one. They had five children together, and spent their lives loving each other and their children. They had a life built on trust, respect, and love, grandma told me.

Life in the South for grandma became too much for her to handle. She tried to be at peace with the constant stares and whispers, but it took a toll on her happiness. She told me she was no longer happy living in Alabama. After two years of living as a married couple with one child, Grandma Ruth told me it was always her desire ever since she was a little girl, to live in Colorado. The crisp, cold air, blue sky, and gorgeous mountains, was where she wanted to be. She begged and pleaded with grandpa to take her there. Eventually, he did. They left their families and modest life behind, to build a new life in Colorado.

Grandma remained in Colorado ever since she moved there in 1954, and getting her to leave the place she was accustomed to, was not happening, no matter how much we begged her to move. I spent as much time with grandma as I could before we were due to leave, because of dad's job. His job made him relocate to Virginia, and we were forced to up-root our lives, and start over. I wasn't excited about leaving, and I expressed to grandma how I felt. In a roundabout way I was sneakily trying to convince grandma to let me stay with her. I was hoping by me confessing the anguish I was feeling about leaving, she would talk to mom and dad, and offer to keep me. However, things didn't turn out the way I wanted them to.

"You have to go with your family," grandma said.

"I don't want to leave, I don't want to start over in a new place," I cried.

"You have no choice. Your life is with your family," grandma told me.

"It's not fair to us. Dad didn't even ask us how we felt about it," I said.

"Sometimes things in life come unexpectedly, and we have to deal with them the best way we know how," Grandma said.

"I don't want to leave. I want to stay!" I revealed.

"If you don't go, and you stay here, you'll regret that decision everyday of your life," she explained.

"I don't think so," I said.

"Trust me, you will. One of the worst things in the world is to be without your family. They're a part of you, and you're a part of them. Even though I loved my life in Colorado, I regretted leaving my family," Grandma confessed.

"Why have you stayed all these years?" I asked.

"I couldn't leave. We had already started a life," Grandma replied.

The years grandma spent away from her family haunted her for a long time. She opened up about the fact that she wished she would've stayed, because even though her life was hard and she resented her parent's, she missed her brothers and sisters. Grandma's leaving drove a wedge between her and her siblings. So much time had passed by that the connection they once shared was broken by years of distance. I was shocked to learn that it would take multiple years before she would even get the chance to speak to her siblings again after she moved away.

Grandma Ruth also revealed that at the time Grandpa Garrison died, she still hadn't forgiven her parent's for her upbringing. She cried on the bed next to me that night, when she told me that she had let so much time pass by, before she was able to truly forgive her parent's.

"After your grandfather died, I realized just how important life was, and how precious time is. I never got the chance to stand face to face to my parent's and tell them all the things I wanted them to know. I ran from my problems," Grandma proclaimed.

"What's wrong with wanting to escape problems," I asked.

"Running never fixes the problem. I found that out the hard way," grandma said.

It had been close to twenty years before grandma was able to reconnect with her sisters. Grandma said she suffered inside, unable to tell grandpa about how she really felt. He made a way for them to move, and it would've broken his heart to have to pick-up and move again. I never quite understood why grandma lived her life in such bondage. From the outside looking in, it appeared as if grandma was a woman who lived her life in fear and resentment. That's probably why she wasn't very happy throughout her life. The only thing I could tell that made her smile, was when she would talk about Grandpa Garrison and her children. Otherwise, it seemed as if she lived a depressed life.

Grandma probably never would've admitted to me the fact that she lived a depressed life, but I knew in my heart there was only a trace of happiness I could find throughout her life. I never asked her if she was unhappy with the way her life turned out, but she made it clear to me so many times she missed her family, and wished she would have stayed in Alabama. With so much time wasted, and the long distance between her and her family, the only people she could depend on were her children and Grandpa Garrison.

My second exposure to death came when my aunt died in a car accident, a couple years after Grandpa Garrison died. Once again Grandma Ruth spent so much time crying and keeping to herself. Two tragedies for Grandma Ruth were hard for her to deal with. She lived long enough to watch her daughter die. I think my aunt's death is what sent her over the edge. My mom spent day and night trying to comfort grandma, but all she wanted to do, was go to the cemetery and spend the day with her daughter. I couldn't imagine what it was like for someone to lose two people they loved, so close together.

I spent so much time with grandma the last month before our move. Almost every day I would cater to whatever she wanted, or needed. I didn't mind. While I was taking care of grandma, I began to notice some changes in her. She wasn't herself. I noticed a sickness about her. She didn't look like herself. I was concerned and told my mom about my concerns. After several trips to the doctor, grandma was diagnosed with Parkinson's disease. I cried for days, because this disease meant grandma's health was going to get worse over time. She already had diabetes, now she was battling this brain disease. I couldn't be optimistic. I had seen two members of my family die, and I just knew it was grandma's time. With her recent diagnosis I was waiting for dad to tell us to unpack so that we could stay and help grandma, but that never happened.

Grandma Ruth didn't show any symptoms at first, but I soon noticed her slow movement, and her shaking sometimes. I didn't want to look at her and stare, but I couldn't help but look at her sometimes, and reflect on the grandma I use to have. My brother, sister and I, did everything we could for grandma in the last couple of weeks we spent with her. At night I spent the night on one side of her bed thinking about how much I was going to miss her. Mom tried her best to get grandma to come and live with us, but she refused to leave her home. Mom hired a nurse to take care of grandma short term. In my mom's mind, she believed grandma was going to come around and eventually want to live with us.

We left for Virginia with grandma still in Colorado. I worried how she would look, or who she would be the next time I saw her. So much time was going to pass by before we would be able to see her again. Mom kept in touch with her, and I wrote to her every week, and tried to talk to her as much as I could, but it wasn't the same. I wasn't able to hear any more of grandma's life stories, and I wasn't able to see her any time I wanted to. It was hard for me to adjust to not having her around, but she didn't want to leave. She didn't want to leave her life. I almost started to become upset with her because I felt she was being selfish. Grandma Ruth had family who was willing to help her, and care for her, but she didn't want it. She didn't want our help for some reason.

On one particular occasion I remember grandma writing to me, and telling me how much she missed us, and wanted us to come and visit her before she passed on. I cried while I read the letter, because I knew also she might not be around much longer either. Death is not something that ever becomes easy to accept. No matter how much someone thinks they are prepared to say good-bye to someone they love, they aren't. I would call anyone a liar who could stand in my face and tell me they've truly accepted, and they're okay with the death of someone important in their life. I wouldn't believe them. There's too much pain involved to be one hundred percent accepting of someone's death *before* they die. Even the strongest of strong, have their times of sorrow and the questions phase. At the very last second of someone's life, it is one of the most heartbreaking things to watch them slip away, or to know you're looking at them for the very last time. That letter was my preparation, but I wasn't aware of it. I didn't understand that grandma was trying to prepare the family for her death. It didn't matter, because nothing would have truly prepared me to lose my grandma. Prepared or not, the pain was still going to be there.

That visit I had hoped for only happened on holidays. Every time we went to see grandma, her health was becoming worse and worse. In addition to her Parkinson's, she was battling diabetes which was taking a toll on her body. The communication never stopped, and although it became harder to see grandma, we never stopped communicating until it became hard for her to write. Her uncontrollable body movements made it difficult for her to complete a full letter without mistakes. She gave up. I understood, and tried to keep in touch through the phone, but even that only lasted a little while. I was losing my grandma right before my eyes.

Grandma's last letter was in response to a letter I had written over a month earlier. She finally wrote me back, and I'm guessing she used the assistance of her nurse or someone else. In the letter I complained about my school and about my home life, but I tried to keep the letter positive for the most part. I wanted to try to raise her spirits, but I also needed that 'confidant' like she had been for so many years when I lived in Colorado.

Towards the end of the letter, I admitted to grandma that I was scared to lose her, and that I didn't want her to die. I was worried that I might not ever see her again. That was a scary thought for me to ponder. Would I ever be able to see Grandma Ruth again? When she died, was that going to be the last time I would ever see her face? What did death mean I thought? I couldn't understand if death just meant, gone just from the earth, or gone forever, as if she never existed. My question to grandma in the letter was, "Will we meet again?"

When I received her reply, I didn't write her any more after that. She needed to focus on getting better, I didn't want to weigh her down with trying to answer me. She started off the letter, by telling me not to be afraid, and to stop thinking about questions I was never going to get the answer to. Grandma Ruth made me realize that the more I questioned things, the longer it was going to take for me to be at peace with the things I had no control over. It was natural that I had questions, and that I didn't understand some things, but my focus should've been on communicating with grandma as much as I could. I was going to make myself sick and depressed, worrying about the obstacles I couldn't move.

I could feel the distance between us, and our relationship wasn't the same as it had been before. It wasn't because of miscommunication, or me turning my back on her, it was due to her health and the many miles that separated us. I had asked grandma in my letter a question that I wanted her to be truthful about when answering. I didn't know much about what people perceived to be the hereafter. I heard stories and read books about where people spend eternity.

Of course I knew evil people went to hell, and I knew good people went to Heaven, but there was more to the afterlife that I didn't know about. There was a lot more I didn't understand. I even heard some people say that when we die, some of us will come back to earth as an animal, or that we come back as ourselves with a new life. It was a bit complex to think about. I certainly didn't know what to believe.

Grandma gave me some comfort that night after I read her letter. She explained to me that I would meet her again, but that I wouldn't know she was my grandmother. As I was reading I grew more confused than ever. I didn't understand what she was talking about. Apparently, the Holy Bible indicates that when we die, and those that make it to Heaven, we will love again in Heaven, but the former things of the world, and the life we lived will be erased from our minds, or passed away. What was the point I pondered to myself?

What benefit would I receive by meeting my grandmother, but not knowing who she is? I didn't want the former things to pass away; I wanted to know exactly who she was, and remember the special times we shared together.

Her answer was yes; we will meet again. I was overjoyed about the fact that we would see each other, but the fact remained that I wasn't thrilled to not know who Grandma Ruth would be. She ended her letter telling me to be strong, and not lose the hope I should have, not only for her sake, but for me as well. It was time for me to start having faith and hope, and believing in the things I was passionate about. Grandma's encouragement touched me in a way I wasn't use to. Nonetheless, I couldn't start to build on my hope just yet. Grandma was going to die, and there was nothing I was going to be able to do about it. Trying to deny this fact was only going to make things worse.

It was like a double-edge sword, dealing with this faith thing. If I didn't have the faith that grandma was going to be okay, and fight this disease, then, I would be looked upon as uncaring, or in some way signaling that I was ready for grandma to pass. Or, if I did have the hope I needed that she was going to be okay, and she ended up dying, I would've never continued believing in faith and hope. There would've been no need for me to believe in anything anymore. I wanted to deny the inevitable, but there were too many signs which lead me to believe grandma was getting worse, before she got better.

"How long do you think grandma has to live," I asked my mom.

"I don't know. Her disease can overtake her any time," mom replied.

"I don't want her to die, but I know she will," I stated.

"We don't know that completely," she answered me.

"All I know is, life will never be the same for us once grandma leaves," I expressed.

"You shouldn't feel that way," Mom told me.

Mom told me I was supposed to carry grandma in my heart, and I was going to be allowed to move on.

"How do I carry her in my heart," I asked.

"Never forgetting who she was, and what she stood for. Keeping the happy memories alive in your heart, and never forgetting her," mom exclaimed.

Wasn't I being heartless and cruel by seemingly waiting for grandma to die? My heart was heavy, my mind was overloaded, and my emotions were up and down. I could never get settled with the idea of letting go of someone you love. There was something in me which grandma believed to be special. She saw something in me which made her draw closer to me more than my brother and sister. I wanted to live up to her high aspirations of me. It was different with grandma. I knew besides my parent's, she was the only person I could go to and tell everything to, without worrying about being judged, or being looked down on.

My mom didn't have any answers for me. Her responses to some of my questions were safe, thoughtful, replies, which allowed her to limit what she wanted to say. I think mom was just upset and trying to fight back the fury she felt inside. If, and when, grandma died, she wouldn't have any parents, and she also had one sister who was dead as well. Mom was tired of tragedy always coming to her door. Things had gone so well in the early part of her life, she would've never expected to lose two very important loved-ones. I could sense that mom was more confused than I was.

I saved that final letter grandma gave me, and I began trying to form my mind to believe all of the things she had mentioned. One particular event in grandma's life came rushing back into my memory. It was after she was married and had three children, that she decided she wanted to take a job and come out of the domestic lifestyle. Grandma had spent a majority of her life working in the home and raising children. She did it for her mother and father, and spent years doing it for her own children. She was ready for a change.

"I've grown tired of spending my life in the home," grandma said one night.

"What do you mean," I asked her.

"I was subjected to other people's command of what I should do, and who I was supposed to be. I didn't want to live like that anymore," she revealed.

"In simplistic terms, are you saying you wanted a career?" I inquired.

She paused for a second.

"I guess you could say that," she answered.

"What did you end up becoming," I asked.

"I worked as a cafeteria cook for almost twenty years," grandma said.

Grandma told me that because of her education background she didn't have very many job options. She took the job which she was qualified for. She started off late in life, and she didn't learn to drive until after she already had two children. She became independent. Making her own money, driving herself to work, and being able to still run the household. Grandma never let fear stop her from attaining everything she had a desire for. That was one of the qualities I liked about her. I could sense her valiant spirit a mile away.

Four solid years had passed, since grandma came to visit us, or we went to see her. Life got in the way of maintaining a close relationship with grandmother. Grandmother became old and weak, and didn't like traveling on the plane anymore. The ride wasn't to her liking either. On holidays she would just stay in Colorado with her other children and grandchildren, and spend time with them. I hated the fact that dad's job moved us away from Colorado. I hated the fact we had to miss out on all the times we could have shared with grandma. So much time was wasted.

I'll never forget where I was that fateful night I learned my grandmother was dead. It was late in the evening around seven or eight when my Aunt Louis in Colorado called my mom crying hysterically. I was right in the room next to my parent's room, and I could hear my mom keep repeating, "Where is she?" Things weren't sounding too pleasant on the phone. Suddenly, I heard mom let out a toe-curling scream. I rushed into the room to see what was going on and I found her on the floor with her legs bent at the knees. Her face was a dazzling red, and her eyes were puffy.

"What?" I yelled.

Mom kept crying and extended the phone to me. I was confused and didn't want to take the phone, but she wouldn't lower her hand.

She sobbed and had the phone daggling from her hand. I kneeled down and reached for the phone.

"Hello," I said.

"Who's this?" some woman replied.

"This is Julie," I replied.

"Julie, darling, this is Aunt Louis," she said.

"What's going on?" I questioned.

"Sweetie, your grandma passed away early this afternoon," Aunt Louis said.

The only thing I could do was hold the phone while my heart stopped for a split second. That wasn't something I was expecting right then and there. My eyes stared heavily at the light brown carpet. I glanced over at my mom, and looked back down at the carpet. I was angry, but didn't know how to express myself just yet. I was silent. Aunt Louis waited for me, and it felt as if she was giving me time to think about what she had just told me.

"I know its hard sweetie, but she's in a better place now," Aunt Louis said. She kept asking me, "Are you going to be okay?"

"Yes I am. I need to go now," I said.

I hung up the phone, and got on the floor right next to my mother and put my arms around her, then rested my head on her shoulders.

"I'm so sorry mom, I'm so sorry," I cried.

All mom could do was cry and rock back and forth. I was mad at the fact that I hadn't seen my grandmother in nearly four years, and that she had died without us by her side. However, I was equally as mad at the fact that my mom had to endure yet another death. How much sadness and grief can one person handle? I didn't leave mom that night. My sister and I stayed with our mom in the same bed, and my brother and father made a few calls to the rest of the family, letting them know what had happened.

Grandma passed in her sleep. Her health had gradually deteriorated, and she was becoming unable to communicate. She was fighting Parkinson's disease and diabetes. The shock wasn't that she had died, it was the way I found out. I was caught off guard, and it hurt to find out in such an unexpected way. I felt even worse because all communication between us had been cut off. I didn't know what grandma was thinking in her last days, and I didn't get a chance to ask her what she was feeling. I had a host of emotions I was unable to deal with effectively.

I would get my chance to say good-bye at the funeral the following week. When we all gathered in the big white cathedral, with family and friends, I could feel grandma's presence moving up and down the aisles. We were reminded of the humble spirit, and loving demeanor she had as a daughter, sister, wife, mother, and grandmother. Ruth Salinas was my grandmother, a peacemaker, and love-giver. I sat on the front row listening to various family members and friends, talking about what kind of person grandma was, and what kind of life she led. They didn't know her the way I knew her, I thought to myself. I actually wanted these people to sit down and stop acting like they had such a special love for her. I bet some of these people didn't even know she had been sick.

After her burial we went as a family to go visit where she lay the next day. It was just a pile of dirt with flowers all over. Her headstone wasn't there yet, so all I could do was leave my letter buried deep inside the dirt hoping the headstone would cover it when it got there. I wrote the last letter this time. I told her how I missed her, and how I was sorry for not keeping in touch. I think grandma knew I loved her unconditionally . . . I'm sure of it.

Our bond could never be broken, not even by death. When you truly love someone, there's nothing in the world that can destroy that love. I valued my grandmother like none other, because she made me believe in myself, and gave me courage I never knew I had. I thank her. Her wisdom was a light to my dark path, and a motivator to keep me fighting. I love Grandma Ruth, and I can't wait to get to Heaven, where I'll meet her again.

CHAPTER SIXTEEN
He, Who Has No Home

There are times when it seems as if life would be much easier if we didn't have family around. The nagging mother, the nonchalant brother, the strict father, the drama-queen sister, and the noisy aunt and uncle, can sometimes cause certain individuals to want to click their heels, close their eyes, and wiggle their noses to make themselves disappear. A good majority of people have been in a situation where they question why they were born into a certain family. Those questions of 'why weren't we put with a different family' arise at various stages in life. If only I would've been placed in another family, we often may say. Do we subconsciously believe this from time to time? Do we believe that things in our life would've turned out better if only we would've had different parents, siblings, or another set of relatives?

It's hard to pinpoint a definite answer to such a simple question, but to the average person who believes this way, they feel things in this life could've turned out better for them if they would've had different circumstances.

Devin Collins didn't believe that way. In fact, it bothered him when he came in contact with people who would joke about hating their families, or wanting to belong somewhere else. It upset him. At age twenty-five, Devin didn't know who he was. His life undeniably had been shaped by the horrible circumstances he had to endure as a child.

By the time Devin was fourteen years old he had been in and out of Juvenile Detention several times. He was a notorious teenager who was either going to end up in prison, or dead on the streets! He was a drug dealer, and he was at the beginning stages of becoming an alcoholic before he was even at the legal age to drink it. His life was a downward spiral ever since he was eight years old. Due to the tragedy which had played a significant role earlier in his life, was it fair to classify Devin as a troubled teenager? Or, was he allowed to act-up, because of his home life?

Most people would agree that somewhere down the line a child has to grow up, and as a teenager and adult, they are responsible for their actions. Devin felt entitled to live his life any way he wanted to. For the early part of his life he believed he was dealt a bad hand in life. He felt sorry for himself, and wanted sympathy anywhere he could get it. Devin hadn't always been such a disaster, but on January 18, 1993, his life was changed forever.

Devin was fast asleep in bed on this cold January night, in his own room, far away from his older brother and parents. At about two-thirty in the morning, the Collins' household was quiet, and all the lights had been turned out. Devin, at eight years old, had been accustomed to sleeping through the night with the lights out, but on this particular night he awoke and was crying out for his dad.

"Daddy!" cried Devin. "Daddy!" he shouted.

Devin's father got up, and went into Devin's room and got in the bed with him, and held him until Devin went back to sleep. Devin remembers this night, and wished that his father would've stayed with him, but his father got out of the bed and went back into his own room. Devin's mother was asleep, knowing that Devin was going to be comforted by his father. It didn't hurt her in the slightest. She knew Devin loved her, but Devin just had a special connection with his father it seemed like.

At three-thirty in the morning smoke began to engulf the Collins home. Devin smelled it first, and quickly jumped out of his bed. He was holding his favorite night cloth, and went to his door and slowly opened it up. It was dark in the long hallway and he couldn't see anyone. He started to cry. He didn't see his mother, father, or brother. Five minutes later, the whole downstairs of their home was overtaken by smoke, and the intense orange fire was blazing fiercely, making its way upstairs. By this time Devin's father had called the police, and the fire department was on their way.

Devin's mother rushed out of her room, and gathered Devin and his brother. She held onto their hands and tried to lead them downstairs and out the door, but the fire was too severe to go through. The flames were shooting up left and right, furniture was burned to the core, and pieces of the house were beginning to fall. Devin, and his eleven year-old brother, had lost contact with their mom as she tried to throw blankets and coats over the flames, to make it easier for them to escape. She tripped on four stairs in the process, and fell right into the burning flames.

After Devin's father got off the phone with the police, he was downstairs trying to figure out what the problem was. However, when he saw how serious the fire was, he tried to make his way back upstairs to get his family. He couldn't make it. The whole downstairs was engulfed with fire. Devin's poor father was trapped, and couldn't escape the hot flames. He burned instantly. Devin and his brother didn't know that both of their parent's had died in a matter of seconds. They stood at the top of the stairs holding hands, crying, and not knowing what to do.

When the firemen arrived, they already saw Devin's parent's bodies, lying in the fire.

"Is there anybody else in here!" the fireman yelled.

Devin tried to run down the stairs, but his brother held him back, and yelled back at the fireman.

"Help us, please!" he cried.

"Mom, Dad! Mom, Dad!" shouted Devin.

"Help me and my brother," said Devin's brother.

The fireman made his way up the stairs, blowing through the fire with some kind of machine that killed the flames as he was going up the stairs.

"Don't move!" he yelled at the boys.

Devin and his brother stood right there, watching the fireman make his way to rescue them. The boys got scared and ran into Devin's room and waited for the fireman to come get them. Devin's brother left Devin in the room and went back to his own room to get one of his favorite toys; he didn't listen to the fireman's advice. He ran out of the room and ran right past the fireman, who grabbed him and had to throw him back towards Devin's room. He was hurt, but at least he was saved from being burned.

Another fireman came and shielded Devin, carried him, and then made his way down the stairs to the front door, and outside. The same fireman, who had thrown Devin's brother, Colton, to the ground in an effort to try to save him, carried him out of the house. Colton was in extreme pain. His back was injured, his face was bruised, and he was suffering from stomach pains. He received timely medical attention, and was taken straight to the hospital.

Devin was sitting all alone outside the house, surrounded by cops, fireman, and neighbors. His eyes searched up and down the street, trying to locate his mom and dad. He got up from the hood of the police car he was sitting on, and headed straight for his front door. One of the officers saw him and grabbed him. Devin began to cry. He wanted his parents. He didn't feel comfortable around all these people.

"Where's my daddy?" Devin cried.

"Son, you're going to have to wait for the firemen to find them, okay? I can't let you got back in there," the officer replied.

The fire had been contained on the first floor, and it tried to spread to the second, but the timely response of the Fire Department, enabled the men to destroy the fire safely and efficiently. If only they could've arrived a few minutes earlier to save Devin and Colton's parent's.

"Any word on the parents?" one of the officers asked the fireman.

"They're in there," he replied.

"It's not good is it?" the officer said.

"They were the first ones to burn. They've been dead for over eight minutes," the fireman said.

"I don't know how I'm going to tell those kids their parents died. I don't know how I'm going to do it," the officer said.

One of the neighbors called Devin and Colton's aunt, to come and see about them, and tell her everything that happened. Since she was the next of kin, Devin was released to her and she took him and went directly to the hospital, to see how Colton was. Devin continued to cry all night long. He wanted his family, and no one was giving him what he wanted. He didn't know where his parent's were, or where his brother was.

Once Devin and his aunt were settled in the hospital room where Colton was, she decided she needed to tell the boys what happened. Colton's condition was serious, and he faced a challenging journey in trying to get better. Fortunately, the doctor didn't mention anything about paralysis. Nevertheless, Colton was far from being all right. Their aunt had every intention on telling them what happened to their parent's, but before she could tell them, both of them were fast asleep. These innocent, adorable little boys had just experienced one the most horrific things a child can go through. They had survived a house fire by the grace of God. They should've been dead, but their lives were spared. It wasn't their time yet.

The Collins home was still standing, but it was burned to a crisp. The whole downstairs had been completely destroyed. The once beautiful home which housed a loving family had been annihilated. Devin and Colton no longer had a home. What was worse, they no longer had their parent's. Devin slept in his aunt's arms that night, dirty from all the smoke. Colton lay helpless in the inclined hospital bed. If only the burned up home would've been the worst of their problems, then they would of at least still had their mom and dad.

Early the next morning, Devin still cried for his dad. Colton awoke to the screams made by Devin. By noon that same day more family members had arrived, and brought food and clothing for Devin and Colton. Devin wasn't himself all day. He knew something was wrong.

He had always been with his parent's at night, and sleeping without mom and dad was not something that ever happened.

"Come here sweetie," Devin's aunt whispered.

Devin hurried over to his aunt and got in the bed next to Colton. Colton was wide-awake and preparing for what his aunt was about to tell them.

"You know there's no more house, right? It's gone, it burned up," she said sadly.

"I know that," replied Colton.

"Well, there's something else I need to tell the both of you. It's about mommy and daddy," she started to say.

"When are they coming to pick us up?" Devin asked.

Their aunt began to cry, she had lost her nerve to tell them as soon as she saw the sadness and worry in Devin's eyes.

"I can't do this," she cried out loud.

One of their uncles came over, and removed their aunt from the room, and motioned for his wife to tell the boys what happened. Their uncle was the brother of their father, and he left the daunting task to his wife. She sat on the bed holding Devin, and rubbing Colton's head.

"Mommy and daddy won't be coming back. They're in Heaven now," she explained.

"What do you mean?" Colton asked.

"They died last night in the fire. You won't get to see them anymore," she cried.

Devin burst into tears and screamed out. He was taking the news the hardest.

"Mom and Dad died? That means I will never ever see them again," sobbed Colton.

"Yes honey, I'm so sorry," Their aunt replied.

After a period of hysterical crying and screaming, Devin became silent. He didn't talk or move for hours. He laid down in the bed next to Colton looking out of the window. His eyes were puffy and bloodshot. Colton was asleep, still trying to recover from the injuries he suffered. The fireman, who had thrown him, came to visit Colton that same day. He brought all kinds of toys for Colton and Devin, but neither boy touched the toys, or even opened their mouths to tell him thank you. They were still in shock.

Devin and Colton's parent's bodies had been severely burned, almost beyond recognition. There was no sense in having a funeral, the family decided. As a result, the boys never got to properly say good-bye to their parent's. They didn't get the chance to see them one last time.

As the days passed, all Devin could do was hold the loving image of his father holding him in the bed one last time. All Colton could think about was his brave mother trying to make a way for them to escape. Both of their parent's had been brave that night, and their lives were taken because of it.

. Hours, days, and then weeks passed, and Devin was finally able to accept the fact his parents weren't coming back. Once Colton left the hospital, he and Devin were staying with their uncle and aunt and their four children. Life was hard for the two boys, and adjusting to new surroundings without parents was even harder. It had been determined by the Fire Department and investigators that a burner had not been turned off properly, and was left on. An accident that could've been avoided thought the family. The boy's uncle had been disappointed in his brother for being so careless, but looking at the bigger picture, two young boys were now without parents. There was no need to point fingers, or be upset with someone who was deceased now.

Devin and Colton remained with their uncle and aunt for four years. So much time had passed by, and all Colton had were distant memories of his parent's. The two boys didn't have much to remind them of their parent's either. Pictures, clothes, keepsakes, personal items, had been destroyed in the fire. All of the precious memories that could have reminded them of their parent's had been taken away by a blazing fire that faithful night. Things didn't get any easier for the Collins boys as time went on. Devin and Colton were soon relocated to foster care, due to Colton's multiple run-ins with the law. His aunt and uncle didn't want the boys living with them and their children. Colton had seen the walls of Juvenile Hall, and the courtroom one too many times. He was fifteen at the time, and Devin was twelve. The family wouldn't step up and take in these boys, so they went to the State.

Soon after, Devin would follow in his brother's footsteps. Only, Devin was much worse than Colton. By the time Devin was fourteen years old, he was dealing drugs, and trying to associate himself with a gang. As part of Devin's treatment while in Juvenile detention, he was ordered to see a counselor. He had desperately wanted to talk to someone about what he was going through, but he never had the opportunity.

"What do you think it is that causes you to do the things you do?" asked the counselor.

"I don't know," Devin replied.

"There has to be some reason why you act out in ways which could actually land you in prison one day. Is that the road you want to head down?" she asked.

"I'm not sure. Maybe that's what I need," Devin said.

"You talk idiotically," she proclaimed.

"I don't know what it is. Maybe my brother," Devin stated.

"Okay, tell me about your brother?" she inquired.

Devin stopped for a brief moment, as if he was trying to cherry-pick his words carefully. He stared at the ground with a confused look on his face.

"What's wrong Devin?" the counselor asked.

"I love my brother. I just wish I knew where he was," Devin answered.

"You don't know where he is?" she questioned.

"No, I have no idea. I haven't seen him in over a year and a half. Last time I saw him it was before I came in here. He was staying with our foster parent's. Now, I don't know where he is," Devin revealed.

Devin made it known to the counselor that he wanted to see his brother. Besides Colton, Devin had no one else to turn to. The same family that had been there for them when their parents died that night had abandoned them. The love that was supposed to be strong between this family was nothing more than a farce. If there was true genuine love for their two nephews, nothing would have come between them. Their deadbeat uncle and aunt, tossed Devin and Colton to the wolves, and sent them into a world in which they were not prepared for. They had no compassion or understanding for the fact that these two boys had lost their parent's, and only had each other. They were selfish just like the rest of the family who turned their backs on Devin and Colton. It was the responsibility of living relatives to take on the role of raising and helping the two brothers become happy, healthy young men. They really didn't have a fighting chance.

Upon Devin's third return to Juvenile detention at the age of fifteen, he had become familiar with the system. This was his life, this is what he knew best, getting in trouble. Colton was eighteen, and had been gone from the house for quite a while. He didn't know where Devin was, and Devin didn't know where Colton was. The bond between the two brothers had been broken. The foster parents Devin lived with since he was twelve would come to see about him occasionally, but it wasn't enough to say they were concerned, or truly even cared about what happened to him.

Devin opened up to the counselor who had been working with him. Even though Devin was notorious, he was still a quiet, calm spirited teenager. It was his bad decisions that affected him and caused him to be taken out of society.

"There's something in my brain which makes me do things I don't want to do," Devin confessed.

"What do you think it is?" the counselor inquired.

"I think it's from my childhood," he replied.

"Tell me about your childhood?" she questioned.

"It was horrible and unbearable!" Devin projected.

"Your whole entire childhood? There wasn't anything pleasant about it?" she asked him.

"I loved it until I was eight, after that, I wished I would've been hit by car, shot, or beaten to death," Devin cried.

"No, you couldn't possibly mean that," she said astonished. "Why, if I may ask?"

"Because my parent's left me and my brother all by ourselves!" Devin blurted out.

The counselor could sense the tension in Devin, and she could see tears begin to form in his eyes. This was the breakthrough she wanted. However, the tragedy he was speaking of was going to undeniably open up wounds which had been covered by years of trouble. The counselor eased her way back into the conversation. She wasn't trying to hurt Devin and have him relive a painful time in his life; she wanted him to open up and have the opportunity to release all the anger he had suppressed for so many years.

"Why did your parents leave?" she asked.

"I mean, it wasn't their choice to leave, they died," Devin muttered.

"I'm sorry, Devin. How did they die, if I can ask?" she said.

"They burned in a fire. A fire I wish I would've burned in too," Devin admitted.

"You don't mean that," she stated.

"I one-hundred percent mean it. I wish I'd died that night. Then, I wouldn't have had to stay in this stupid world and be raised by an uncle who threw me out, and by people who didn't even want me," Devin proclaimed.

Devin was trying to be brave, and he was trying to hold back from crying in front of the counselor. She wouldn't have minded though, she wanted to see some emotion. The emotion was the first step in letting go, and moving on. Devin hadn't moved on. He was still carrying around a weight which needed to be lifted off. He was mad at his parent's for leaving him alone in the world, and he was in distress over where his brother was. And he was packing abhorrence for his aunt and uncle.

They ended their session with a mix of emotions that day. The counselor felt they had made great progress because Devin was opening up. On the other hand, it was hard for Devin to have to express how he was feeling. He hadn't gotten the chance to before, and it was like a flood of emotion that came pouring out of him. Although the counselor had been sympathetic to Devin, and all that he had been through, not everyone felt the same way she did. Devin's judge was one of them. She felt Devin was using the death of his parent's as a way to gain sympathy points, and that his loss gave him an excuse to participate in radical behavior. The judge called it, 'his crutch.' If *she* felt that way, there had to be more people which felt the exact same way.

After six months in Juvenile Detention, Devin returned home to be with his foster parent's. It was on the day of his return, he learned that Colton had died in a car accident about a month ago. Another family member Devin was unable to say good-bye to. He wept on the kitchen floor that night in the dark by himself. He didn't understand why his foster parents didn't tell him sooner. They claimed they didn't find out until a little over a week ago, that he had been dead for close to a month. Devin didn't know whether or not to believe them. All he knew was that he needed to see where his brother lay.

The two brothers had been living in the same city and didn't even know it. Colton tried his best to clean his life up, and he was working hard to come out of the lifestyle he was in. When he was coming out of Juvenile Hall, Devin was going in. It was such a sad life for a little boy who had grown-up to be consumed with a host of problems and circumstances.

One sunny afternoon, Devin was able to get to the cemetery and see Colton's grave. Unlike his parent's, there was actually a place for Devin to go, and visibly see his brother's resting place. It wasn't the best cemetery, but it was the resting home of his late brother. He knelt down, and only saw a small wooden cross standing straight up with Colton's name engraved into the cross. There were no flowers, and the grass looked like it hadn't been cut in weeks. Devin came empty handed, but he poured out his heart to Colton that day.

If Devin didn't hate this world before, he sure hated it now. Colton was the only close family he had left. Everyone else didn't want anything to do with the Collins boys. Devin wondered why that was. As he was sitting in the cemetery next to Colton's grave, he was reflecting on what went wrong in his uncle's house that caused him to throw Colton out. The problem wasn't Devin, it was Colton. The *one* good thing their uncle did, was keeping them together. He didn't want them to be separated, so when Colton was put out, he sent Devin right along with him.

Devin then found himself mad at Colton, for breaking up the little family they did have left. He wished Colton hadn't messed-up, because maybe things would've turned out differently for them, if Colton had of been a normal teenager. Devin remembered one of the incidents which lead up to them being kicked out, and how their uncle made it clear he wasn't going to be putting up with anymore of Colton's "bull crap." Why did he even take them in, Devin thought to himself? Their cousins weren't the perfect angels, but their uncle still found a way to get rid of him and Colton. It was unjust he thought. We needed to be loved just like anyone else.

Conversely, that special love wasn't going to come from an aunt or uncle. There is no love like the true, warm, affectionate, and unconditional love like mom and dad's. Devin soon realized this as time went on. He saw the difference their aunt and uncle made between him and Colton, and their cousins. It should've been expected that their cousins were always going to be first, and the most loved in the house. At times Devin felt he wasn't wanted. It was evident in Colton and his treatment. They were not mistreated, but their uncle's actions made them feel as if they were a burden and a chore. After the brothers began to grow up, and the freshness of their parent's death passed, their uncle and aunt made them feel like their decision to take them in was a mistake.

Colton's actions had caused some trouble for the family, and Uncle Mitch was not happy with the way Colton was turning out.

"I don't understand you, boy," Mitch said. "You act like you're running things in my house. Coming home when you feel like it, getting my boys involved in stuff they would have never even thought about getting into. I'm sick of it," Mitch stated.

"I didn't know I was such a problem," Colton stated.

"What's wrong with you? I don't get why you're acting like a heathen," Mitch uttered.

"I'm trying my best," Colton stated.

"Things are going to have to change, and fast," his uncle said.

Devin had been listening at the bottom of the stairs that night, and had been scared of what his uncle was going to do to Colton.

The only thing his uncle did was give an ultimatum. Either Colton straightened up, or he was going to send him packing.

"All I can do is try, Uncle Mitch. Believe me, I don't like being how I am. I want to change and do good, I just don't know how," Colton revealed.

"It's time to figure it out. I'm not your daddy, I'm not going to raise you," Mitch said.

Those comments are exactly what Colton and Devin didn't need to hear. Of course Mitch wasn't their father, and maybe that was part of the problem. Colton and Devin needed a strong male figure who was going to love them, care for them, and teach them. Their father was dead. They didn't get that chance. Perhaps Mitch didn't understand Colton because he didn't want to. It seemed as if he took in the brothers out of some sense of obligation to his brother. However, if he wasn't going to treat his nephews like his own children, he should have let them go with other relatives, or let the State take them.

A couple of days after the fire and when Colton was still in the hospital, the family decided that since Mitch had kids around Devin and Colton's age, it was best if they moved in with his family. Mitch's wife, Lisa, wasn't too thrilled about the idea since they already had four kids of their own. It was Mitch who stepped up and felt he had to take them in. Besides Mitch and Lisa, no one else really offered to take the misplaced boys in, and raise them and love them. It's funny how everyone in the family was sympathetic for the first couple of weeks, but when it came time to make decisions about where the boys should go, it was hard to get a family member to take on the task, and face that responsibility.

Devin left the cemetery that day feeling better than he had in a long time. At least he was able to have a place to go to anytime he wanted to remember the memory of Colton. While he was there that day, all those old emotions soared to his mind, and he had no choice but to remember all the fights Colton and his uncle had. Things really wouldn't have turned out any better even if Colton and Devin had stayed with their aunt and uncle, because the unconditional love wasn't there. Obligation overruled love, and set precedence in their upbringing. Devin felt his life was one big mistake, and he had even thought about killing himself. Maybe that was the answer to end this painful life.

Devin didn't get the chance to heal properly. He was forced just like Colton was, to seemingly forget about their parent's, and their memory, and start a new life. Uncle Mitch and Aunt Lisa didn't talk about the boy's parents that often, and if Devin did mention them, they would quickly remove themselves from the conversation. Maybe that's why Devin felt ashamed of talking about his parent's. He had no one to talk to, and no one would let him talk about it. The pain became rooted deep inside of his heart and he had anger he didn't know how to release.

Who was going to understand him with all he had been though. It was a sad life for Devin. He had no biological parents, and his only brother had died as well. He felt as if he had nowhere, or no one, to turn to. He was without a home. He became socially awkward and withdrawn as he finished the remaining stages of his teenage years. He stayed in trouble, and soon upgraded to more devious and dangerous crimes. He hung around a group of guys that liked to break into cars, destroying property, and stealing out of stores. Until Devin turned eighteen years old he remained in Juvenile Detention. This had been his longest stint there since he was fourteen. He spent two years of his life in there. It didn't bother him, he was used to it.

"Devin do you understand that your next step is jail, then prison," his counselor informed him.

"I know," he said.

"Why do you keep messing-up? I thought we had an understanding that you were going to start doing better?" she stated.

"I *was* doing good, I just slipped up," he confessed.

"Don't you care about what this is doing to your parent's?" she asked.

Devin grew silent, not sure how to answer her question.

"I don't have any parents," Devin replied.

"Yes, you do. Your foster parents," she exclaimed.

"If they thought of me as a son, they would've adopted me and my brother a long time ago. They didn't want to, so they could get rid of us any time they wanted," Devin proclaimed.

"If that were true they would've given you up by now," the counselor answered.

"I don't know why they keep me around, but when I turn eighteen I'm not their problem anymore," said Devin.

"You wish you could live with your uncle again?" she questioned.

"No!" Devin replied.

"Why's that?"

"Because he kicked us out years ago. I didn't even do anything, and he still kicked my brother and I out. I hate him, and hope to God I never have to see him again. If my real dad were alive, he would've taken in my uncle's kids no questions asked," Devin said firmly.

"You believe that?" she asked.

"Yes, I do. My dad was a much better man than my uncle could ever be. So was my brother. My uncle tore my brother apart, but the truth is, Colton was a better man than him too," Devin stated.

Devin didn't feel like his bad actions were affecting anyone. There was no one to chastise him with love, like he knew his parent's would've. He missed that structure of having a loving mother and father. Two days after the fire, a couple of uncles and aunts went to Colton and Devin's home to see if anything was salvageable. Unfortunately, most of everything was burned, or covered in ashes. The entire downstairs was burned up and only a small portion of the upstairs was still intact. The back half of the house upstairs seemed to be minimally touched, and the aunts and uncles were allowed to grab anything they could find that was worth saving.

The boys never received the few photos which were recovered that day by the family members. Where were all the memories? There was nothing left to remind Devin of his mother, father, and now his brother. During his time in Juvenile Detention, Devin began writing down his thoughts as some sort of therapy, when he was unable to see his counselor. He wrote how he didn't understand why so many bad things had happened to him. Life started great for the first eight years he could remember. A fire one night changed everything. It changed everything in the worst possible way. All it took was one mistake on his parent's part, to break up the loving home he once had. It was their fault for not checking the kitchen that night. All those years, Devin felt they had skated by untouched from the numerous dangers of this world, and one night destroyed everything.

Devin knew in his heart what it was like to have good parents. His foster parents weren't the worst, but they weren't the best either. At least he and Colton were able to stay together for the short time they did have together. However, their time would be cut short by multiple arrests, time spent in Juvenile Hall, and finally, a long period of separation. It plagued Devin that the family could be so cruel and turn their back on him and Colton. Everyone was understanding and loving, buying them clothes, toys, and being warm and affectionate. Suddenly, all the concern stopped, and people moved on with their lives.

The pain other family members and friends felt was only for a short while. Colton and Devin had a reserved place in their hearts for the grief of their mom and dad that would never be taken away. It was a permanent fixture until the day they died. It happened too fast. That very morning their parents were with them, and that night they were taken away. What if the family wasn't being heartless? Maybe they backed off because they didn't know how to approach the grieving boys. It took months before Devin could rest at night without crying for his mom and dad. He wondered why they wouldn't come to him. No matter how much he begged, shouted, and cried for his parent's, he didn't know they weren't ever coming back to comfort him again.

To have a mother and father's love stopped at such a young age, was hard for Colton and Devin. Eventually, the boys had no choice but to move on. There was no other alternative for them. Both boys had grown up in a loving nurturing environment, and knew they weren't getting the same kind of love from their aunt and uncle. Things were stable for the most part, but they went downhill when Colton decided he wanted to rebel against his uncle and aunt. He was just a teenager, and some of his behavior was to be expected.

After Devin was released from Juvenile Detention four months after his eighteenth birthday, he never went back again. He made great efforts to clean up his life and honor his mother, father and brother. Where would he begin, he thought? For someone who was without a home, Devin returned to his foster parent's until he was able to get on his feet. They really did try their best to love the two brothers, but they knew they would be competing for the love of their real parent's. A love neither Colton nor Devin ever experienced again.

Devin would find himself jealous of other people who still had their biological parents around. It would hurt him even more, when he would see other people with their brothers, like his cousins for example. It appeared as if they had the perfect life. All their siblings were alive, and so were their parent's. Devin felt he couldn't be happy in this life anymore. There was no need to be happy. He felt he had nothing.

Aside from trying to move on with his life, Devin had to work through the pain of getting the visual memory of standing in a burning house, out of his head. It was something he had dealt with for a long time. It was a memory he was trying hard to forget. He witnessed his mother fall into the flames, but it never occurred to him in that moment, that she was dying. Standing in the midst of burning flames was something he couldn't overcome. It was a traumatic experience that he will always carry with him. He realized a true mother's love years later. His mother died trying to save him and Colton. That was a mother who truly loved her children.

Losing his whole family is something Devin will never get over, and it's not even probable to say that time will make it easier and bearable. All he can do is take one day at a time, and make the most of his life while he is still living. The grief he has to go through can never be measured, or felt, by anyone else who thinks they know what he's going through, until they themselves have experienced it. His grieving period may take years for him to overcome, but it's at his own time and his pace.

Maybe Devin Collins was dealt a bad hand in life, and maybe his suffering was more intense than someone else's, but if he believes with all his heart that he was truly loved by his family, then, he will never be without a home, because his family will remain in his heart forever.

CHAPTER SEVENTEEN
His Stained Blacks

Standing in the mirror looking at myself dressed in a black dress, hose and pumps, with a tilted black and white hat on my head, was not how I envisioned I would be spending my thirty-seventh birthday. I needed something to distract me this morning, and my birthday was all I could think about to keep my mind focused on something else. I was supposed to be resting today until about noon. My day would have consisted of me getting up to a house decorated with happy birthday balloons, streamers and banners all around the house, like last year. After I stepped out of bed and showered, I would've sat down to a nice brunch, which would of consisted of steamed sugared rice, buttered toast with strawberry preserves, four banana pancakes topped with whipped cream, fresh oranges and apples, and blazing black coffee.

After brunch, Trevor and the kids would've taken me to the mall and bought me clothes, and jewelry. Then, we would go to a movie and dinner, and come back and eat cake. None of that would be happening today. It was seven-thirty in the morning, and I was standing in the mirror putting on lipstick with tears in my eyes. I didn't dare fix my face up, because I knew my make-up would get ruined once the tears flowed from my eyes. I was going to dwell in a sad place today, and I wasn't looking to impress anyone. I honestly didn't care how I looked.

After I was dressed and ready to go, I went to make sure my three children were getting ready. My oldest son, Ryan, was the one I could count on to help me out whenever I needed it. I knew he would be ready on time like I was. Clara, my middle child, was a struggle to get up in the mornings. I have to fight with her morning after morning to get her up for school. She was nine years old now, and she still acted as if she was three years old. However, on this particular morning, I quietly walked into her room, came to the side of her bed and gently caressed her back and said, "You need to get up now please. We don't want to be late."

Without argument or battle, she simply replied, "Okay." Trevor had told me over and over it was the way I was waking her, which made her fight with me. He told me to be more loving and gentle when waking her up, and his advice was golden.

Isaiah, who was six, was like his brother. He was quiet and always did what I asked him. When I peeked into the boy's room, Ryan was helping his brother get dressed. I didn't know how to feel today. I didn't know if I was supposed to be sad first, and express all of my emotions, or hold everything in for my children's sake. I didn't know what to do. Seeing them get ready for this dark day was something they should've never had to have experienced at such an early age.

I sat in the white rocking chair on the porch, dressed in my black clothes waiting for the family and the limousines to arrive. This house didn't mean anything anymore to me. It was a two-story brick disaster, filled with misery and heartache. I didn't want to live here anymore, now that Trevor wouldn't be living here. However, I couldn't bring myself to just pick-up and move. This was the only house my children had ever known. It wasn't fair for me to move into a two-bedroom apartment all because I was an emotional wreck.

I have to admit today was a beautiful day. It was early October, and the wind was blowing peacefully, causing the tree leaves to gently hit the ground. The sun was bright and there wasn't a trace of dark clouds, or a hint of rain in sight. I swayed back and forth in the rocking chair staring into the street. As I was sitting on the porch waiting, I reflected back to when Trevor and I first moved into this neighborhood. When we were one of four couples that lived on this street years ago. It remained that way for quite some time. Soon, everyone started moving into our subdivision, and on our street.

"I love this house," I told Trevor.

"Of course you do, it's only got three other houses on this street," he replied.

"If we take this house, I know we're going to have some happy times here," I said.

"Define happy, Rachelle?" Trevor asked.

"You know, lots of kids, good careers, health, and so on," I stated.

"So you really think this is the house for us?" Trevor asked.

"I know it is!" I answered.

I remember that conversation we had after we got married, and we were looking for a place of our own. When we first met two years earlier, Trevor was in police training, and I was just finishing up my last year of college. It had been a long-standing dream of mine to become a nurse. My mother had been a nurse for over thirty years. I wanted to follow in her footsteps. I wondered why Trevor wanted to be a cop so bad. Every time I would ask him, he would just tell me he felt like it was his calling to be a policeman. I thought he was a liar. No one wakes up one day and realizes their calling in life is to be put in harm's way. I was misinformed back then. After seeing the amount of hard work and dedication Trevor had put into the police force, I started to believe maybe it *was* his calling.

Things didn't become tough for us until after we had Ryan a year later. We weren't even married a good solid year before I was pregnant. My mom thought I should've waited before having kids. Her philosophy was to test out the marriage first, then, see if this is someone I would want to spend the rest of my life with, and if this was someone I wanted to have kids with. Her philosophy didn't work on me, because I already knew Trevor was the one for me. Besides being the most gorgeous man I had ever laid eyes on, he was a hard worker and loved me for who I was.

Family started arriving and I had to snap out of my daydreaming. My relatives began piling into my home one by one, carrying cakes, pies, drinks, and pans of food. Most of all, they brought their love.

"Rachelle, I'm so sorry, darling," one of my aunts said.

"Thank you," I replied.

"I know what it's like. I went through the same thing fifteen years ago," she stated.

"I know, and I thank you for being here," I said.

The limousines eased next to the curb in front of my house, and all I could do was sit there for a brief second. Everything was happening fast, this was really about to happen. I could hardly believe it. I stood up, and took off my hat, and walked down the stairs to the curb. I saw four shiny black, stretched limousines parked right in front of me. A blonde-haired woman, dressed in black, got out and walked over to me.

"Hi, Mrs. Cramer," she said with a bright smile.

"I um . . . um . . . we aren't quite ready yet," I blurted coarsely.

"That's fine, ma'am. We're here for you today. We came a few minutes early so let us know when you are," she replied.

"Thank you," I said.

I went back up the stairs and into house, to make sure Ryan, Clara and Isaiah were ready. When I got back into the house they were at the table eating breakfast. Ryan, at age fourteen, was much more responsible and mature than I had given him credit for. There he was fixing breakfast for his brother and sister. I immediately began crying. Everything just hit me at once. My poor children didn't know how tough things were going to be from here on out. A cloud of sadness was about to cover us for the rest of our lives. Things in the Cramer home were never going to be the same, and I didn't know how to tell my kids this.

As we got into the limousines, my mom was holding my hand and I was holding Clara's hand. I walked down the stairs thinking about all the happy times we had up until this point, in this house. I got into the limousine, and on the ride to the church I closed my eyes and let the tears just fall onto my dress. Had I been wrong fourteen years ago? Was this house not the house for us? I didn't know. I was confused. Everything had ended in tragedy. I didn't get the happy ending I had planned for. I started to reminisce again.

The last vacation we had as a family was just a few months ago this past August. I wanted to return to happier times when my children had smiles on their faces, and reflect on how Trevor was playing with them all night long. I was never going to get that back. My world was over I thought. How was I supposed to go on now? I was a good mother, but not the best mother. There were much better mothers than I, and it was scary for me to have to play two roles now. I remember the conversation I had with my mother when I became a mother for the first time.

"I'm scared to death," I confessed.

"You don't have to be scared. Do you love Ryan?" she asked.

"Of course," I replied.

"Then you have the first step mastered. Everything else is easy," Mom told me.

"What's easy about being a mother?" I inquired.

"Because if you have love for your child, everything else will come natural. Trust me. Being a mother isn't anything to be sacred of," she said.

"I just don't want to make any mistakes," I revealed.

"Sorry to tell you, but you will. There isn't a perfect mother. All you're required to do is love your child, be there for him, and learn along the way," Mom said.

Those words stuck with me every time I had a child, but I also had help. Trevor was my backbone. Trevor was the one who held me and comforted me when I believed I was a screw-up. It was him who gave me the confidence to believe in myself when I felt all my confidence was gone. I thought I had such a great life that I didn't deserve. Sometimes I believed it would all be taken away from me. I was right. This tragedy that struck my family was just the beginning. What if I lost everything? I didn't know what I would do with myself if one of my children died.

My mom softly touched me, signaling for me to come back to my present self. We were at the church. I got a sickening feeling in my stomach. Something came over me I couldn't explain. I didn't want to go inside the church. I didn't want to have to see a casket. I hadn't prepared myself. Whether or not I was ready, it was going forth. The church looked enormous from inside of the limousine. Red brick covered the Classic Gothic style church. There were so many cars in the parking lot. So many people were here. I was becoming more upset minute by minute.

Before we entered the church, we were lined-up and told this was how we were going to walk into the church. My mom and I were in front, and I was holding Clara's hand. Ryan held Isaiah's hand, and they walked behind us. It was the longest walk I had ever taken in my life I thought. When we approached the sanctuary's double doors, my emotions overtook me. My mom and one of my brothers had to hold me up, and keep me from falling to the ground. I could hear Isaiah crying behind me. All the people who told me everything was going to be alright had lied to me. Everything was *not* going to be alright. The pain was still embedded in my heart.

We walked into the church, and all I could see was the russet colored casket situated in the front of the church, and resting in front of the podium. As my mom and brother walked me hand in hand to the front bench, I couldn't see clearly. Tears had filled my eyes, and I felt as if I had been blinded by a wave of tears. Once I dried my eyes, I saw a row full of policemen dressed in their uniforms. Some were standing on both sides of the casket, and others were sitting on the pews across the aisle from Trevor's family and mine. There were even men dressed in military uniforms standing by the casket. My heart was filled with such heaviness. I had all of my children sitting next to me. Ryan was trying to be brave, but I knew he wanted to cry. My mind went back to the night when I first got the call about Trevor. I sat on the front pew thinking about this calamity which had consumed my family's happiness.

It was about ten o'clock at night, when the phone kept ringing and ringing. I was exhausted from a long, strenuous workday. My normal routine was to pick-up Isaiah and Clara from the babysitter's house, bring them home sometime between six and seven in the evening, and start dinner. Ryan would already be at home starting his homework and sometimes watching television until I came home. I usually went into work around five or six in the morning, and expected to be home no later than eight o'clock. As a family, we could always expect Trevor home by nine o'clock. The way his schedule worked, he was home in time to spend the remainder of the night with us.

I had been so tired that September night that I forget I had dinner in the oven, and that Trevor wasn't even home yet. As the phone rang off the hook, Ryan dashed in the room and asked me, was I going to get the phone, or did I want him to answer it. I told him to go ahead and answer it, and that I would be in the kitchen trying to salvage the portion of dinner that wasn't ruined. I awoke for two reasons that night. Not only did I respond to Ryan calling out to me, but also I could smell burnt food.

I had turned over and it took me a moment to come to myself and realize where I was, and who I was. I was so tired that night I hadn't even taken off my uniform yet. My youngest two kids had fallen asleep without even eating for the night.

Ryan fiercely yelled for me to come back into the living room, telling me it was the hospital. I dumped all the food I had in my hand in the trashcan, placed the pans in the sink, and hurried back into the living room.

"It's St. John's Hospital, mom," Ryan said frantically.

I dried my hands on my uniform, and unintentionally snatched the phone out of Ryan's hand. He stepped back and allowed me some space. He looked just as worried as I was.

"Hello," I said.

"Is this Mrs. Cramer?" a woman asked.

"Yes, yes it is," I replied.

"Hi, ma'am. I'm a nurse here at St. Johns' Hospital over on Gretchen and Fifty-Third Street, we need you to come down as soon as possible," she requested.

"Oh my God, what happened?" I cried.

"It's about your husband, Trevor," she answered.

"What about Trevor? Is he hurt? What happened to him?" I demanded.

"He's in critical condition, and we need you to come to the hospital right now, please," she told me.

"Okay, thank you," I said gently.

I hung up the phone, and took a seat on the couch. The nurse had just told me to move swiftly and come down to the hospital as soon as I could, but I was in a state of shock at the moment. Ryan kept staring at me. He knew something was wrong.

"What's wrong with dad?" Ryan asked.

"I don't know. All she would tell me is that he's in critical condition," I replied.

"Can we go see him?" he asked.

I kept looking at the phone without blinking, and concentrating on what I needed to do next.

"Yes, but I need you to call your grandma and tell her to meet us at St. John's hospital. Then, wake up your brother and sister please," I said.

Ryan did everything I asked of him, and he did it promptly. All I could think about was one of the greatest fears I had as a wife being married to a policeman. So many years had gone by without an incident, or any violence. Now, our time was up. There wasn't any more protection for us. Trevor's time had come. I wanted to get to the hospital as fast as I could, but another part of me didn't want to go and have to face what might be waiting for me. I didn't want the bad news. By procrastinating as long as I could, I was saving myself from heartache, and my kids from pain.

However, if I didn't go, I wouldn't know anything about Trevor's condition and I would be wasting precious time by not being at the hospital. I got on my knees by the couch, and said a little prayer to myself. I was no stranger to calling on God in times of trouble. I literally begged and pleaded for God to make Trevor okay. I didn't know what kind of condition he was in, but I knew if I wanted Trevor to be okay, I needed to pray. I said my silent quick prayer, got up, got the kids, and headed out the door.

It was totally silent on the way to the hospital. I think the kids knew something was wrong. Ryan knew Trevor was in bad shape, and I believe Clara and Isaiah knew as well. I didn't talk about anything until I was able to get to the hospital and see Trevor for myself. I needed to see what kind of condition he was in. Critical condition wasn't good. Being a nurse, I knew exactly what that meant. No matter how badly I wanted to imagine that Trevor wasn't in any real danger, I knew that he was. What happened, I thought to myself as I was driving? Was he stabbed, shot, beaten up, hit by a car, all sorts of things ran through my mind. This wasn't like Trevor, he was always careful on the job. Twelve plus years he's been a cop, he's never been injured or had to fire his gun. Why had things changed all of a sudden?

I drove up to the emergency side of the hospital, parked the car and told the children to get out quickly. Almost forty-five minutes had passed between the time I was on the phone with the nurse, and the time we actually arrived. As we were walking in through the automatic doors, my pace began to change. I was thinking like an irrational woman. My husband could be losing his life, and here I was thinking about all the ways this awful situation was affecting me. I was thinking about my feelings and what I was going through. This wasn't about me, and it took twenty minutes on the way to the hospital for me to realize this.

Before the children and I could get to the information station, I saw Officer Jordan Redden. He had been Trevor's former partner for a while, and they had maintained a close friendship ever since. Even though they were no longer partners, if I saw him here, I knew things couldn't have been good.

"Rachelle!" Jordan called.

I made my way over to him quickly.

"How is he, Jordan?" I asked in fear.

"I'm not going to lie to you, it's not good. He's barely hanging on," Jordan said.

I put my hand to my face and sighed. The tears were falling from my eyes.

"What happened?" I asked.

"All I know is that he . . ."

I interrupted Jordan, and told Ryan to take Isaiah and Clara over to sit down. I didn't want them to hear any gruesome details about their father. I didn't know what was going to come out of Jordan's mouth.

"Rachelle," Jordan said softly.

"I don't think I want to know," I cried.

"Rachelle, they said he was shot in the head and chest," Jordan revealed.

"Oh God!" I screamed. "Oh God! Oh God!"

Ryan ran over to me.

"Mom, what's wrong?" Ryan cried.

Jordan pulled me over to a chair and sat me down. I wanted to collapse right in the emergency room. I tried my best to fight Jordan. I didn't want to sit-down, I wanted to fall flat to the ground. I could hear Isaiah and Clara crying.

"Did dad die," Ryan asked.

All I could do was cry.

"Mom is he dead!" Ryan yelled.

I couldn't answer.

"He's still holding on, son," Jordan told Ryan.

"Why is my Mom acting like this?" I heard Ryan say.

"She's just in shock," Jordan replied.

Ryan began to cry. The strong young man I knew, who was use to being brave, was crying.

"What's going on?" he cried.

Jordan sat with me, until my mom arrived at the emergency room. We all moved to the Intensive Care Unit. Trevor had been moved to ICU once he was out of surgery. I saw so many policemen gather outside the ICU, I didn't know what to think. What did all of this mean? Did they know something bad was going to happen? The doctor wouldn't let us see him just yet. My mom pulled the kids aside, and told them what happened to Trevor. That was *my* job, but I was too distraught to find the words to tell them their father was shot in the head and in the chest. These were serious injuries, but this wasn't like Trevor. Something wasn't making sense to me. Trevor was the most cautious person I knew. He was always extra careful on the job.

I remember a conversation we had years ago when I got scared just from him being threatened. I made it clear to him that I didn't know how long I could be married to a cop.

"My job has nothing to do with you," Trevor said.

"It does, Trevor. We have two children now, and it's not safe for you to put your life on the line every day. I don't know how much more I can take," I confessed.

"Take! What do you mean you don't know how much more *you* can take?" Trevor asked me.

"This . . . this violence, worry, and living on edge every day of my life, wondering if something is going to happen to you," I said.

"Being a cop is a dangerous job, but it's something I love doing. I don't think I'm ever going to give it up," Trevor replied.

"So what you're saying is that our marriage and our family aren't important enough for you to quit being a cop! Is that what you're telling me?" I asked.

"No, I'm saying that my calling in life is to protect and serve others. I love being a cop, and this is what I want to do. I can't just give it up because you worry and get scared," Trevor told me.

"What if you die?" I blurted out.

Trevor got silent, and looked directly in my face. He approached me and kissed me on the forehead, and then gave me a hug.

"I won't die. I'm not going to die. You don't have to worry about that. I have a guardian angel watching over me every day I'm on the job," Trevor stated.

"Promise me you won't get killed on the job. Right here, right this moment. Promise me," I demanded.

"I promise you with everything that's in me, I don't plan on dying anytime soon. I'll be here for you and the kids, that I promise," Trevor said.

We hugged and kissed that night, and I felt at ease. I truly believed in Trevor's promise to me; his promise to be here for me and the children. I held on to the promise from that day on, believing he was always going to be here for us. My faith wasn't shaky, and I didn't have any doubt about what I believed. Trevor's promise had been fulfilled all the way up until this night. Something went wrong this time. No one had any details for me, and I wasn't quite ready to hear the bad news anyway.

I sat peacefully with mom, and with my three children beside me. Officers kept coming up to us telling us Trevor was going to be okay. I really wanted them to leave me alone. They didn't know anything, they didn't know if Trevor was going to survive. Furthermore, I was upset with the whole Police Department. Why didn't anyone protect Trevor tonight? All these stupid cops are here now showing their concern, where were they when Trevor was getting shot in the head and chest, I thought to myself? I didn't want them coming up to me, and pretending like they cared.

A tall skinny Hispanic male, dressed in his police uniform came up to me, and asked if he could speak to me privately. I didn't want to get up and leave in case the doctor came out and said we could go in to see Trevor. My mother nudged me, and gave me a look to let me know I needed to get up and go with the man.

"I'm not even going to ask how you're doing, because I can only imagine what you're going through," he started off.

I just looked at him.

"I'm Ricky Hernandez, I was one of the responding officers on the scene tonight where Trevor was shot," Ricky said.

My eyes lit up. I was finally able to talk to someone who was able to give me some insight.

"What happened?" I asked.

"Well, come over here and sit down," Ricky insisted.

I followed him further down the hall until we reached a set of chairs.

"Your husband was responding to a domestic call tonight. Apparently, a woman made a claim that her husband was getting ready to stab her," Ricky said.

"Did Trevor go by himself?" I asked.

"He arrived on the scene by himself, but he called for back-up when he found drugs in the couple's home. The husband tried to flee the scene," Ricky stated.

"I don't understand how he was shot in the head?" I stated.

Ricky went on to explain that he and another officer arrived at the couple's home to help assist Trevor. The same woman who called for the police, called for her two brothers in the back room to come out, and get the cops off of her husband. Trevor had to hold the husband down, because he tried to leave the home. When the other two cops arrived at the home, everything turned to total chaos. One of the brothers had a gun and began shooting at the two responding officers. The other brother fled the scene, and the husband remained in Trevor's grip. In an effort to protect his brother-in-law, the woman's brother shot Trevor directly in the head. Once he was down, he shot him once more in the chest. Ricky explained that he fired his gun, and shot the man in the arm and shoulder, making him fall to the ground.

The husband got up and ran out the door. The only two people who remained in the house, was the wife and her brother, the shooter. The second officer chased the husband down and placed him under arrest. The wife was also arrested that night.

"Where is that coward now?" I asked.

"You mean Joe Vasquez, the shooter?" Ricky asked.

"Yes," I answered.

"He's at the hospital being treated for his wounds, and then he's on his way to the Police Station once he's well," Ricky told me.

"I've never hated anyone in my entire life, but I hate him. I hate this Joe! I hate him, I hate him, I hate him!" I revealed.

Before Ricky could give me any more information about what happened tonight, my mother called for me to come quickly to her. I left Ricky right where he was sitting, and ran to the other side of the hall.

"What?" I yelled.

"The doctor wants to talk to you. You're his wife and he won't give us any information until he tells you first," my mom said.

"Are you Mrs. Cramer?" The doctor asked.

"Yes," I replied.

"I need to speak with you," he said.

I followed him to the entrance of the ICU.

"Ma'am I sorry to tell you, but your husband passed away ten minutes ago," he said sympathetically.

I could feel my facial expressions turn to sorrow. I closed my eyes and put my hands to my face. There was nothing I could do. I cried loudly. I felt arms around my neck. I could feel someone trying to comfort me. At last I opened my eyes, and saw my mom. She was whispering to me it was going to be okay. I continued to shake my head from side to side in disbelief.

"I'm sorry for your loss, ma'am," the doctor said gently. He rubbed my shoulder briefly, and excused himself.

His promise, I thought to myself. His promise!

"He promised me, Mom!" I shouted.

"What? Who promised what?" she asked.

"Trevor promised he would never leave me. He promised me," I kept saying.

"He didn't want to leave you. He was taken away from us," mom explained.

I heard what she was saying to me, but I didn't want to receive what she was telling me.

Ricky finally caught up to me, and I could hear him talking quietly with my mother, asking her what happened. I was resting in the arms of my mother, forgetting that I needed to tell the children their father just died. My mom held me up, and told me to at least pull myself together just for tonight, and to be strong for them. She was right. I got up with her, dried my eyes, and tried my best to put on a brave face.

"Come here," I signaled for them.

They gathered around me, and I told them I had something important to tell them.

"I want all three of you to know I love you, and daddy will always love you too. Something happened to daddy tonight," I said.

"Mom, what happened?" Ryan asked.

"Kids, daddy died tonight," I cried.

They all just kind of looked at me, not really knowing whether or not they should believe me.

"When?" Ryan began to cry.

"Ten minutes ago," I answered.

"Died?" Isaiah said.

"Yes, honey, he died from some very bad injuries," I replied.

Clara immediately fell into my mother's arms.

"I know, baby," mom said.

Clara began crying uncontrollably. I grabbed a hold of Isaiah and Ryan and put my arms around them. We all cried. The pain was too strong for any one of us to try and be strong. We couldn't, and the kids didn't expect me to be strong. Besides, I couldn't hold back my emotions. The news hit me like a ton of bricks to the face. The kids wanted to see him, and so did I. The doctor didn't advise the children to see Trevor, but I told him they needed to.

"There's no way we can leave tonight without my kids being able to see their father. That's not happening! So you need to let us in there, please!" I insisted.

The doctor gave his approval and let us in to see Trevor. I explained to them daddy didn't look the same and they could only see him for a moment. We went in, the kids, my mother and I, and stood next to the bed. Trevor was bandaged on his head, and the bandage looked like it had been soaked in red punch. It was full of blood. I told Mom to take Isaiah and Clara out, they didn't need to remember their father in that way. If they had stayed in there any longer, those images would have haunted them forever. They saw him for a second, and that's all I was comfortable with. Ryan stayed with me because he said he was able to handle it.

Trevor's chest was wrapped up as well. The life had been sucked out of his face. His skin resembled a light blue, his body was plotted firmly to the bed, and he looked like he had been in some sort of altercation. That wasn't the Trevor I knew. I told Ryan to leave, so I could have a moment alone. He left and I began to weep more and more. I took Trevor's hand in my hand, and kissed it.

"You promised me!" I said to him. "You promised you wouldn't leave us. Why Trevor?" I asked.

In my heart I already knew the answer. He didn't know. Today was like any other day for him. When he got up this morning to go into work, he didn't know today was going to be his last day on this earth. Everything happened so fast, right before my eyes. My life and the life of our children changed so fast. It was completely unexpected, my husband, Officer Trevor Cramer, was gone. He had died in the line of duty.

One of the nurses came up to me and asked me, did I want anything of my husband's before he was to be taken away.

"Where's his uniform," I asked.

"I can get that ma'am, but it's ripped and stained," she explained to me.

"That's alright, I still want it," I said.

The nurse soon returned to me holding a bag with Trevor's uniform; watch; neck chain he wore around his neck; wallet; keys, and his bloody badge.

"This is all we can release to you Mrs. Cramer," she told me.

"I understand, thank you," I said.

It seemed like every police officer in the world was at the hospital that night hugging my family and I. If I heard, "I'm so sorry for your loss he was a good brave man," one more time, I was going to lose it. If I never heard, "I'm sorry for your loss" ever again, it would be too soon. My mom drove us back to the house that night. The kids spent the night in our bed, my mom took Ryan's room, and I didn't go to sleep that night at all. I couldn't rest my eyes knowing Trevor wasn't coming home. I didn't even get a chance to process anything. I got the call to go to the hospital, I came, and Trevor died. Nothing made sense to me.

I took out Trevor's uniform, laid it out on the living room floor, and rested my head on it. I cried all night long on his uniform. Besides pictures, three children, and wonderful memories, all I had to remind me of Trevor was his blood-stained black uniform. His 'stained blacks' I called it. I could see the blood from where he was shot in the chest. I put a piece of cloth over the blood and tried to clean it off as much as I could. I wasn't going to dare wash it. It still had Trevor's scent, and I didn't want to erase that last scent I had.

I came back to myself with a jolt, and realized I was sitting at the funeral. After I was presented with a folded United States flag, and a plaque, I was ready for the funeral to be over. I couldn't stand to look at Trevor's large picture of him in his uniform, displayed next to the casket. I got sad all over again. I had an open casket because I wanted everyone to see the heroic man who was taken away. Some people appreciated it, and others didn't understand why I did it, being that Trevor had been shot in the head. However, as I was looking at him lying in the casket, all I saw was Trevor Cramer, the man I fell in love with fifteen years ago.

The Police Chief and a couple of other officers on the force said some nice words at the funeral, and revealed to everyone what a loving, humorous, caring, and courageous person Trevor was. These were things I already knew about my husband. I didn't need them to tell me that. Nonetheless, it was still nice to hear. At the burial site, I placed some roses on his coffin, and told the children they didn't have to. At this point I was beyond crying, I was just going through the motions. My emotions had ceased for a split second, and all I could think about was the happy times I spent with Trevor.

We got back to the house later that evening, and all of Trevor's family and my family, was at our house. I didn't want to be bothered, but I knew they were here to support us and see us through this difficult time. The kids had been silent all day long. All of this was still a shock to them. My mom said to give it some time, and pretty soon they would be willing to talk about Trevor and his death. I know what it's like growing up without a father, and I didn't want my kids to have to go through what I went through. But no matter how hard I tried, I couldn't outdo death. Now they would know the pain of losing a father.

The man that actually killed my husband, Joe Vasquez, was officially charged with murder. He sits in jail waiting to go to trial. I can't wait to see his face, and express the amount of pain he inflicted on me and three innocent children, who now have to go through this life without a father, all because he was an ignoramus. I hope he's sentenced to death, and knocks the bottom out of hell!

As night fell, I sat out on the porch thinking about what the rest of my life was going to mean. In the days before the funeral, I didn't want to do anything. I didn't want to be around anyone, except my children and my mother. I was in a confused state, and just doing what I needed to, in order to make it through. I wondered what life was going to be like now that I lost my husband. I had never anticipated on living my life without Trevor. I knew it was possible, but I never envisaged it. I was a part of setting up the memorial fund in honor of Trevor, and I know Trevor would be proud of me.

In no way do I resent Trevor for the kind of career he chose, but I have to watch myself, because some days I would get angry with him that he left us. It will take some time before we are able to accept Trevor's death, and live with it. It will never be something that's easy to live with, but I hope in due time we are able to accept his death peacefully, and understand why God had to take him away.

The grief has only just begun for us as a family, but as I sat on this porch, I thought about the one thing I have which I am able to share with Ryan, Clara, and Isaiah, anytime they miss their father, and need to feel close to him, I have his 'stained blacks.'

CHAPTER EIGHTEEN
Sophia

Andrea Clothson was sitting in the big blue reclining chair in her living room, staring out of the window. She was wrapped in a warm pretty pink blanket she had been given as a gift for her younger daughter. Andrea had awakened from a restless night, but she was unexplainably tired. Her pattern for the past four weeks was to spend the night tossing and turning, constantly getting up to check the news on the Internet, checking her phone messages, and spend her days sleeping on her lunch break. She occasionally fell asleep behind the wheel. Andrea couldn't help her actions, and everyone she knew was sympathetic to her because of what she was going through.

Four weeks, Andrea kept thinking to herself every time she would see something that reminded her of the pain her and her husband, and oldest daughter were going through. Unfortunately, Andrea was the only one who hadn't lost hope. She was still clinging to the possibility that the authorities would find something that would give her the happy ending she had so desperately hoped for.

Forest, Andrea's husband, had quietly slipped back into his normal routine two weeks before Andrea even thought about resuming her normal life. Forest went back to work, and it was 'business as usual' to him, once he felt there was no reason to believe in miracles.

That's exactly what it was going to take in order for the Clothson family to be in a blissful state of mind again. Even though they still lived in the same house, they each had gone their own separate ways. Andrea spent her mornings at the police station, Forest spent a good majority of his time at work, fixing the cars people brought in, and their eldest daughter, Amelia, resumed her last year of college. From the outside, it looked as if Andrea was the only person who was still fighting to bring Sophia home. True, everyone suffers in their own way, but there was something uniquely different about a mother, and the connection she has with her children.

Forest undoubtedly loved his daughter, but he felt as if trying to bring her home was like looking for a needle in a haystack. The police had lost hope, and so had he. It wasn't that Amelia didn't care about her sister, she was just like her father in believing that there was no way anyone could find her little sister. Her optimism had ceased when the police turned the search for Sophia from 'search and rescue,' to 'recovery.' Amelia had even joined in on the search for her sister, but after days and days went by, and there was no trace of Sophia, she gave up just like the police had.

So much time had been lost in the search for ten year-old Sophia Clothson, because Andrea and Forest focused their attention on something much smaller than the true reality of the circumstance. They believed Sophia had gone off somewhere. They believed she was being adventurous, or curious about something, and lost her way to come home. It never entered their mind that perhaps Sophia was abducted, held captive, or even killed. They couldn't bring their minds to consider these horrible possibilities, because nothing like this had ever happened to them before, nor did they think it was possible for something like this to happen.

"Who would want to take a little girl away from her family?" Andrea said multiple times to a detective.

The police made Andrea go down her family, and ponder whether or not it was possible for anyone in her family to take Sophia. Andrea felt insulted, and couldn't believe the police were actually serious.

Andrea knew in her heart no one on either side of the family would take Sophia from them.

"We have to consider everyone, ma'am," a detective said to Andrea.

"There's no one in my family who would kidnap our daughter," Andrea cried.

"I know, but we must investigate everyone. I'm sorry to tell you this, but eventually you and your husband might be asked some questions as well," the detective informed Andrea.

"You mean question us as if we had something to do with it?" she asked in horror.

"Well, yes. We must eliminate everyone close to Sophia first, before we move outside," the detective explained.

"I want you to listen to me very carefully detective," Andrea said sternly.

On this particular day, a day after the abduction of Sophia, Andrea revealed some things to this detective. She didn't want him to be misinformed about the situation at hand. When she got finished spilling her personal story, she wanted him to feel mortified that he could even conjure up the notion that her and Forest, could even be remotely responsible for the disappearance of their daughter.

"I don't make it a point to go around telling people my personal business, but since this has to do with my daughter, and her life, and the police investigation to find her, I feel it's relevant," Andrea stated. "Because I don't want you, or anyone else, wasting time focusing on us, when the real perpetrator is out there with my daughter," she told the detective.

Andrea told the detective to sit down with her. She began by telling the detective how Sophia was the miracle she never expected. Due to certain complications after the birth of her first child, Amelia, Andrea was told she would never be able to carry a baby to full term again. Andrea went years without another baby, believing that she would miscarry, and that devastation was conceivably worse than not being able to have another child again. Twelve long years passed, before Andrea would conceive again. She told the detective that she lived each day in fear for eight months, worrying that she might lose her baby. It was a tough eight months for her because she knew what the risk was if she got pregnant. Against what she and Forest had been told, she still went forth with the pregnancy at age thirty-eight.

Although she had multiple complications with the delivery of Sophia, she believed Sophia was a blessing she and Forest were not supposed to receive.

"There's no way I would harm the blessing that was given to my husband and I ten years ago! I just wouldn't do it," Andrea cried.

"I understand what you're saying, but that doesn't mean we can automatically rule you out just because you're the mother, and your husband is the father. We come across tons of cases where demented, twisted, parents harm their own children every day," the detective explained.

"I'm just asking this Department, not to spend time searching for answers in my home, because there *are* none," Andrea proclaimed.

Andrea's attempt to convince the detective that she and her husband were innocent didn't do much good. They were both called down to the Police Station two days after their daughter had been abducted, and were questioned separately. Andrea couldn't believe she was being questioned as a possible suspect in the disappearance of her daughter. She wanted to yell at the top of her lungs that she had nothing to do with it, but showing that she could fly off the handle was not going to persuade officers that she had nothing to do with this kidnapping.

"Please state your name?" the detective asked her.

"Andrea Clothson," she replied.

"Mrs. Clothson, what's your daughter's full name and age?" the detective asked.

"Sophia Angelica Clothson, and she's ten years old," Andrea replied.

"And when was the last time you saw your daughter, Sophia?" the detective questioned.

"It would've had to have been the morning of April 5th," she answered.

"Tell me under what circumstances you had seen her?" the detective inquired.

"It was about seven in the morning, and she was getting ready for school. It was just a morning like any other morning. Nothing was strange about that day," Andrea told the detective.

The detective asked her what she had done that day, and where she was when she first learned about what happened to Sophia. Andrea told the detective that she had gone into work as normal. She had spent the majority of the day working in the dentist's office where she was a receptionist, and left around six in the evening, like she had always done. She got home expecting Sophia to already be there like she was use to. Andrea said she wouldn't be expecting Forest home until about seven that evening.

Andrea said she didn't notice Sophia's bicycle out in front of the house, like it had always been whenever she got home. Andrea admitted that this was strange, because Andrea had told Sophia to never operate the garage when she wasn't home. Sophia had obeyed her mother, but that day seemed peculiar to Andrea. She told the detective that she got out of her car, opened the door, and called for Sophia. Andrea said she called multiple times for her daughter, but she didn't get a response.

School was out at two-thirty, and Sophia was always home no later than two-forty, or two forty-five, when she rode her bike. Andrea said she went upstairs to Sophia's room and didn't find her in there either. She said she searched the house from top to bottom, and didn't find her anywhere. She then checked at the neighbor's house, and she even got back in her car and went to the neighborhood park, and then to Sophia's school. She couldn't find Sophia. Andrea said she waited until Forest got home, to ask him did he know where she was. Maybe he had picked her up and took her somewhere. There was no room for panic just yet. It had never even crossed Andrea's mind that something was decisively wrong.

However, when Forest got home, and told Andrea that he didn't know where Sophia was, the fear rose in Andrea, and she didn't know why her daughter wasn't home.

"Where in the world could she be?" she thought to herself.

After Andrea had been questioned by the detective Forest was questioned moments later. He had gone through the same questions as Andrea. He told police he went into work around seven that morning, and worked at the mechanic shop like he had always done, he took his two hour break, finished up his day, and headed home around six-thirty that evening. Both Andrea and Forest's whereabouts checked out after investigators got in contact with their co-workers and managers. Forest had a timesheet that cleared him, and Andrea and a computerized clock-in, and clock-out, system that verified she was at work at the time of Sophia's disappearance. The dental office even provided a security camera that showed Andrea at the front desk during work hours. Both parents were ruled out as potential suspects.

The detectives were able to verify that Sophia did indeed show-up to school that morning by talking to her teacher, other students, and confirming that day's attendance roster.

"I can't even believe we were even considered, what kind of sick parents do you think we are?" Andrea said to the detectives that day.

"It's only a precaution," he replied.

Forest had become visibly removed from the situation that day. He was hurting inside, and was often caught by police shedding some tears.

"What about your oldest daughter, would she . . . ?"

Andrea interrupted the detective, "Um, no sir, don't even think it. Amelia is all the way in another state in college. I doubt she would have time to fly here, get her sister, and fly back. Don't even consider her," Andrea stated.

When Andrea and Forest returned home that night, they didn't eat dinner or watch television, and they didn't rest easy. Andrea spent the night crying on the couch, and Forest was making calls to people. Andrea rocked herself back and forth with her eyes closed, trying to imagine where Sophia could possibly be. It didn't make sense to her that someone would take her. Andrea believed in her mind that Sophia ran off somewhere. It wasn't in her to believe that her daughter was the victim of a kidnapping. The street and neighborhood they resided in was safe, and there was never even a spot of trouble. People who lived in this neighborhood followed the school zones, stopped at stop signs, helped each other out, and most importantly, almost every single person on the street had at least one child. Nothing was connecting in Andrea's mind. When she finally did fall asleep, the only thing she could think about was the first night they spent without Sophia.

After Forest arrived home, Andrea began to question him about Sophia.

"Do you have Sophia? Did you pick her up?" Andrea asked.

"No, I've been at the shop all day," Forest replied.

"I can't find her, and its seven o'clock, and she's always here every day when I get home at six. Plus, her bike is gone," Andrea said frantically.

"Did you call the babysitter . . . did she get her by mistake? I already checked with Faye. I even checked neighbors and Sophia friend's house. No one has seen her," Andrea exclaimed.

"What are you saying, Andrea?" Forest asked.

Andrea stared at Forest for a second, with a look of fright on her face. "Maybe she wondered off somewhere," Andrea suggested.

"She knows she's supposed to come straight home after school, we already had this talk with her in September. Sophia knows she's not to go anywhere but to school, and home," Forest stated.

"I think we need to call the police," Forest said.

"What! She's not missing, I just think she went off somewhere and we need to find her," Andrea said.

"Andrea, we need to call the police. Neither of us knows where Sophia is. You call the police, and I'll go search the school and the neighborhood," Forest instructed.

"Forest . . ." Andrea started.

"Do as I say, please!" Forest demanded.

Forest stormed out of the house, got in his car, and looked for Sophia in every possible place he could think of. Andrea made the dreaded call to the police to inform them that their daughter, Sophia was missing and she was supposed to be home at three o'clock. The officer, who took the call, asked Andrea had she talked to the school and Sophia's teacher to see if she had shown up to school, and did she leave at the end of the day? Andrea explained that by the time she got home from work, the school was already closed for the day, but that she was going to try to call Sophia's teacher at home. The officer reluctantly told Andrea that there wasn't much they could do until Sophia had been missing for at least twenty-four hours, then, she and Forest could make a 'missing person's report.' Once Andrea received the bad news from the police, she hung up the phone and called Sophia's teacher. Her teacher explained that Sophia had indeed been in class that day, and she watched Sophia get on her bike and pedal home. Sophia's teacher began crying, and told Andrea she would do anything to help find Sophia. However, there was nothing she could do to help, the same way the police couldn't even help, until tomorrow around this time.

Forest arrived home looking tired, helpless, and scared out of his mind. He walked in the house and ran to Andrea, and collapsed in her arms.

"I can't find her," he cried uncontrollably.

Once Andrea saw the tears roll down Forest's eyes, she knew just how serious the situation was. Andrea hadn't let her mind go to that dark place yet, and she wouldn't allow herself to believe anything had happened to Sophia. Yet, when she saw the anguish in Forest, and that he couldn't stop crying, she had no choice but to relinquish her denial. It was real, and no one knew where dear Sophia Clothson was. Andrea and Forest's angel girl was missing!

The first night they spent without Sophia was the hardest. Neither one of them could sleep. They spent the night trying to think of any place to look for Sophia. They even got back in their cars, and went looking for Sophia again at three o'clock in the morning. They once again found nothing. When they arrived home again, Andrea went straight to Sophia's bed and spent the remainder of the night in her bed. Andrea and Forest hadn't called anyone in the family just yet, they didn't want to alarm anyone. Amelia didn't even know anything.

The next morning when Andrea and Forest awoke, there was still no sign of Sophia. Later that day they went to the police together and filed a missing person's report. They spent a good part of the evening at the police station talking to police and answering questions. The questions at this stage they had been subjected to were only informational questions, not questions to clear them as potential suspects. They both answered questions and headed home. Later, a detective came to their house and did some investigating and some searching. Andrea was too distraught to make any calls to family, so Forest took on the task, and called Amelia, Sophia's aunts and uncles, cousins and friends, and asked them to pray for Sophia's return. No one in the family could believe that this was happening to Andrea and Forest. Everyone knew what loving parents they were to both Amelia and Sophia. Additionally, they knew how hard this was on Andrea, being that she was never supposed to have kids again. Amelia got on the first flight home, then, Andrea's sisters came, Forest's mother and father showed up. No one could believe something like this was actually taking place in the family.

"This is something you only read about in newspapers, and see other people go through. I never thought we would be going through this," Andrea told her oldest sister.

As of April 7th, police were officially searching for Sophia, and they had organized an entire team to look for the missing ten year-old. Besides authorities, the entire community in which Andrea and Forest lived joined in on the search for Sophia. Sophia's school was also helping in the search. With so many able bodies, and vigilance on board, it was hopeful that someone would find Sophia somewhere. Day and night people were searching for Sophia. Authorities searched creeks, ponds, parks, back-woods, shelters, they questioned neighbors, checked the city morgue, and called hospitals. Sophia's picture was posted all over the community, in stores, businesses, schools, hospitals, and on the local television news. There was still no sign of Sophia.

After a full week and a half of searching for Sophia, Andrea and Forest were called into the Police Station. They expected to have some good news going into the station that day.

"Good morning Mr. and Mrs. Clothson," a detective said.

"Hello," they both replied.

"We just needed to inform you that despite all the efforts we have put into searching for Sophia, we have to turn this search into a recovery," the detective explained.

"Recovery?" Andrea looked horrified.

"This was a search and rescue, but now we're trying to recover Sophia," the detective said.

"That means you think she's dead?" Forest muttered loudly.

"No! No, no, no. She's not dead. How could you think that?" Andrea cried.

"We have to be realistic, madam. We're still hoping for the best, but at this stage it's not likely were going to find anything good. We don't want to give you false hope," the detective said.

"Oh God, oh God, oh God!" Andrea sighed.

Forest took a hold of Andrea, and comforted her the best way he knew how. They didn't want to listen to anything else the detective had to say. Forest and Andrea left the room with Forest holding Andrea up. As Forest drove home, Andrea cried all the way. Once they got home that night, Andrea and Forest spent the night in Sophia's room. It seemed like the right thing to do after they got this devastating news from the police. All the sympathy cards, words of encouragement, and prayers had stopped from family and friends.

"Do you think she's dead?" Andrea asked Forest.

Forest took a second to respond to Andrea, as if he was stunned that she had just asked him this question.

"I don't know what to think Andrea. One minute I'm kissing my daughter on the forehead before I go into work, and the next I am looking in creeks for her," Forest responded.

"Where is she, Forest?" Andrea asked.

"I wish I knew. I wish I knew," Forest said.

Two whole weeks had passed, and there was still no sign of Sophia. Everyone in the community knew about Sophia Clothson, but no one knew anything about where she was. No one had any answers. People who saw Andrea and Forest would stop them, and pray with them, hug them, and tell them that their thoughts and prayers were with them. Andrea didn't want prayers and hugs, she wanted her daughter back, but there was nothing she could do. She felt helpless as a mother. Andrea felt she had let her daughter down, and that she had failed as a mother in some way. All sorts of dangerous and sadistic things ran through her head about where Sophia was, or what was happening to her. She felt Sophia was calling on her to rescue her, but Andrea couldn't get to her.

Andrea's spirits were lowered when she heard gossip in the community that she and Forest should have never let Sophia ride her bike to and from school. People were saying Andrea and Forest were to blame, because a ten year-old girl had no business riding her bike to school by herself. Those nasty comments got back to Andrea, and all she could do was cry herself to sleep at night, believing that whoever said that about her and Forest was right. Andrea never would have thought in a million years something like this would have happened to her and Forest. At the request of Sophia, Andrea and Forest let her ride her bike to and from school, because it was something that she wanted to do. They figured there was nothing wrong with giving their ten year-old daughter a little independence. In Andrea's mind the school wasn't even that far away from where they lived, and they felt safe letting her travel on her own.

It had been three long weeks, and the search efforts for Sophia had already stopped. The case seemed to have waxed cold. All the search efforts had been ceased it felt like to Andrea. Although she continued to check in at the Police Station every day, the police never had any positive leads as to where Sophia was. Andrea felt like everyone had given up on finding Sophia. No one took an interest anymore. Everyone probably believed the way the detectives had, that Sophia was most likely dead by now. When it takes weeks and weeks to locate a missing person, and the missing person is not found, the general consensus is that the person has passed on.

The tension was thick in the Clothson household. Andrea and Forest were not on the same team any longer. Although Andrea and Forest shared in each other's pain and suffering, Andrea didn't agree with the decision Forest made to continue his life as if they didn't have a missing child.

"I can't even fall asleep at night without crying, and I can barely stand to get up in the morning. There's no way it's possible for me to go to work and act like everything is okay, but you sure can," Andrea said to Forest.

"You think I don't care Andrea?"

"I don't know, do you?" Andrea replied.

"How can you even ask me something like that? I don't understand you Andrea!" Forest uttered.

"I don't understand how you're able to go to work and come home and not think about Sophia. She's gone, Forest. Do you get that? Our daughter is missing, presumed dead, and we don't know where she is!" Andrea shouted.

"Don't you think I know that? But what can I do? What can we do that hasn't already been done?" Forest yelled. "Everyone in this neighborhood has searched every inch of this city. All we can do is keep praying God brings her back home!" Forest proclaimed.

"It's not enough. We have to do more. Sophia is out there somewhere, and the longer we sit back and wait for someone else to look for her, we lose valuable time," Andrea explained.

"So you want us to lose our house and everything we own, on top of losing our daughter?" Forest asked. "Because if one of us doesn't go to work, we'll have no place to live," he cried.

"I guess I'll never be able to understand you," Andrea said softly.

In a way Forest was right in what he was saying, and Andrea knew this, but she was mad at herself more than anything, because she wasn't able to accept Sophia's disappearance the way Forest had. She wasn't able to move on, and leave the rest up to the authorities. She had spent too many nights without her little angel and she felt helpless. Andrea knew in her heart there was nothing she could do to bring Sophia home again. It didn't matter how many posters were plastered all over town, and how many times Sophia's picture appeared on the Internet, or the news . . . no one knew anything.

Andrea didn't know what to do with herself from day to day. She had taken a leave of absence from her job, and told her supervisor it would be awhile before she would return. He told her he understood, and that when she was ready to come back, she was welcome to. Andrea spent three and a half weeks away, but she decided to return one day in an effort to get her mind off of her situation. She was greeted with a warmness she desperately needed. Every minute of the day Andrea was thinking about Sophia. Working didn't take her mind off her daughter's kidnapping.

Things weren't supposed to have happened this way. Sophia was supposed to be home by now. What made Andrea upset the most, and what made her cry every day and night, was the fact that she didn't know whether or not Sophia was dead or alive. At least if she was dead she wouldn't have to hold on to the hope of her returning home, and she could have acceptance in her heart of her daughter's death. Also, she would be able to visit the cemetery any time she wanted to be with Sophia. Conversely, by her not knowing if she was still alive, Andrea didn't know what she should've been praying for. Should her prayer have been for a safe return home, or the ability to accept her daughter's death? Some people say no news is good news, but in Andrea and Forest's case, this didn't apply. Andrea couldn't function in her everyday life not knowing where Sophia was.

A full four weeks had passed, and there was still no sign of Sophia. Andrea had grown more distressed that everyone she once counted on had moved on with their lives. Even Forest was able to produce a smile or two at times. This bothered Andrea to no end. What did he have to smile about she thought to herself? Andrea no longer slept in the bed with Forest. She spent her nights either in the rocking chair in the living room, or in Sophia's bed. All communication between Andrea and Forest had almost completely stopped. Instead of coming together, and bonding through this tragedy, they grew further and further apart. The only thing that could possibly bring these two back together was the safe return of Sophia. However, that would never happen.

Come June, two months after Sophia had gone missing, a break came in the case. Andrea received a phone call from the Police Station one day around four o'clock in the afternoon, telling her that she and Forest needed to come down to the station immediately. There wasn't any excitement in Forest's eyes, it was like he knew the news wasn't good. On the other hand, Andrea beamed with joy and optimism as she rushed to get into the car to make it to the Police Station. It was the longest fifteen-minute ride she had ever taken.

"What they have to tell us might not be good," Forest warned.

Andrea ignored Forest, and continued to act as if she was gathering her belongings. She didn't pay him any attention.

"I know you heard me," Forest said.

"So what! So what Forest! Let's just see what they have to tell us. Leave me alone!" Andrea shouted.

Andrea and Forest walked in the Police Department side by side, and they were both thinking about different circumstances. Andrea had hope Sophia was alive, and Forest didn't want to be informed his daughter's death was brutal.

"Good afternoon, Mr. and Mrs. Clothson, follow me over here please?" the officer requested.

Andrea noticed the officer had a large manila folder that was half open, and there was a seemingly large picture sticking out. All Andrea could put together from the folder was a white paper with red in the background. Andrea stopped in her tracks and wouldn't go any further.

"What's that?" Andrea said, pointing at the envelope.

The officer stopped and looked at Andrea.

"Excuse me," he asked.

"What's in the envelope? Is it about Sophia?" Andrea inquired.

"Andrea!" Forest said.

"Please be quiet, Forest!" Andrea demanded.

"We'll explain everything to you in the interview room," the officer replied.

"Tell me now! Let me see what's in that envelope please?" Andrea asked.

"Ma'am, please wait. Come with me," the officer begged.

"Are those pictures of Sophia?" Andrea questioned.

The officer hesitated in his response, because he knew he wasn't going to be able to get Andrea to come with him unless he answered her question truthfully and convincingly.

"Yes, yes these pictures are of Sophia," the officer said.

Tears surfaced in Andrea's eyes.

"Let me see them!" Andrea said loudly.

"No, Andrea!" Forest said.

"Let me see the pictures officer!" Andrea shouted.

"I don't think you want to see these pictures," the officer answered.

"Let me see the pictures!" Andrea yelled again.

Everyone in the Police Department couldn't help but focus on Andrea and her demands to see the envelope, which contained pictures of Sophia. Several police officers stood up and eased their way over to Andrea and Forest thinking that Andrea might become irate, and try to harm someone.

"You don't want to see these pictures," the officer said frustrated.

"Let's just go in the room, Andrea," Forest said silently. He gently tried to push Andrea towards the interview room.

"I'm her mother, and I have a right to see the pictures, show me the pictures!" Andrea screamed.

"Okay, ma'am, you need to calm down right now," another officer stepped in.

"Give me the pictures, I have a right!" she yelled.

Before the officer could react, Andrea grabbed the envelope out of his hand and ran swiftly into the nearby interrogation room with tears rolling down her eyes. Forest and the officer ran after her, and they both tried to grab the envelope out of her hand. The two men struggled with Andrea, but there was an undefined strength within Andrea at this particular moment, that didn't allow Forest or the officer to overpower her. Andrea opened the envelope. She screamed in pain, as if she was being tortured, when she had the pictures in front of her.

"No, Sophia! No Sophia! This isn't her. This isn't my child!" Andrea cried in pain.

As Andrea was slipping, Forest caught her by the arms and tried to keep her from falling.

"This isn't my baby. This isn't her!" Andrea proclaimed.

The officer forcefully regained control of the photos and stuffed them back into the envelope. He handed the envelope over to another officer, and helped Forest pick-up Andrea from the floor. She had collapsed in her distress. Andrea was seated in a chair. She had passed out.

"I want to see the photos officer?" Forest requested.

"No, sir. That's not a good idea," the officer replied.

"Please. It's sad to say, but I've accepted my daughter's death two months ago. This will give me the end I need to sleep better at night. I need to see it," Forest explained.

The officer looked at Andrea in the chair passed out, and looked in Forest's eyes. He could see the pain of a dad who just wanted this nightmare to be over. He went against his better judgment, and asked the other officer to bring the photos back over to him. Forest opened the envelope and pulled out three large photos. The first photo showed a badly decomposed body with what looked like dried spots of blood around it. The body was almost unrecognizable. The second photo showed a close-up of the decomposed body. Forest couldn't take anymore. He began to cry.

When Andrea came-to, the officer pulled Andrea and Forest into a room, and explained to them what happened to Sophia. He explained that a woman, who was jogging by in a park, could smell an unusual order. She came upon the odor, and noticed the decomposed body situated between a couple of trees.

"We searched every inch of the park in our neighborhood," Forest stated.

"We didn't find your daughter's body here. She was spotted about thirty miles from here," the detective said.

"How did she die?" Forest asked.

"Sophia's body was too decomposed to determine a cause of death. We were able to secure dental records, and match them to the teeth we found on site. It was Sophia," the officer said.

"I can't believe this!" Andrea cried.

"We did find a piece of cloth tied to her eyes, which let us know that she had been blindfolded at the time of her death," the officer added.

Andrea began to throw-up in the trashcan. Forest helped her out of the room.

"We can't hear anymore. I just want to know if you caught the sick person who did this," Forest asked.

"No we haven't," the officer said.

"Figures," Forest replied.

Andrea and Forest left the Police Station that evening, grief-stricken from the news about their daughter. There was no comforting Andrea when she got home, she ran straight to Sophia's room and fell in the center of the floor crying her heart out.

"Who would do this? I don't understand who would do this to our angel," Andrea sobbed.

Forest stood in the doorway of Sophia's room and looked around her room. He looked at all her drawings, her clothes, her shoes, her bed, and couldn't believe she wasn't here anymore. All those months just to find out his daughter had been blindfolded, killed and thrown out in a wooded park.

Andrea took it really hard. She never gave up hope that Sophia was alive. Her miracle child had been taken away from her in such a tragic way, and there was no one to pay for this senseless crime.

A full year had passed, and no one was ever charged with the kidnapping and murder of Sophia Clothson. Andrea tried grief counseling, and joined a support group for women who lost their children. However, nothing seemed to work for her. She missed Sophia every day and challenged God with questions as to why He took her ten year-old daughter away.

Some advice came from a mother who had lost her child as well. She told Andrea that our children are God's first, and he simply provides us with them until he sees fit to take them back with him. She encouraged Andrea to reflect on the positive side of Sophia's death. She wanted Andrea to remember that Sophia is in Heaven and away from anymore hurt, harm, and danger from this cold and wicked world. The person who committed this crime may have gotten away with their misdeed in this life, but one day they will undeniably suffer, and reap the painful punishment they are due, because everyone must pay for their wrong. Knowing this gets Forest through the day.

It's been a struggle for Andrea and Forest to move on without their youngest daughter in their lives, but they hold on to the reassurance that God doesn't make mistakes, and that Sophia was His before she belonged to them. Sophia will always remain in their hearts. Unlike her physical body that was taken away, her loving spirit will never die, and she will be waiting for her parent's in Heaven.

CHAPTER NINETEEN
May this grudge pass?

"**I** hate the sight of you, you're dead to me, never talk to me again!" Those are words I'll never forget for as long as I live. Maybe it wouldn't have hurt as bad if it had came from a complete stranger, or just an associate that I knew, but those words burned deep in my heart and mind when I stood before my sister and brother-in-law. If I could go back and change what happened two years ago, I would.

How I desperately wish I could go back and change what happened that June summer day. I can't, and with my sister shutting me out, I'm reminded every day of just how damaged our relationship is.

I can't move forward, or even begin to find acceptance with what happened, because it's too painful to think about. My heart won't allow me to be at rest, and besides the internal scars, my family won't allow me to be at rest. Whatever happened to, 'we all make mistakes,' or, 'no one's perfect?' My family has forgotten all about forgiveness, understanding and compassion. I wasn't looking for sympathy, but I wanted somebody to be on my side. I needed someone to look me in the eye and tell me it's going to be okay. Stupid me, I should have known there was no way I would get sympathy after what happened.

My own husband stopped talking to me for a period of time. I felt all alone in the world. I contemplated suicide on multiple occasions. I figured if I cut my life off, people would feel somewhat relieved because I was gone from this earth, especially my sister. She would be the main one enthused at my passing. I wished my father were still alive, I knew he would probably be the only one to give me the understanding I needed. My mother was down my throat and highly upset with me when she found out what happened. I needed consoling as well, but no one thought twice about comforting me. One of the only reasons why I didn't take my life was because of my children. I loved my three children very much, and didn't want them to suffer and feel the pain of growing up without a mother.

I tried to reach out to my sister numerous times, her birthday, holidays, family gatherings, but she wanted nothing to do with me. As we were approaching the anniversary of the accident, I made another attempt to reach out to her again. I was lucky enough to have some of the family speaking to me again as we approached this two-year mark, but there were a few cousins and other relatives who shunned me out-right. My older brother Kline wrote me a beautiful letter a couple of weeks ago, and said he wanted to repair our relationship. He said it wasn't in him to have such resentment in his heart any longer. Before I made the phone call to my sister, I prepared myself mentally for more verbal bashing, and emotional abuse. I called her the night before the anniversary.

"Hello," my sister answered.

"It's Hope," I said.

"Hi, Hope. I know why you're calling," Veronica replied.

"Please don't hang up in my face," I pleaded.

"I'm not. I'm actually glad you called. I wanted to ask you something," Veronica informed me.

"What?" I asked.

"I need you to tell me what you remember about his last words?" Veronica inquired.

I put the phone down away from my mouth, and sighed. Why was she bringing this up, I didn't want to talk about this and have her get angry at me all over again.

"Veronica, why do you want to bring this up again? I'm trying to re-connect with you, and I don't want you to think about those bad memories," I insisted.

"It'll be two years tomorrow, and I still can't get those images out of my head," Veronica said.

"I wanted to know if you wanted to go to church this Sunday with Teagan and I?" I asked.

"Let me think about it, and I'll let you know," she answered back.

"Okay," I said.

I was about to say I love you, but I didn't know if she was ready for that. We were two of the closest sisters growing up, and even into our adult years, and our relationship was torn apart by a senseless tragedy in which the whole family blamed me for. As I went to bed that night, I rested my head on my pillow, laid next to my husband, and thought about June 17th. The more I thought about that day, I wish I would have never taken on the responsibility of being in charge of all those kids that day. My mind was in so many different places that day I couldn't focus on anything. I was trying to be the best aunt, the cool mom, and the hero big sister. I needed help that day, and I was too proud to ask for it.

Veronica arrived early that morning with her four kids. Her oldest was only nine years old, and her youngest was four. She was dropping them off because she had to work, and so did her husband, and the kids wanted to play in my pool. She had promised them they could play after school was out for the summer, as long as it was okay with me. I scheduled the date and time, and told Veronica I would also take them home at the end of the day. On top of having her four kids there, I had my three kids, two daughters and my son. My oldest daughter was thirteen and my son was eight years old. Lastly, my oldest daughter invited three of her friends over. The day started off with a hot blaze of air, a shining sun, and layers of blue sky everywhere I looked.

Teagan had gone to work that day, and it was just me alone with ten children. That day had progressed rather nicely. It wasn't until around three in the afternoon when one of my daughter's friends told me she needed a ride home because she needed to be somewhere, and her mom wasn't going to be able to come by and pick her up. I knew in my heart I didn't want her to walk all the way home, but I also couldn't fit all of the kids in my car. I didn't know what to do.

"Are you sure your mom can't pick you up," I asked.

"No, ma'am, I should've been home already," she replied.

I kept glancing at my watch trying to figure out what to do. All the kids were outside still playing in the pool. There was no way all of those kids were going to fit in my car. I made a brainless decision that day that I have to live with for the rest of my life. I pulled my oldest, Grace, aside, and told her she was in charge while I drove her friend home. The drive was about fifteen to twenty minutes away.

"Bring all your cousins in the house until I get back home," I told Grace.

"Mom, they're not going to listen to me," Grace said.

"I'll talk to them before I go," I replied.

I went outside and told my nieces and nephews and Grace's friends, they needed to come in the house for about fifteen minutes. I met some resistance, but I told them they could play outside once I got back home. They all went inside as if they understood.

"Don't let anyone go outside until I get back, Grace, you understand?" I told her.

"Yes ma'am," Grace answered.

I trusted my thirteen year-old daughter, because she had proven herself to be a trustworthy teenager. There was no reason for me to not trust her. It hurt me in my heart that I was leaving her with all of these kids, but I felt okay because she had two of her other friends who were the same age as her. They could help her. I tried to justify the fact that I was leaving them alone with these kids by telling myself that it was just like they were babysitting. I went against what I believed was right, and left home.

As I was driving my daughter's friend home, all I could think about was how guilty I felt. I hadn't prepared myself to think about anything negative because I was only going to be gone fifteen minutes. Still, there was something in the back of my mind that wouldn't allow me to be at ease with what I had done. I felt I was doing a good deed by not letting this young girl walk all the way home by herself. Who knows what could have happened to her if she would've walked home all alone. Due to my speeding the drive actually only took about ten minutes. I dropped her off and raced for my life back home.

I pulled up in the driveway and felt a sense of relief, because I was back home.

No sign of a fire or any perceivable danger. I dashed to the front of the house, opened the front door, and locked it behind me. I headed to the back of the house where the kitchen was.

"Grace!" I shouted.

I didn't see the kids in the kitchen where I thought they would be.

"Grace!" I shouted again.

I swiftly moved to the living room where I thought they would be watching television. I didn't see anyone in the living room either. My body wouldn't allow me to even head out to the pool, because in my mind I consciously knew where they were. I knew they were out there. I was more upset than relieved, because it was as if Grace had disobeyed me. After checking upstairs, I went back downstairs and made my way to the back of the house again. This time I went to the sliding door which led to the backyard. Before I could brace myself, I saw Grace reaching down in the pool laying on her stomach acting as if she was reaching for something. Tears filled my eyes and I ran outside feeling my legs already giving out on me. I ran in a limping motion, yelling and screaming.

"Oh God, oh God, what happened!" I yelled.

"Mommy!" Grace cried.

"Grace! Grace, what happened?" I asked.

"Hamilton fell in the pool!" Grace screamed.

With tears in my eyes I fell to my knees scraping them on the cement. I looked for all of the other children. I saw the rest of my sister's children over by the fence crying. My other two children where coming up out of the pool as if they had been looking for something.

"Get out! Get out! Get out of the pool," I yelled at my children.

My daughter's other two friends were in the pool as well. They looked liked they had been searching for something as well. Once

I yelled for everyone to get out of the pool, everyone got out and immediately ran over to me.

"Grace, go call the police," I ordered.

Grace got up and ran into the house. As I was trying to get off my knees, I fell on my back and scrapped my elbows. I got in the pool and tried to look for Hamilton. I couldn't find him. I had to come up and wipe my eyes. In addition to the water, and because I was crying and very emotional, I wasn't able to effectively look for him. Where was he? I thought to myself. I couldn't locate him. When I went down deeper, I found him floating face down. He wasn't moving. My heart literally stopped. I had to swim almost to the bottom of the pool to get Hamilton. I got a hold of him, and with everything I had I pulled him to the cement.

"The police are on their way," Grace shouted.

Poor Hamilton was blue in the face. He wasn't moving, and there was water rushing out of his nose. I didn't know what to do. I didn't know CPR; all I could do was wait for the paramedics to arrive. I cried and cried, and tried not to think about how serious his condition was. I could hear the ambulance piercing our neighborhood with the sound of their sirens. I was relieved, so I stood up holding Hamilton in my arms. I walked to the fence and asked Grace to open it. The other children followed behind me.

"Grace, take everyone inside!" I ordered.

Grace did as I asked, and she and her two friends walked the children inside the house. I stood on the lawn with the fence gate open. I saw the white ambulance turn the corner speeding as if there was a rush of fire coming after them. I was holding Hamilton with both arms, and he was lying across my arms on his back. I tried to elevate his head, but I was scared that if I touched him anymore I was going to hurt him. Three men hastily jumped out the truck and ran to me at the fence where I was holding Hamilton.

"Is he breathing ma'am?" one the EMT's asked me.

"No, sir," I replied.

"How long as he been unconscious?" he questioned.

"I don't know. I was only gone for about ten or twelve minutes," I answered.

I didn't want to be honest with the EMT, but I knew Hamilton's life was in danger. I feared that I was going to be in trouble. Were they going to call the police and have me arrested? Were they going to call Child Protective Services, and take my children away? I didn't know what was going to happen once they found out I left nine children here by themselves.

"Grace!" I yelled. "Grace! Grace come out here," I yelled again.

Grace ran to me with a disturbed look on her face.

"What's wrong?" she inquired.

"How long was he in the pool?" I asked.

Grace began to cry.

"I don't know mom, I did what you said and told . . ."

I interrupted her, "Grace, how long after I left did you find Hamilton in the pool?" I asked.

"I don't know, Mom, it was like five minutes after you left," Grace cried.

I ran up to the EMT's and told them what Grace had told me. They were still there trying to revive Hamilton. They kept trying and trying, but Hamilton wouldn't respond. They loaded him up on a stretcher, and placed him in the back on the ambulance.

"How old is he ma'am?" one of the EMT's asked me.

"He's five years old," I answered.

"Is he going to be okay?" I demanded to know.

"It doesn't look like it. We can't get a pulse ma'am," he replied regretfully.

I closed my eyes and took a deep breath.

"Do you know of any medications your son is allergic to?" one of the EMT's asked me.

"He's not my son," I answered back.

The EMT didn't say anything.

"He's my nephew. I don't know if he's allergic to anything," I said.

"Okay, we need to get him to the hospital," he said.

"Which hospital are you taking him to?"

"On Benedict Street," he said.

The ambulance fled my house at full speed, with the sirens sounding off strong and strident. I rushed back into the house and told all the children to get dressed. I ran upstairs and called my husband. I wasn't ready to call my sister. I couldn't call her just yet. I was hysterical and out of my mind with grief. Teagan's phone rang repeatedly. Just before I was about to hang up, he answered his phone.

"Hello," he said.

"Teagan," I whimpered in distress.

He could hear the fear in my voice.

"Hope? Hope what's wrong?" he asked. I cried right there on the phone with him.

"Hope answer me! What's wrong?" he uttered.

"Teagan," I cried.

"Hope, tell me what's wrong?" he demanded.

"We had an accident, and I need you to come home right now," I blurted out.

"Are the kids okay?" he shouted.

"Yes, it's Veronica's son," I replied.

"You're scaring me. What's wrong with Veronica's son?"

"I think he's hurt really bad. He was in the pool face down," I said softly.

"What?" Teagan screamed.

The sound of his voice made me feel even worse in that moment. I wanted to kill myself right then and there. How could I have been so stupid? Why did I do what I did I thought to myself.

"I'm on my way," Teagan said.

After I got off the phone with Teagan, I went downstairs to make sure all of the kids were dressed. My two other nieces and nephew were crying on the couch. Grace's friends had already left. My two other children looked terrified, and didn't know what was going on. They had never witnessed anything like that before with an ambulance, stretcher, and seeing their cousin lying face down in a pool. All this was because of me. No one was going to have to tell me this was my fault. I already knew in my heart and head who was responsible.

On the drive to the hospital, I tried to be angry with Grace because I wanted someone else to blame as well. I told her specifically not to let those kids go outside until I got back. Hamilton should have never been out there in the water. We arrived at the emergency room, and took a seat while the nurse checked on Hamilton's condition.

"Grace, what happened?" I asked.

"I did what you told me to do. I made sure we were all in the house until you got home," Grace answered.

"Why was Hamilton outside Grace?" I demanded to know.

She paused for a second. "He told me he forgot his bear and he wanted to get it. I didn't know he meant outside," Grace said.

"You let him go outside?" I asked her.

"I just told him to go get it," she replied.

"Oh Grace," I sobbed.

Grace began crying and put her hands over her face.

"It's not your fault," I comforted her.

My nieces and nephew cried to me that they wanted their mom. I tried to avoid having to tell her, hoping I would get some good news first, but I had to make the call. I was so petrified. This was the first time in my life I was actually scared to death. I didn't want to have to tell another mother her child was in the hospital fighting for his life, all because of my ignorance. Nonetheless, there was no way around it. I got my cell phone and went outside, and stood by the entrance of the emergency room.

"Hello," Veronica answered.

"Veronica, its Hope. Sorry to bother you at work," I cringed.

"Its okay, what's going on?" she asked.

"Um, um, I don't know how to tell you this . . ."

"Hope, what's wrong? Are my children okay?" Veronica questioned.

"I need you to get to North Shire Hospital, on Benedict Street. Hamilton had an accident in the pool," I said hurriedly.

I could hear my sister crying heavily on the phone.

"I'm on my way," she said.

Telling my sister that her five year-old son was in the hospital was the most difficult thing I ever had to do. There was no way on God's green earth that Veronica was going to understand why Hamilton ended up in the hospital. She put me in charge of her kids, and I let her down. I had watched my nieces and nephews so many times before, and today of all days, tragedy hits. My only hope now was that Hamilton would be okay. At least the hate that was going to come between my sister and I could be minimized if the extent of Hamilton's injuries weren't that severe. However, fate was not on my side at all. The doctor came out and pulled me aside.

"Ma'am, we did everything we could," he started telling me.

"Oh God, please no," I cried.

Heaviness raced through by body and centered itself right across my heart. I knew this doctor was getting ready to tell me my sister's son was dead. My heart literally couldn't take any more disastrous events today. Surely God wasn't about to make me suffer the wrath of my sister. Not only was she my sister, but also a mother who had a child in the hospital. It's one thing for a child to have an accident while their parents are around, or they're in their parent's care, but it's a completely different thing when a child had an accident while someone else was supposed to be watching them, and taking care of them. Mother's rarely get the chance to release their rage on the guilty individual, but Veronica was going to have total access to me to hurt me verbally, and maybe even physically.

"We're terribly sorry ma'am, but he drowned. We tried everything, but between the damage to his head, and the amount of water in his lungs, we got to him too late," the doctor said.

"What damage to his head?" I asked.

"Your son had swelling on the left side of his head. He was either hit with a heavy object, or he hit his head on his way into the pool," the doctor explained.

How was I going to face Veronica? I wanted to run and hide . . . forget my husband, children and everybody. I wanted to escape, but there was nowhere for me to go.

Teagan arrived shortly after the doctor gave me the bad news. He found us all sitting in the emergency room. I had a blank stare. I couldn't look Teagan in the face when he called out to me.

"Hope! Hope! Hope!" he kept calling.

I gazed up at my husband, and reached out for him to hug me.
"How is he?" Teagan asked.

I looked into his eyes, and by the sorrowful look on my face, Teagan knew the answer to his own question. He kissed my forehead. He hugged our children, and then comforted our nieces and nephew. He sat with them until their parent's came. The only people who knew what was going on was Teagan and I. I stood by the big square glass window with my arms folded, looking out and waiting for Veronica and Kale. I was going over what I was going to say in my head, and how I was going to try to justify my reasoning for leaving the kid's home alone. In my mind I felt I had done a good deed by giving a young teenage girl a ride home, but no one was going to care. A lovely five year-old boy had just died.

Twenty minutes was all I got to mentally prepare for what was coming my way. I saw Veronica and Kale running to the emergency room. They were hand and hand. I could see my sister running frantically. Kale couldn't keep up with her, and at one point they let go of each other's hand. I moved to the sliding door to be the first one to greet my sister. Veronica dashed into the emergency room with sweat dripping from her forehead and tears in her eyes.

"How's Hamilton?" Veronica said.

I stretched out my hands to hug Veronica. She backed up from me, letting me know she didn't want a hug.

"Hope, where's Hamilton?" she asked.

All I could do was fall to the floor crying hysterically.

Veronica looked confused, and glanced over at Teagan sitting with her kids. Kale knew what happened. I looked up at Veronica, and I could see her chest furiously beating up and down.

"My baby is dead?" Veronica shouted.

I turned my head to avoid her falling tears from hitting the top of my head.

"Tell me he's not dead. Tell me he's still alive! He's not dead, he can't be dead!" Veronica yelled.

Tears rushed from Veronica's eyes. Kale had to hold her up, because it seemed as if Veronica was about to faint.

"Teagan!" Kale called.

Teagan rushed over, and helped Kale to keep Veronica from falling. Veronica's kids ran to their mom and kept screaming. They were scared and didn't understand why their dad was struggling with their mother. Their scared little faces and agonizing screams are forever etched in my memory. I'll never forget the look they had on their faces. Eventually, Kale and Teagan let Veronica slip to the floor. A horde of doctors and nurses raced over to tend to Veronica and I, because we were both on the floor crying. I had my arms around my sister. She was sobbing in my arms with her eyes open, and her kids were beside her rubbing her back, stroking her hair, yet, not knowing that their brother had passed away about thirty-minutes ago.

Kale spent the remainder of the afternoon talking to the doctors, and making phone calls to some family members. Veronica wouldn't let me take her children home with me, so Kale called my mother to come and get them. From that afternoon on, Veronica didn't speak to me for a long time. She had basically put in her mind that I didn't exist. I understood why she was furious with me. Things changed drastically that night. I could only imagine what she must have been feeling. She blamed me for what happened, because I took away the opportunity for her to say good-bye to her child. I didn't allow her to be with him one last time. She entrusted me to watch over her kids, and the worst possible thing that could happen, took place that day.

Kale was a little bit more forgiving than Veronica. Before I left the hospital that night he hugged me, and told me he didn't blame me. He said he knew it was an accident and that I would never do anything purposefully to hurt his children. I just wish Veronica had been able to see that. Veronica was inconsolable, she was admitted into the hospital the same night for high blood pressure, and she was having heart problems. I stayed as long as I could with her, but my kids needed to go home. They had been through a traumatic experience that day, and they needed to be at home now. I told Kale to tell Veronica I loved her, and I would be back tomorrow to see her. He said he would give her the message. When I got home that evening, things took a turn for the worse. My husband was beyond upset with me at what happened.

"I don't get you Hope! Why would you leave Grace to watch a five, and four year-old?" Teagan asked me.

"I didn't know things were going to turn out like this," I replied.

"I'm so mad at you, Hope!" Teagan said.

"I hate myself for what I did. I have to live with this for the rest of my life. I have to feel the pain," I stammered.

"What do you think about Veronica and Kale's pain? Their son died at our house. That's something they're never going to get over!" Teagan explained.

"Everything went perfect until I took that girl home," I said.

"This has to be one of the stupidest things you've ever done in your life," Teagan stated.

I could see how visibly upset Teagan was with me. I knew if he felt this way, and Hamilton wasn't even his son, I just knew Veronica hated me to the core. One of the few things I never wanted to happen was for someone else's child to be in danger because of me. This innocent, sweet little boy, was taken from this earth all because I wasn't there supervising him.

"I already feel horrible as it is Teagan. You don't have to make me feel any worse," I said.

"I just don't know how the family is going to move past this. Wait until the rest of them find out what happened. They're not going to believe it," Teagan exclaimed.

Teagan and I stood together, united, when we told our children about Hamilton's passing. They cried and didn't understand. Luckily, I think my three children were the only ones who didn't see Hamilton's death as my fault. In their minds Hamilton had an accident. They didn't blame me, and didn't shut me out. We cried together that night. All they knew was that one of their cousins had died. I wanted so badly for my sister to have a mind like my children, and not see this accident as my fault, but I knew the truth. I was responsible for not only my children, but my sister's children as well.

Things didn't get any better for me after that night. The next day I went to the hospital to see Veronica, but she wouldn't see me. She did not want to have any type of communication with me. I talked to Kale, and explained to him what happened, and why I was gone.

"I know it doesn't bring Hamilton back, but I was only gone for ten minutes. I was trying to do something nice for my daughter's friend, by not letting her walk home in the heat. Now that I look back, maybe I should've just taken the younger kids with me," I explained to Kale.

"There's no sense in trying to think about what you should've done, Hamilton's gone," Kale said.

"Sorry will never make up for what happened, and I feel such a tremendous amount of guilt on me. From the bottom of my heart Kale, I'm sorry for your loss. I hate myself right now as we speak," I said to him.

"I know it was an accident Hope. I loved my son and miss him already, but I know personally you would've never done anything to intentionally hurt my children," Kale stated.

"Veronica doesn't want to see me?" I asked.

"No, she doesn't want to," Kale replied.

"Okay. Just tell her I love her, and I'm willing to do whatever it takes to help her," I proclaimed.

After the police did their investigation, and questioned my children, they were temporarily taken away from Teagan and I. They didn't like the fact that I left all those children home alone. This pulled Teagan and I further apart. Child Services had to come into our home, investigate, and our children stayed with Teagan's parents. Being without my children for those couple of days was one of the worst feelings I had ever experienced when it came to my own kids. I didn't know exactly how Veronica felt, because all my children were alive, but I knew what it felt like to have them missing. My dear sister was going to have to live with this pain until the day she died.

Our children would eventually be returned to us once the investigation was over, and Grace's story seemed to match the injuries reported by the medical examiner, and Child Services learned Teagan and I weren't bad and neglectful people. Through that process I felt like a criminal having to go to court and explain my parenting. The judge declared that having to live with what happened was punishment enough.

Hamilton's death was ruled an accident. The same story Grace told me was the same exact story she told the police and Child Services.

The back door wasn't locked, and Hamilton walked right outside. Grace thought he wanted something inside the house. If she had of known what he wanted was outside, she would have gotten it for him. As he was reaching for his bear his head hit the cement, and he fell into the water. All this transpired only about four or five minutes after I left. It was one of Graces' friends who noticed that Hamilton hadn't returned. When they called for him and searched the house, Grace noticed the back door was open. They didn't instantly see Hamilton because by the time they got there he was sinking further and further to the bottom of the pool. No one knows if he struggled to get back to the top.

Kale made a conscious decision not to tell Veronica the details about Hamilton's death. It would send her over the edge he thought. After two days in the hospital, Veronica was released and went to go stay with our Mom. Kale took care of the children, they missed their brother, and now their mother. Veronica was a wreck and she would never be the same again. Kale told me when we left that night, Veronica was hysterical, and it took a shot to calm her down and to control her emotions. She had been sedated, but even so, Kale told me he could hear her calling for Hamilton throughout the night.

Teagan's assumptions proved to be right. When we had the funeral a week later, family members barely wanted to speak to me, friends acted as if they didn't know me, and Veronica gave me a few choice words afterwards. I know people hated me, and I stayed in the back the entire time. My nieces and nephews also didn't blame me as well, they ran up to me after the funeral, and hugged and kissed me. I needed those warm embraces that day. So many people had been cold to me, and it was nice not to feel like a monster for three minutes.

As I listened to the Minister speak at the cemetery, I could hear Veronica crying, and speaking to the casket, telling Hamilton to wake-up.

"Wake-up, son. Get up before it's too late," Veronica said.

People just looked, and felt sorry for her. I had to excuse myself, because seeing my sister in such pain hurt me deeply. Hamilton was buried in the same cemetery as my father, a few plots over. It was a beautiful sunny day, and yet there was so much sadness.

It took months before family was even ready to speak to me. I still remember Veronica standing right in front of me after the funeral going to the cemetery. She looked directly into my eyes, her eyes were filled with tears, and she said, "I hate the sight of you, you're dead to me, never talk to me again!"

I stood there not knowing if she was going to slap me, spit in my face, or curse me. She didn't, but I wish she would have. Then, at least she would have released some of her anger towards me, and not develop hate for me. However, she had a deep grudge rooted in her heart for me, that she's carried for the past two years.

After waking up the next morning, and trying to forget about the horrible dream I had about that dreadful period in my life two years ago, I received a call from my sister.

"Hello," I answered.

"Hi, Hope," Veronica said.

"How are you doing?" I asked.

"I'm okay. Listen, I was calling to tell you that Kale, the kids and I would like to come to church with you and your family if you still want us to," Veronica exclaimed.

I put the phone aside, and began to cry.

"I would love that, Veronica," I said.

"I think I'm ready to talk now," Veronica stated.

"Do you think we could ever get back to where we use to be?" I asked.

"Nothing will ever go back to what it used to be, because my son is gone. But I'm willing to talk to you," Veronica said.

"So, do you think this grudge may pass?" I questioned her.

"I truly hope so," she said.

I'll never be able to bring Hamilton back, and even though he's not my child, I will love him the rest of my life. I visit his grave every day. My only hope is that God can forgive me. But before I can forgive myself, I need my sister to forgive me first. By her coming to church with me, this is a step in the right direction. May this grudge pass? I believe in my heart it is possible, and my sister can love me again.

CHAPTER TWENTY
I'm At Peace

W hen Maura first came to us and told us she was getting married the whole family was stunned beyond belief. No one understood why she was in such a rush to get married and lose the little bit of freedom she had left in her life. My philosophy was simple, a woman who gets married, loses any kind of freedom she once had. This wasn't something I conjured up in my head. I knew first hand, because I myself had been married for five years, and shamefully, I was constantly looking for a way out. It wasn't that I didn't love my husband, but the idea of being a submissive wife, and a virtuous woman wasn't something I wanted for myself any longer. However, I wasn't about to leave my husband and have to start all over again. Advertently, I was trying to save my sister from making the same stupid mistake I made when I was just a little older than she was.

Maura hadn't even finished college yet, and instead of focusing on completing her junior year in college, she was worrying about where to get her wedding dress, and how many people she was going to invite to her wedding. I was so upset with Maura that there were times I didn't even want to be in the same room with her. No matter what I said, or how many negative stories I told her about being married, she wouldn't rescind her engagement.

I could see the hurt in our parent's eyes when she sat them down and told them she was getting married. Mom and dad both cried that warm spring day back in May. We as a family couldn't understand what the rush was and why she felt as if she had to leave college and give-up everything she had worked so hard for. No one understood. Countless times I begged Maura to rethink what she was about to do, but my pleas went unheard. Besides, it wasn't like Maura was going to marry some rich, good-looking, business executive. My sweet, innocent sister ended up marrying a backwoods, country boy named Spencer Grady.

From the minute I laid eyes on Spencer, I knew he wasn't the one for Maura. Not only was he unfriendly to my family and I, but also he was nothing but a sloppy farm boy. I'll never to this day be able to piece together what it was Maura saw in him that allowed her to leave her comfortable, prosperous life, to go and spend her days with a pale, bony, boot wearing, nut-job. I could tell within five minutes of meeting him that he was a *nutcase*. Nonetheless, Maura saw something else in him that the rest of us didn't see. After Maura's announcement about her engagement, my parents wanted to meet Spencer and invited him over for dinner one night. My parents wanted all of us to be there. That night is forever burned within my mind. I couldn't forget meeting Spencer even if I wanted to.

I arrived at my parent's house a little before six o'clock that night. Dinner was at seven and I wanted to help with anything I could. My older brother and his wife arrived shortly after me, and our youngest brother, Wes, showed-up exactly at seven. There we were, the whole family sitting in the living room waiting on Maura and Spencer to show-up. Forty-five minutes had passed and the two of them still hadn't arrived yet. I was pissed, and tried to call Maura several times on her cell phone. She wouldn't answer her phone. When eight thirty rolled around, dinner was cold, the family was tired, and Maura and her fiancée finally showed-up. We were all upset, but for the sake of our parent's we pretended as if their tardiness hadn't irritated us in the slightest.

"Sorry were late mom and dad." Maura stated.

I could see the look of embarrassment plastered all over Maura's face. She knew she had messed-up, and to see all of her family waiting on her made her gently lower her head every time she would look one of us in the eye.

"It's quite alright darling. What happened if you don't mind me asking?" Mom asked.

Maura hesitated to speak and rushed to the window, pulled back the curtains, and looked frantically out into the driveway. As Maura was looking out of the window she tried to answer mom's question in the best way possible.

"Please, don't make a big scene and ask a whole lot of questions when Spencer gets in here. Please don't!" Maura requested.

"Maura, you're an hour and thirty minutes late. What in the world took so long?" I demanded.

"Jen please, for me, don't embarrass me in front of him." Maura asked.

"Where is he anyway?" Dad said.

"He's taking a call, he'll be in shortly." She replied.

Maura knew out of all of her siblings that I was sort of crazy and outspoken. I didn't mean to be, but other people's stupidity stirs something in me, and it causes me to react in a hostile manner. None of our brothers were going to say anything, but I would've questioned Spencer if Maura hadn't stopped me before hand. He was already giving a bad impression. What kind of lamebrain idiot takes a call outside completely ignoring his future in-laws knowing he's already an hour and thirty-minutes late?

We all gathered around the dining-room table hugging and kissing, and trying to understand why our baby sister wanted to get married at twenty-one. We all took a seat and mom brought in the food one item at a time. The four of us caught up with each other about what was going on in each other's lives. I kept glancing over at dad wondering why he had a smile on his face. He was probably happy to see all of his children around a table; an occasion which rarely happened except for on holidays. After another grueling fifteen minutes, the man of the hour finally walked into our living room holding his cowboy hat in one hand, and his cell phone in the other.

"Hello, how y'all doin this evenin?" Spencer uttered.

One gaze at him and I wanted to throw-up in my mouth. I gave Maura a piercing look. She couldn't understand why I was staring at her with such intensity. This little bony butt, pale skinned, country boy is who my sister wanted to marry. I understand that being in a relationship isn't always about looks, but there's something to be said for wanting a little happiness in one's life, and I didn't see how my sister could be happy with this horse riding, boot wearing, redneck.

"Come on in son and take a seat," dad insisted.

When mom walked in she put down a plate of food and walked over to Spencer and gave him a hug.

"Welcome Spencer." Mom said.

Spencer got back up and went around the table shaking my brother's hands and my husband's hand, but when he got to me, I swiftly used my hands to stuff my face with food so he wouldn't want to shake my hand. *Luckily*, it worked. He made his way back to his seat. There was something about him that bothered me. I didn't like him. There was just something I couldn't quite figure out, but I knew in my heart there was something wrong with this boy.

"So Spencer, Maura tells us you work with your father. What kind of work?" Mom asked politely.

We were all eating our food anticipating Spencer's answer, but after about ten seconds, there was no answer. I looked up from my plate and wondered what this boy's problem was. Poor mom, she kept eating her food acting as if she hadn't just asked Spencer a question. The whole table was silent, and no one would say a word. Even my father didn't speak. I became enraged at that very moment. The pep talk Maura had given us earlier was about to go out of the window. Spencer was not getting ready to disrespect my mother in her own home.

"Excuse me Spencer!" I muttered.

Spencer looked up at me as if he couldn't believe that I had basically just yelled his name. He looked at me like he was confused.

"Yeah, you. My mother asked you a question and you never responded to her. She's waiting on an answer, and quite frantically the rest of the family would like to know the answer to that question as well." I said.

Spencer put his fork down and he turned red. I could literally see his neck veins protruding out.

"What's your name?" Spencer asked.

"The family calls me Jen, but you can call me Jennifer." I replied.

"Well, Jennifer, I assumed Maura told your mother what kind of work I did. I wasn't trying to be rude, I thought she was just making small talk." He answered.

"That has got to be the dumbest answer I've ever heard!" I shouted.

"Jen stop, please!" Maura begged.

"He's rude and inconsiderate Maura. I sure hope you know what you're getting yourself into. I can't stay here." I said.

"Sit down Jen!" Dad ordered.

"Joey and I are leaving!" I said. My husband and I got up from the table and excused ourselves.

Maura got up from the table and ran to the door and grabbed my arm as Joey and I were heading out of the front door.

"You just couldn't keep your mouth shut and be happy for me could you?" Maura whispered.

"Maura he disrespected mom in front of everybody. Not to mention the fact he was an hour and a half late on the day he's supposed to be making a decent first impression. Then, he keeps us waiting even longer while he stands outside taking some 'urgent' phone call. I honestly don't know what it is you see in him!" I stated.

"I can't believe you would do this to me." Maura cried.

"I'm sorry, but I don't like him. I can't be in the same room with him." I said.

From that night on Maura and I weren't on speaking terms for what seemed like months. She was angry with me because she felt I didn't try hard enough to get along with her fiancée. In the back of my mind I replayed over and over what I could have done different that night. Joey even told me I could have tried harder, but my emotions wouldn't let me keep quiet. I paid dearly for a few months. Maura was beyond upset, and any communication between the two of us was done between our mother and father. Even though Maura was upset with me, I still loved my sister and I wanted the best for her. Of course she didn't see that, she was too busy believing that I was trying to ruin her life. She didn't know my true intentions. I was actually trying to save her.

After a year had passed, Maura was twenty-two, and she married Spencer in a quiet outdoor ceremony with Spencer's family and our family in attendance. It was a beautiful spring day and Maura looked absolutely stunning. Her long, silky, blonde hair was blowing in the wind, and the sun beaming down made her appear as if she were glowing. I had never seen my sister look so lovely. Her gorgeous, white, sleeveless gown draped her body as if she were an angel. As I stood next to her watching her crying, I could no longer deny the fact that she was truly in love. All those months I had spent convincing myself she was just in love with the idea of being in love, and that Spencer was nothing more than a fill-in until the right guy came along. After watching Spencer and Maura say their vows, and gaze into each other's eyes, I knew I was wrong. I knew for the first time in a long time, I wasn't right. I felt discomfited.

Two months before the wedding took place Maura and I had patched things up. We put all the trivial things behind us and reconnected as sisters. It took my mother to tell me what I was doing was wrong. Mom had made a special trip to my house one Sunday evening and told me that if I didn't back-off, I was going to be at odds with Maura for a long time.

"She's your only sister, and you two have got to stay close." Mom cried.

"I'm trying to look out for her. I don't want her to make a mistake." I explained.

"Making mistakes is a part of life. I'm not a big fan of Spencer, but in order for me to have a quality relationship with my daughter and be in her life, I have to go along to get along." Mom told me.

"It doesn't seem worth it to me. What's wrong with trying to save her?" I asked.

"There's nothing to save her from. Look, Spencer is twenty-eight years old, he works in his father's construction business and has a nice family. He may need to work on his social skills, but I can't stand here and tell you he's a bad guy." Mom proclaimed.

"You and dad don't like him anymore than I do, and I'm mad that you and him are pretending to care for Spencer." I said.

"We have to Jen. You don't understand. Once they get married, Spencer could very well take Maura away from us, move to god knows where, and we would probably never see her." Mom said.

"I hate this." I stated.

"Well, you need to get over it, and fix the relationship with your sister. Besides, it's her life. She's the one who has to sleep next to him every night, and see his face every morning, not you." She uttered.

I found myself laughing.

"And, it's not like she has to be tied to him forever. If things don't work out, she can always divorce him." Mom told me.

After my talk with mom I felt as if it was time to reach out to Maura and ask her to forgive me. Mom was right, I didn't want to keep going months and months not talking to my sister over something as stupid as a man. Additionally, I really hadn't taken the time to actually get to know Spencer. Maybe I judged him to fast. If the worst thing about him was the fact that he had very little people skills, Maura was doing all right for herself. A week after my conversation with mom I broke down and called Maura. She was shocked and emotionally moved that I made the first step. My whole family knows that I'm stubborn and when I want things my way I don't budge. However, this situation was different, this was my little sister, and I didn't want to be excluded from her wedding.

We talked for hours that night and I could hear the relief in Maura's voice as she explained to me that she was happy that I wanted to put things behind us. With an overwhelming amount of fear within her, she asked me did I still want to be her maid of honor. She was even more relieved when I accepted for the second time. Even though Maura seemed to be overjoyed on the phone, there was something wrong with her. Her sentences were choppy and she would often pause before answering my questions. I asked her what was wrong, but Maura vehemently denied there was anything wrong with her. I let it go, but I knew deep down there was something wrong with her and even though she ultimately passed it off as her being tired and drained, I knew she was lying. Nevertheless, in order to keep peace and to remain on good terms with my sister, I let it go and tried to take on the new role of being a supportive, quiet sister.

After a year and half of marriage Maura and Spencer had their first child, a little boy named Weldon, named after Spencer's grandfather. Life appeared to be going well for Spencer and my sister. They bought a nice home about twenty minutes away from our parent's home. Maura finally graduated from college and took a teaching job as a second grade teacher. No one in our family really knew what it was Spencer did at his dad's constructing company. Every time we would ask he would start talking about random things trying to avoid the subject. At one point Spencer's mom said something about him being the financial brains of the company. I knew she was a liar, because her son didn't even look smart enough to be a dog trainer. Whatever he did it was enough to take care of my sister and my nephew.

Things in our family for some time seemed to be falling into place. There wasn't any tension mounting and no one was at odds. Maura and Spencer spent holidays with us and strangely enough, everyone grew to like Spencer. I still had my reservations about him, but anything I felt or thought I kept to myself. I pretended to like Spencer for the sake of my sister. I don't know if anyone else felt the way I did, but we all got along with Spencer Grady.

It wasn't until one cold night in January when I tried to call my sister that I began to fear for Maura and Weldon. I tried for over two and half hours to get in contact with Maura, but no one would answer the phone. Even if Spencer would've answered I would have been satisfied. I called my mom and asked her had she or anyone else been in contact with Maura and she told me she hadn't. I grew worried and told Joey to drive me over to Maura's house. It wasn't like Maura to not answer her phone, and I wasn't content with resting my head not knowing if my sister and nephew were okay.

Joey didn't want to drive me over to their house, but once he saw I was determined to go with our without him, he got dressed and started up the car. I called mom and dad and told them Joey and I were headed over to Maura's, and if they didn't hear from us in an hour they should assume something happened to us, and they should call the police. They agreed, and I hung-up the phone. Joey made it a point to keep insisting that nothing was wrong, and I was getting myself worked-up over nothing.

"This isn't like Maura, Joey. She's a school teacher, she should be at home." I said.

"Maybe the family is asleep." Joey proclaimed.

"Even so, Maura would still answer her phone. Something is wrong, I know it is," I stated.

"I just think you're going to be embarrassed and feel like an idiot when you realize everything is okay," Joey murmured.

"Well then I guess I need to prepare myself to look like a fool, because I'm not going home until I find out what's happened." I cried.

When we pulled up to the curb outside of Maura and Spencer's house all of the lights were off, and there weren't any cars in the driveway. Joey asked me was this unusual, and I couldn't give him a definitive answer. The cars could have been in the garage, and as far as the lights being off, maybe they were asleep like Joey suggested. To cure my curiosity I made the brave decision to get out of the car, go up to the door, and ring the doorbell. Joey got out and stood literally only a few inches behind me. I rang the doorbell once, and I waited for someone to come to the door. After standing there for at least a minute, I rang it again. Then, I knocked long and hard on the door, I even found myself beating the door. No matter how hard I knocked or how long I rang the doorbell, no one would come to the door.

Joey turned to me and I could see fear in his eyes. He didn't want to admit it, but I think he was beginning to realize that maybe, just maybe, I was right and something was wrong. Even if the whole family was asleep the amount of commotion and noise I made should have been enough of an incentive for either Spencer or Maura to get up and come to the door to see who it was. Joey and I stood outside for at least thirty minutes. We tried to look in windows, raise the garage doors from the outside, and I kept calling Maura. We couldn't reach them. I eventually called mom and dad and told them what the situation was. Mom automatically began to go into hysterics, and dad was trying to hold himself together. No one in the family knew where Maura and Weldon were. I kept hoping that even if I was wrong and nothing serious had happened, I at least wanted them to be okay. I could stand some embarrassment for a while from the family. I just wanted to know where Maura was.

Come the seven o'clock hour the next morning Joey and I moved up closer to the house. We had spent the night outside Maura's house the whole night hoping she would come home, but once we realized no one was coming home we moved our car from in front of their house to a couple of houses down so Spencer wouldn't be irate. I got out of the car and rang the doorbell again. No answer. This time as I walked around to the back of the house I thought I could get a better look into the windows since it was daylight. I peered heavily through a mid-sized square window hoping to see something. I didn't see anything eccentric or bewildering. As I continued to look inside moving my eyes up and down all sorts of things were going through my head. Where in the world is Maura I kept thinking to myself. When I was finished gazing into the window, I turned from the window looking down and saw someone standing in front of me wearing rusted, old, worn-out, cowboy boots. I looked up slowly, and saw Spencer.

"What you doing?" Spencer asked firmly.

I needed to come to myself, gather my thoughts, and move past my shock. In a way I was relieved to see Spencer, but I wanted to see Maura standing in front of me. I was relieved to see him because that meant everything was okay and I had excited myself with worry for no good reason. I was caught off-guard, because all night I wanted a response from someone, and now I was getting it.

"What, you can't hear and speak this morning?" Spencer teased.

"Where's Maura?" I asked hurriedly.

Spencer looked at me with intensity and guilt and ignored me.

"Oh, so you can't hear either?" I said comically.

I was so caught up in the moment and glad to see Spencer, because I knew Maura and Weldon were okay, I didn't even realize Spencer wasn't wearing a jacket and that he was holding a black laundry bag half-way full.

"Why aren't you wearing a jacket in thirty degree weather? I know your bony butt has got to be freezing." I said.

"Get off my property!" Spencer yelled at me.

By this time Joey came running around the side of the house.

"What is this? Why are y'all here?" Spencer said angrily.

"Where is Maura, Spencer? I'm tired of asking!" I uttered.

"Where is Maura?" Joey repeated.

"I don't have to tell y'all nothing!" Spencer stated.

"Where's Weldon?" I asked.

"The two of you have one second to get off my property before I call the cops! Get off my property now!" Spencer yelled.

I could see Spencer's face change from lily white to bright red. He was enraged.

"Let's go Jen. He's not going to tell us anything. We'll just go back to your parent's house." Joey said calmly.

"Let him call the cops. Then, maybe they can figure out where my sister and nephew are." I shouted.

I reached for Spencer's black laundry bag. "What's in the bag?" I said.

Spencer lunged at me and struck me right across the face, and violently grabbed his bag back. Joey attacked Spencer and punched him in the stomach.

"Don't you ever touch my wife!" Joey screamed.

"I'm not scared of him." I cried. I held my right cheek trying to calm the sting I felt.

"Maybe y'all don't understand reason. Let me get my gun!" Spencer shouted.

Spencer, holding on to his bag as if his life depended on it, ran past Joey and I, and headed for his front door. We knew it was time to go. No matter how tough I thought I was, I was no match for a deadly weapon. Furthermore, Spencer was actually right. Joey and I had no right to be on his property. Spencer could shoot us and claim he had every right because we trespassed. Joey took me by the hand and we ran as fast as our legs could carry us. We got in the car, and as we began to drive away, I threw a bottle in Spencer's driveway. All those feelings I had for Spencer, which I thought, I had suppressed, silently resurfaced. I hated Spencer Grady.

That same morning we rushed over to mom and dad's to tell them what happened with Spencer. No one could believe Spencer's actions, and how he wouldn't tell us where Maura was.

"He wouldn't tell you where she is?" Mom asked.

"No. He stood there ignoring me." I replied.

"Something's going on with him and I think we should call the police." Joey suggested.

"Has anyone called Maura's school to see if she showed-up to work?" Dad asked.

"I'll do that." Mom insisted.

"While she's doing that, I'll call Weldon's babysitter and see if Maura dropped him off." I said.

For about fifteen minutes we all clung to the little hope that everything was just a misunderstanding, and we prayed that Maura would turn up. When mom got off the phone with Maura's school she told us Maura hadn't been to work in two days and the principal wasn't able to get a hold of her. Likewise, Weldon's babysitter informed me Maura hadn't dropped him off for the past three days. My heart sank, I began to sweat, and I felt as if I was going to faint. I knew something was wrong. People in the family constantly label me as bitter and evil, but I don't just make assertions about things I don't feel strongly about. They may say what they will, but when I'm right, I know I'm right. Now, I felt stupid because I let my sister marry this man knowing that I didn't like him.

"What's next?" Asked Joey.

No one said anything, and we all looked at each other wondering which one of us had an answer to this horrifying dilemma. Surprisingly, I was shocked at how well mom was taking this news that no one knew where Maura was. I expected her to immediately go crazy, but there she was optimistic, and having faith.

"We need to call the police." Dad uttered.

"Guys what if she's on a trip or she was in that house, and Spencer just didn't want to tell us?" Joey suggested.

"I love you Joey, but now's not the time to be brainless. We need to stop pretending like we don't know what's going on!" I shouted.

"What Jen. What's going on?" Dad cried.

"Spencer hurt Maura and Weldon." I said carefully.

"What!" Mom said in disbelief.

"Hurt, what do you mean hurt?" Joey asked.

"I think he killed them." I proclaimed.

"You shut-up Jennifer! Shut your mouth! Don't you say that! You're going to burn in hell for thinking that!" Mom exclaimed.

Mom removed herself from the living-room where we were all gathered and left the rest of us in there to try to sort through my bombshell revelation.

"Jen that's a little bit extreme." Joey said.

I grew silent. I didn't want to carry on with my accusations just to have everyone else mad at me like mom was. I closed my mouth and waited to see what Joey and my father were going to do next. I wanted to just grab my mom and shake her and tell her Spencer got rid of Maura and Weldon. I thought my mom was going to be the one I could confide in and tell her everything I was thinking, but no such luck. She was highly upset with me, and I wasn't about to approach her.

After Joey informed my brothers about what was going on, Wes was ready to storm Spencer's home and find out what happened to Maura. I knew there had to be at least one other person who felt the way I did. I plotted with Wes on how we were going to ambush Spencer, but in the midst of my planning I realized how dangerous Spencer was and I couldn't risk my nineteen-year-old brother's life. If Joey and I didn't leave that morning off of Spencer's property, he probably would have shot both of us. Instead, I did what no one else in the family was willing or brave enough to do. I called the police.

"911 what's your emergency?" A lady said quickly.

"Yes I need to report a missing person. Well, actually two missing people." I said.

"Okay ma'am, are you sure their missing, because a report can't be filed for at least . . ."

I interrupted her.

"It's been three days. The police need to go to 5491 Gollin Lake Drive. My sister and my nephew have been missing for three days." I cried.

"Are you sure ma'am?" She asked.

"Yes. Spencer Grady is her husband and I think he killed them. I saw him this morning with a black laundry bag in his hand." I stated.

"Okay ma'am I'll send an officer out there." She informed me.

As soon as I got off the phone with the dispatcher I rallied the whole family to come with me over to Maura's house. Everyone came and as we pulled close to Maura's house we could see Spencer outside already talking to an officer. Before Joey could stop the car I rushed out and headed over to Spencer and the officer.

"You tell them what you did to my sister you redneck!" I yelled.

"See officer, this is the kind of abuse I've been putting up with all day. Tell her to leave!" Spencer requested.

"I'm not going anywhere." I said bravely.

"Yes you are." The officer replied. He told me to go back and wait in my car, and I did as I was told, but by no means did I leave.

A few minutes later four more officers arrived at Spencer and Maura's house. No one in the family left, we all waited to see what was going on. One of the officers' refused to talk to me claiming I was unstable and borderline on way to being arrested for disorderly conduct. Joey and my father pleaded with me to calm down and wait in the car. I rested my head and kept my eyes locked on Spencer. Everything I thought was playing out right before me. I was to angry to be hurt and cry, because I knew from the time I saw Spencer he was no good and I didn't do anything to stop my sister from marrying him.

Finally, the police entered Spencer and Maura's home after securing a search warrant. From what one of the officers' told dad the message relayed to me was that Spencer reported Maura and Weldon missing a day ago, but nothing was done because he was told he had to wait before an official search could be conducted. He said when he came back from his business trip with his father, Maura and Weldon were nowhere to be found. I didn't buy his story.

"It doesn't make sense Joey." I said.

"It sounds plausible to me." Joey replied.

"No it isn't. Even if it was true and he did report Maura and Weldon missing, why didn't he contact the family to find out where she is? Even if he didn't call you or me, he still could have called mom, dad, Wes, or Rex. He called no one. Plus, why would Maura leave to go somewhere in the middle of a school week?" I explained.

Spencer told the officer's he was embarrassed to call the family, because he didn't want us to think Maura had left him, and he was insecure about the marriage. Mom and dad believed Spencer's story, and so did my older brother Rex. Wes and I knew better. Joey was in-between. He couldn't make up his mind about what he believed. After what seemed like hours the police left and didn't take Spencer with them. They found nothing to suggest that Spencer had in any way harmed Maura or Weldon. Additionally, after they reviewed police records a report was filed by Spencer a day ago claiming that Maura and Weldon were missing.

Now, as a family, we began to mourn. It was official not only in our eyes, but in the eyes of the law, Maura and Weldon were gone. The most baffling thing was trying to piece together why Maura would run away, or who would want to kidnap a mother and a child. I lead the way for conducting the first unofficial search for Maura and Weldon. Night and day I was looking for my sister and nephew. The only piece of information I thought could help me determine if Maura was dead or not was to get into Spencer's house and search for that black laundry bag. I knew there had to be a clue in there. The police didn't do a careful job of looking through the home, because that black laundry bag as all of the answers. I knew it did. I just couldn't get my hands on it.

Eventually, things seemed liked they were looking up when Spencer was arrested for Maura and Weldon's murder. Everyone in the family was shocked but me. My mom was beside herself, and dad wanted to kill Spencer. The pieces of the puzzle came together when investigators found traces of blood in the entryway of Spencer and Maura's home, and Spencer's truck contained small amounts of blood and hair on the passenger side of the car. Spencer was charged with two counts of first-degree murder. Mom didn't want to believe it at first, because she thought that just because Spencer and contacted the police and reported Maura and Weldon missing that meant he was innocent. The reason Spencer wasn't arrested that first night was because they didn't have enough evidence to charge him with anything, but after police got the okay to search his car, that's when they found Maura's hair and blood in the front seat. Police were able to match the hair in the car with hair from one of Maura's hairbrushes, and it proved to be her hair.

All the time I spent searching night and day wasn't enough. I needed to know where Maura and Weldon were. Maybe the police were satisfied with going ahead and arresting Spencer, but I needed to see a body. I needed to know for my own sake where my sister was. Spencer's trial started a year later. An official search was conducted, but nothing was discovered. The prosecution wanted to have Maura and Weldon's bodies to present to the court, but decided not to waste anymore time. So, they proceeded. Instead of going to the trial I used that time to continue to search for my sister and nephew. I did everything I could think of except break into Spencer's home. His trial lasted for weeks, and the family felt confident that Spencer was going to prison for what he did.

The only time I came to Spencer's trial was on the day of the verdict. I wasn't there for the trial and relied on Joey to keep me up to date on what took place. He wasn't confident like the rest of the family that Spencer would be found guilty. He said the defense team presented strong doubt throughout the case. I didn't listen to Joey he didn't know what he was talking about. Deep in my heart I knew Spencer was going to prison. I could feel it. Besides, the evidence against him was too strong to ignore.

After the lunch hour that same day court was back in session and the jury had reached a verdict. The whole family held hands and we braced ourselves. I closed my eyes and saw Maura's beautiful face. I pictured Weldon in her arms, and a smile came to my face. As I was getting ready to open my eyes I heard a voice clearly and strongly say "not guilty."

The whole family gasped and I yelled out.

"What!" I screamed.

My mom fell out of her chair and on to the floor with her hands over her eyes, and she hit the floor on her left side. My brothers grabbed her, pulled her up, and took her out of the courtroom. She was crying beyond control. I saw dad put his head down and walk out behind mom and my brothers.

"You got away with murder you psychotic, repugnant animal. I hope your rot in hell!" I shouted.

I was removed from the courtroom immediately when I ran to the defense table and tried to attack Spencer. Two bailiffs took a hold of me and literally dragged me out of the courtroom. Once I was out of the courtroom I broke down for the first time. All those months I wouldn't allow myself to cry and feel the pain, because I was too mad. Now, all I could do was weep into my husband's arms. Shockingly, I can still see that look on Spencer's face. He wasn't happy, but he didn't look sad.

The family was told later that there were too many holes in the case, and circumstances which were ultimately dismissed. For instance, the defense passed off the dry blood in the entryway and Spencer's truck from when Maura was rushed to the hospital the night she gave birth. Maura's obstetrician testified that on the night she gave birth she was in fact bleeding, and an emergency delivery was needed in order to save both Weldon and Maura. The hair in the truck was passed off as Maura just being a frequent passenger in her husband's truck. The biggest piece was locating the bodies. No one knows where Maura and Weldon are, and the jury didn't feel comfortable sending Spencer to prison and there weren't even bodies. They also claimed there was no motive on Spencer's part.

No matter what anyone says I know Spencer Grady killed my sister and nephew. I spent the next two years searching for them whenever I could. I haven't lost hope that I'll find their remains somewhere. I'm the first to admit that Maura and Weldon are dead, but I still want to know where their bodies are. I couldn't find peace and contentment, because it disturbed me that Spencer was a free man and my sister was gone from this world. I think after the first few months mom, dad, and my brothers all accepted the fact Maura and Weldon were gone, and even though I accepted the fact Maura died before anyone else did, I just couldn't find peace with the situation. Maura and Weldon are an unfinished situation I couldn't let go of. It wasn't until my mother came to me and told me I was hindering myself from moving on. It was impossible for me to change or fix what had already taken place, and I was going to make myself sick trying to resolve a situation I had no control over. What she said made sense to me and I was never going to be content if I let what Spencer did control my mind and my actions. I had to move on.

I had to accept what mom told me, because if she was able to encourage me after having lost a daughter, I knew it was possible for me to embrace the fact that Maura and Weldon were gone, and to just grieve for them.

We may never know what physically happened to Maura and Weldon, and where their bodies reside, but they will remain alive in our hearts forever. There isn't a grave I can go and visit my sister, but the memories I have with her will have to suffice until I see her again. I often wondered if God was punishing my family for something that we had done, or maybe Maura was doing something wrong and that's why this happened to her. I had to stop thinking that way, and anyone else who thought that way obviously hadn't experienced what it meant to lose someone close to them, because if they knew, they wouldn't be foolish enough to spew those kind of comments or ponder those kind of thoughts. I realized this was a situation that the only person at fault was Spencer Grady.

As I live out the rest of my life, I may never know where Maura and Weldon are. However, I'm content with that, because I'm at peace.

CONCLUSION

The people of this world are granted the right to believe however they see necessary when it comes to coping with death. The goal in life is for us to live our lives to the fullest, each and every day without regret, to be thankful for the time here on this earth, and start to look at death as a reward. This will be a hard task for some people who view death as either a punishment, or a final act meant to bring unbearable pain to the fallen, and those of us who are left behind.

I now have a different perspective when I think about death. I am aware that leaving this natural life is simply a transition into the afterlife.

Afterlife seems like a fairytale to some individuals, and there are some who believe that after we die we are merely non-existent. True, once we die we are no longer on this earth, and only our memory remains behind. However, certain religions like the Christian faith, believes in a judgment and a final resting place in either Heaven or Hell. I believe in my heart there is a final resting place, and it's up to God to determine who goes where. No one can decide or prejudge where they think someone will spend eternity. Everyone's life is different, and we have all dealt with our own struggles. Victorious, an over-comer, or not, it's not up for anyone to say where someone will spend eternity, because no one knows.

Each one of these stories dealt with real life death issues that families and friends go through on a daily basis whether it is how to prepare for a funeral, how to cope with a death by receiving grief counseling, or how to move on. People face these issues every day. Death is a part of life. I hate that it is, but this is the way the world was formed. It bothers me when I am not able to have a natural conversation or to physically see me brother. I understand it when everyone says, I'll see him again in the afterlife, but it's not the same to me. Before I had a death in the family, I knew death was real, but I didn't comprehend the actual pain and the separation that comes with losing someone.

Some of us are granted the opportunity to prepare for the death of someone we love, or know, well in advance, and others are left to be stunned and hurt when they receive the news of a death of a loved-one or friend. Either way, when they take their final breath, it's still just as hard to say good-bye. Even if we are not given the opportunity to say good-bye, we should have enough memories, love, and kindness in our hearts to keep us satisfied until we are able to see them again.

God is not mean when he allows death to take someone away from us that we love. We forget that they were His first, and as the Creator of the world, who are we to question the decisions He makes? All we can do is cherish each other while we are still on this earth, and not let inconsequential things cause separation, animosity, and hatred to overtake the time we should love one another. Of course it's inevitable to go through our life without having disagreements and misunderstandings, and trying to act like we don't get upset with those who are close to us, but the key is too swiftly, and lovingly, release those negative feelings and be quick to find peace and forgiveness in our hearts. One of the worse things in the world is to let someone pass on without having forgiven them, or us asking for forgiveness. It's important for all of us to love even those people who are a thorn to us. We must, we need to, and if we are to be worthy to spend our life in Heaven, God requires us to.

This life is filled with so much trouble, heartache, pain, and to make things even worse, we have to deal with the death of parents, children, siblings, spouses, and friends. Some of us may see more sunshine in our lives, and the rest of us only see dark clouds, but as humans who have raw emotions and feelings, we each know the emotional damage of what death can do to us if we have experienced a loss. People are different in how they deal with their grief and sorrow. Some take it out on others, some people grow bitter, some withdraw from society, or their families, and some are able to just deal and move on gradually.

It use to upset me when people would treat me with malice, and feel as if they were justified. I wanted to scream at them, and tell them, "You don't know what I'm going through. My brother died." In my short time on this earth I've realized that certain people don't care about others situations or what someone else is dealing with. People don't have time to say a prayer for their neighbor, or to actively take an interest in how someone's doing. People want sympathy and understanding for their situations, but few of us are willing to reciprocate. Coming to this conclusion several months after the passing of my brother, I didn't look for others to comfort me, or to care about the pain my family and I were going through. They hadn't experienced it, and couldn't offer anything more than a, "I'm sorry for your loss." Those of us who have experienced the death of someone significant in our lives, shouldn't look for comfort from others, or for others to help us through this difficult time, if they aren't genuinely concerned and actively willing to listen to us convey all the things we need to express.

Let's pray for one another, and try to look for the best in those we come in contact with, whether they are family members, friends, or individuals we are meeting for the first time. We never know when we are seeing someone for the last time. Death is real, and unlike some people in this world, it's not prejudiced. It should be in each and every one of us, to live our lives to the fullest in accordance with morals, values, and the purest of hearts.

To any and all those who mourn, I want to express my deepest sympathies, and give you hope that one day there will be a sweet peace after you have moved past your grief. We will see our loved-ones again after this life. God Bless, and may God comfort you in your time of sorrow.